ED'S COLLEGE

Lordship and the
urban community

Illustration of Laurence the monk of Durham, taken from Cosin MS.V.III.I,
by kind permission of the Durham University Library

Lordship and the urban community

Durham and its overlords 1250–1540

MARGARET BONNEY

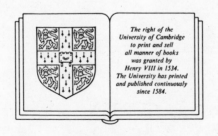

The right of the
University of Cambridge
to print and sell
all manner of books
was granted by
Henry VIII in 1534.
The University has printed
and published continuously
since 1584.

CAMBRIDGE UNIVERSITY PRESS

Cambridge
New York   Port Chester
Melbourne   Sydney

Published by the Press Syndicate of the University of Cambridge
The Pitt Building, Trumpington Street, Cambridge CB2 1RP
40 West 20th Street, New York, NY 10011, USA
10 Stamford Road, Oakleigh, Melbourne 3166, Australia

First published 1990

Printed in Great Britain by the University Press, Cambridge

British Library cataloguing in publication data
Bonney, Margaret
Lordship and the urban community: Durham and
its overlords, 1250–1540 –
1. Durham (County). Durham, history
1. Title
942.8'65

Library of Congress cataloguing in publication data
Bonney, Margaret.
Lordship and the urban community: Durham and its overlords
1250–1540 / Margaret Bonney.
p.   cm.
Bibliography.
Includes index.
ISBN 0-521-36287-3
1. Durham (England) – History. 2. Feudalism – England – Durham –
History. 3. Durham (England) – History. 4. Land tenure –
England – Durham – History – Church History. 1. Title.
DA690.D96B66 1989
942.8'65 – dc20   89-7084 CIP

ISBN 0 521 36287 3

In memory of my parents
Arthur and Mary Camsell

Contents

Contents

viii

Contents

Acknowledgements

During the long gestation of this book, many friends and colleagues have assisted me greatly with advice and encouragement. The original inspiration to work on medieval towns, and in particular, on those of northern England in the later medieval period, came from Miss Ann Kettle. Professor Barrie Dobson nobly undertook to supervise my doctoral thesis and under his expert and rigorous guidance, medieval Durham has taken on a more coherent and disciplined shape. I owe him a considerable debt for time so unselfishly given over the years. The Durham documents have made and moulded the direction taken by the book, and I gratefully acknowledge the help and assistance I have received from their custodians, the inmates of the Prior's Kitchen in Durham. Of these, Mr Martin Snape and Mr Alan Piper have made many valuable comments on earlier stages of my research. They also prevented me from frittering away my time on barren sources by sharing their cumulative knowledge and experience of the documents with me. There can be few record offices which are so evocative of the medieval period, surrounded by the modern successor of the Benedictine priory, and whose documents lie particularly, and ironically, secure from fire or other damage within the confines of the priory kitchen!

I am grateful to the Department of Palaeography and Diplomatic, Durham University, for permitting me to reproduce the three medieval maps in appendix 1 (nos. 5, 6 and 11) and to Durham University Library for the reproduction of John Wood's plan of Durham (appendix 1, no. 2) and the illustration of Laurence the monk, taken from Cosin MS.v.iii.i (frontispiece). The geological plan of Durham and its region (appendix 1, no. 9) is based on figure 2 of D. Pocock and R. Gazzard, *Durham: portrait of a cathedral city* (University of Durham, 1986), with their kind permission. My thanks must go to Mrs Ruth Pollington of the Department of Geography, University of Leicester, for her advice and expert cartography in compiling maps 3, 4, 7, 8 and 10 in appendix 1. The list of the bishops of Durham, which appears as appendix 3, is based on that which appears in *Handbook of British chronology*, ed. E. B. Fryde, D. E. Greenway, S. Porter and I. Roy (3rd edn, London, 1986), pp. 216, 241–2.

Finally, and above all, I should like to offer my heartfelt thanks to my husband, Richard, who has read the whole book from cover to cover with a critical eye during its various stages. He has prevented more than one urban crisis over the last four years, and he has injected liberal doses of moral fibre when it appeared that Durham would never see the light of day.

Department of History,   MARGARET BONNEY
University of Leicester

Abbreviations

For the abbreviations used in references to the muniments of the dean and chapter of Durham, see the bibliography, manuscript sources.

ArchAel	Archaeologia Aeliana
BAA	British Archaeological Association
CBA	Council for British Archaeology
CChR	Calendar of Charter Rolls
CClR	Calendar of Close Rolls
CPR	Calendar of Patent Rolls
DUJ	Durham University Journal
EETS	Early English Text Society
EcHR	Economic History Review
EHR	English Historical Review
Feodarium Dunelm	Feodarium Prioratus Dunelmensis, ed. W. Greenwell, Surtees Society, vol. 58, 1872
Hutchinson, Durham	W. Hutchinson, The History and Antiquities of the County Palatine of Durham, 3 vols., Newcastle, 1785–94
Laurence	Dialogi Laurentii Dunelmensis Monachi ac Prioris, ed. J. Raine, Surtees Society, vol. 70, 1880
MedArch	Medieval Archaeology
PRO	Public Record Office
RegPalDun	Registrum Palatinum Dunelmense, ed. T. D. Hardy, 4 vols., Rolls Series, 62, 1873–8
Reginald, St Cuthbert	Reginaldi Monachi Dunelmensis Libellus de Admirandis Beati Cuthberti Virtutibus, ed. J. Raine, Surtees Society, vol. 1, 1835
Reginald, St Godric	Libellus de Vita et Miraculis S. Godrici, Heremitae de Finchale, ed. J. Stevenson, Surtees Society, vol. 20, 1845

Scrip Tres	*Historiae Dunelmensis Scriptores Tres*, ed. J. Raine, Surtees Society, vol. 9, 1839
Surtees, *Durham*	R. Surtees, *The History and Antiquities of the County Palatine of Durham*, 4 vols., London, 1816–40
Symeon, *HistEcclesDun*	*Historia Ecclesiae Dunhelmensis*, in T. Arnold (ed.), *Symeonis Monachi Opera Omnia*, Rolls Series, 75, vol. 1, 1882
Symeon, *HistRegum*	*Historia Regum*, in T. Arnold (ed.), *Symeonis Monachi Opera Omnia*, Rolls Series, 75, vol. 2, 1885
TAASDN	*Transactions of the Architectural and Archaeological Society of Durham and Northumberland*
TRHS	*Transactions of the Royal Historical Society*
VCH	*Victoria County History*

Introduction

Many writers have been moved to eloquence by the dramatic site of Durham. The Barnard Castle lawyer, William Hutchinson, writing in the late eighteenth century, remarked on its

elegant situation, and the grandeur of some of its public buildings. A few paces from the south road, this English Zion makes a noble appearance. In the centre, the castle and cathedral crown a very lofty eminence, girt by the two streets called the Baileys, enclosed with the remains of the ancient city walls and skirted with hanging gardens and plantations which descend to the river Were, in this point of view exhibiting the figure of a horse-shoe.[1]

Other writers compared Durham with Jerusalem: 'he that hath seene the situation of this Citty, hath seene the map of *Sion*, and may save a Journey to the *Jerusalem*'.[2] Yet, somewhat surprisingly, Durham has received scant attention from modern historians, perhaps discouraged by remarks such as those made by Professor Hoskins who thought that 'we can form almost no idea' of the economic importance of Durham at the end of the middle ages.[3] Also, as others have commented, it is undoubtedly true that the glamour of the bishops and the cathedral church has often distracted attention away from serious research on the city itself.[4] The present study attempts to remedy this omission, at least in part, by surveying all the surviving documentary, visual and archaeological evidence concerning the urban community.

Despite this recent neglect, Durham has been well served by a long sequence of historical writers, starting with the twelfth-century chroniclers Symeon and Reginald of Durham, on whose accounts much of the evidence for the origins and the early

[1] Hutchinson, *Durham* 2, p. 1.
[2] Robert Hegge, *The legend of St Cuthbert* (1626), ed. George Smith (Darlington, 1777), p. 22.
[3] W. G. Hoskins, *Provincial England* (London, 1963), pp. 70–1.
[4] R. B. Dobson, *Durham Priory, 1400–1450* (Cambridge, 1973), p. 35.

growth of the town depends.[5] Although the central themes of these writers were far from urban, the first being the history of the monastery at Durham, and the second the lives and miracles of Saints Cuthbert and Godric, both provided descriptive details of the appearance of Durham as a backcloth to their work. Some six or more centuries separate these two monks from the next significant contributors to the medieval history of the town. These were the two worthy and reputable antiquarian historians, William Hutchinson and Robert Surtees, who both accumulated an impressive amount of material about the government, institutions and appearance of the town, based on their research in the bishop's archive – long before it was carried off to the Public Record Office – and among the documents of the cathedral priory. Hutchinson's *The History and Antiquities of the County Palatine of Durham*, published between 1785 and 1794, and Surtees' similarly entitled *History*, published between 1816 and 1840, present a valuable and systematic – if uncritical – account of the origins and development of the town which has formed the foundation of work by more recent scholars such as the contributors to the three Durham volumes of the *Victoria County History* (completed between 1905 and 1928).[6]

Several modern historians have elected to specialise in particular themes or periods of Durham's early history. The office of the bishop and the extent of his temporal and spiritual powers has been the subject of heated debate since the turn of this century, with G. T. Lapsley's thesis that the bishop of Durham ruled supreme over a mini-kingdom (a palatinate) in the north being challenged by several eminent writers.[7] More recently, the debate has moved on to a discussion of the shifting balance of political power within the bishopric after the middle of the fifteenth

[5] *Historia Ecclesiae Dunhelmensis* and *Continuatio Prima* in *Symeonis Monachi Opera Omnia*, ed. T. Arnold, Rolls Series, 75, vol. 1 (1882); *Historia Regum* in *Symeonis Monachi Opera Omnia*, ed. T. Arnold, Rolls Series, 75, vol. 2 (1885); *Reginaldi Monachi Dunelmensis Libellus de Admirandis Beati Cuthberti Virtutibus*, ed. J. Raine, Surtees Society, vol. 1, (1835); and *Libellus de Vita et Miraculis S. Godrici, Heremitae de Finchale*, ed. J. Stevenson, Surtees Society, vol. 20 (1845).

[6] *VCH Durham*, ed. W. Page (3 vols., London, 1905–28). See, in particular, the section on city jurisdictions, written by K. C. Bayley (vol. 3, pp. 53–64).

[7] G. T. Lapsley, *The county palatine of Durham*, Harvard Historical Studies, vol. 8 (New York, 1900). Professors Barlow and Offler and Mrs Scammell criticise this interpretation by drawing attention to the limitations on the bishop's power: see F. Barlow, *Durham jurisdictional peculiars* (Oxford, 1950); *Durham Episcopal Charters, 1071–1152*, ed. H. S. Offler, Surtees Society, vol. 179 (1968); J. Scammell, 'The origin and limitations of the liberty of Durham', *EHR*, 81 (1966), 449–73.

century, the reduction of its autonomy, and the gradual acceptance of the Reformation throughout northern England.[8] In all of this, however, Durham city, the seat of episcopal power, has played a very minor role. The careers of individual bishops such as Puiset, Bek and Langley (see appendix 3) have been analysed in studies which have added greatly to our knowledge of administrative and ecclesiastical developments in the area and of the relationship between the bishop and the wealthy Benedictine priory situated in the heart of the town.[9] The history of this priory itself has generated considerable interest among scholars, starting with James Raine, the chapter librarian at Durham, who edited a number of key primary sources in the middle of the nineteenth century.[10] Its most recent exponent, Professor Dobson, concentrated on one crucial priorate, that of John Wessington, in his book entitled *Durham Priory, 1400–1450*. So the chief protagonists in the history of the medieval town – the bishop, the prior and the monastic office-holders, the obedientiaries of the priory, who held the majority of properties in and around the urban area and were the temporal as well as the spiritual overlords of the townsmen – have been exposed to some critical scrutiny by historians. But recent work on Durham has not been confined to personalities, politics and religion. The economic history of the estates of the medieval priory has been studied, and comparable work on the estates of the bishop in the north is in train.[11] Again, the town has formed an interesting element of those studies already completed, but it has been treated very much as one small and not very significant part of a primarily rural economy. None

---

[8] David Marcombe (ed.), *The last principality: politics, religion and society in the bishopric of Durham, 1494–1660*, Studies in Regional and Local History, vol. 1 (Nottingham, 1987).

[9] G. V. Scammell, *Hugh du Puiset, bishop of Durham* (Cambridge, 1956); C. M. Fraser, *A history of Antony Bek, bishop of Durham, 1283–1311* (Oxford, 1957); R. L. Storey, *Thomas Langley and the bishopric of Durham, 1406–1437* (London, 1961).

[10] See, for example, *ScripTres; Depositions and other ecclesiastical proceedings from the courts of Durham*, ed. J. Raine, Surtees Society, vol. 21 (1845); Reginald, *St Cuthbert*. See Dobson, *Durham Priory*, pp. 7–8.

[11] E. M. Halcrow, 'The administration and agrarian policy of the manors of Durham Cathedral Priory', unpublished BLitt thesis, University of Oxford, 1949; E. M. Halcrow, 'The decline of demesne farming on the estates of Durham Cathedral Priory', *EcHR*, 2nd ser., 7 (1955), 345–56; R. A. Lomas, 'Durham Cathedral Priory as landowner and landlord, 1290–1540', unpublished PhD thesis, University of Durham, 1973; R. A. Lomas, 'The Priory of Durham and its demesnes in the 14th and 15th centuries', *EcHR*, 2nd ser., 31 (1978), 339–53; T. Lomas, 'Land and people in south-east Durham in the later middle ages', unpublished PhD thesis, Council for National Academic Awards, 1977; work in progress by Dr R. H. Britnell.

of these writers has explored the urban theme and so the development of Durham itself has remained largely uncharted.

The hope has been expressed recently that more detailed studies comparable to the work on Winchester will be undertaken, because 'they would not only broaden our understanding of the hierarchical network of towns which served medieval England, but also do much to assist us in identifying the nature of their regions and in separating those features which were purely regional in character from those which had a national or wider origin'.[12] Durham may not provide all the documentation or the archaeological potential for a survey as thorough as that of medieval Winchester, but nonetheless it makes an appropriate case study in a northern region where few urban communities have as yet been scrutinised by historians. Medieval Carlisle has been the subject of an archaeological report and some preliminary documentary research has been undertaken.[13] There is still no adequate account of medieval Newcastle, although archaeological excavations have demonstrated its potential, and work on rent movements in the fifteenth century throws more light on the murky waters of the controversial theme of late-medieval urban decline.[14] A topographical study of the development of Alnwick was completed and analysed by a historical geographer in the 1960s and a preliminary survey of the documentary and archaeological evidence for Darlington has been made.[15] York has, naturally enough, received the fullest treatment so far, with its valuable *Victoria County History* volume; and recent work relating the documentary record to newly discovered archaeological evidence at the college of the Vicars Choral, Bedern, should reveal some interesting insights into the medieval city,

[12] D. J. Keene, *Survey of medieval Winchester*, vol. 1, part 1 (Oxford, 1985), p. 4.

[13] B. C. Jones, 'The topography of medieval Carlisle', *Transactions of the Cumberland and Westmorland Antiquarian and Archaeological Society*, 76 (1976), 77–96; P. F. Gosling, 'Carlisle – an archaeological survey of the historic town', in P. A. G. Clack and P. F. Gosling (eds.), *Archaeology in the north: the report of the Northern Archaeological Survey*, (HMSO, 1976), pp. 165–85.

[14] B. Harbottle and P. A. G. Clack, 'Newcastle-upon-Tyne: archaeology and development', in P. A. G. Clack and P. G. Gosling (eds.), *Archaeology in the north: the report of the Northern Archaeological Survey* (HMSO, 1976), pp. 111–31; A. E. Butcher, 'Rent, population and economic change in late medieval Newcastle', *Northern History*, 14 (1978), 67–77.

[15] M. R. G. Conzen, *Alnwick, Northumberland: a study in town plan analysis*, Transactions of the Institute of British Geographers, vol. 27 (London, 1960); P. A. G. Clack, 'The origins and growth of Darlington', in P. Riden (ed.), *The medieval town in Britain*, Gregnyog Seminars in Local History, no. 1 (Cardiff, 1980), pp. 67–84.

perhaps along the same lines as the Winchester evidence.[16] A detailed study of Durham will provide at least additional evidence for urban activity in the medieval north and for the standard of town life in the region. Further, it is hoped that this work will help to indicate Durham's place in the hierarchy of towns in medieval England as regards its size, its population and the range of its occupations.

Moreover, the historian of medieval Durham has an undoubted advantage over urban historians working on many other English towns because of the almost indigestible richness of the documentary sources. Through the good offices of the Surtees Society in particular, the value of the Durham Priory account rolls and rentals has been known for some time, and historians have used them in a variety of ways to provide information of demographic, economic or administrative interest.[17] The large collection of medieval property deeds held in the Prior's Kitchen in Durham is far less well known, primarily because it has not been published, although it is hoped to remedy this in the near future.[18] In its size and value, this collection is comparable with that used by the Rev. H. E. Salter in Oxford or W. Urry in Canterbury, although it is more limited in scope than the Winchester and Norwich collections, which benefit from not being derived simply from one or two property-owning institutions.[19] The original title deeds relate to property which was acquired by Durham Priory within Durham and in some cases they provide a history of tenure from the late thirteenth century to the early sixteenth century. They contain some quite

[16] *VCH City of York* (Oxford, 1961); D. Palliser, 'The medieval period', in J. Schofield and R. Leech (eds), *Urban archaeology in Britain*, CBA research report no. 61 (London, 1987), p. 62; S. Rees Jones, 'Property, tenure and rents: some aspects of the topography and economy of medieval York', unpublished DPhil thesis, University of York, 1988.

[17] *Extracts from the account rolls of the abbey of Durham*, ed. J. T. Fowler, Surtees Society, vols. 99, 100, 103 (1898–1901); *Feodarium Dunelm*, ed. W. Greenwell, Surtees Society, vol. 58 (1872). An edition of three bursar's rentals, edited by R. A. Lomas and A. J. Piper, will form the next volume of the Surtees Society's publications.

[18] A complete edition of the medieval deeds relating to the town is being prepared for the Surtees Society by the present writer.

[19] H. E. Salter, *Medieval Oxford*, Oxford Historical Society, vol. 100 (1936); H. E. Salter, *Survey of Oxford*, ed. W. A. Pantin and W. T. Mitchell, 2 vols., Oxford Historical Society, new ser., vols. 14, 20 (1960, 1969); W. Urry, *Canterbury under the Angevin kings* (London, 1967); Keene, *Winchester*, vol. 1, part 1, p. 6; S. Kelly, E. Rutledge and M. Tillyard, *Men of property: an analysis of the Norwich enrolled deeds, 1285–1311* (Norwich, 1983).

detailed descriptions of land and property and in a few cases they include the exact dimensions of tenements. This evidence can be used to reconstruct an approximate street plan of the medieval city.[20] The deeds also provide a wealth of information about rents, occupations and family structure, all of which can be related to the rentals and account rolls to provide a remarkably full picture of urban society.

Few of Durham's surviving deeds, and indeed any documentary sources, date from before 1250, and hence a natural starting date is imposed, by default, on this study. The whole approach to the subject will be thematic rather than strictly chronological or narrative, and the nature of the surviving evidence, with its heavy emphasis on property ownership and its obligations, has meant that the central theme is landholding, and the relationship between landlords and their tenants. In particular, the rich documentation of Durham Priory's urban holdings has shaped the whole study, and consequently, the natural *terminus ad quem* of the work is the dissolution of the priory on 31 December 1539 and the subsequent dispersal of its estates. This event was of far more significance for the history of the town than, for example, Scottish invasions, pestilence and inflation. Durham was affected by all of these circumstances, but they were not as dramatic or revolutionary as the legal and social changes brought about by the dissolution.

Some themes of more general interest to urban historians emerge from this detailed study of medieval Durham. The attitude of Durham landlords towards their urban property can be compared with, for example, the policy of the Percy family – not only in their northern estates but throughout the country – or the attempts of other religious houses, such as Westminster Abbey or Ely and Peterborough, to cope with hardship. The obvious difficulties in maintaining rent income which were faced by landlords in the early fifteenth century are confirmed by the movement of rents which can be charted in the Durham evidence; but there seems to have been no dramatic urban crisis in Durham as there was, it has been suggested, in towns such as Lincoln, Coventry or Stamford in the fifteenth and early sixteenth centuries. One reason for Durham's comparative prosperity in the early sixteenth century may have been that, like Norwich or York, it had a diversity of trades: however, it will emerge that

[20] For an example of such a reconstruction, see appendix 1, map 4.

none of these was particularly important by national standards or employed many inhabitants. This in turn might help to account for the fact that Durham never expanded greatly in population or physical size after 1250. Indeed, it is suggested in the first chapter that Durham may have been at its most prosperous before 1250, no matter how sparse is the surviving documentary evidence to prove this case. But of equal importance at least to any economic arguments for the small size of Durham in the later medieval period is the influence of topography on the urban site; the craggy peninsula surrounded on three sides by the gorge of the River Wear may have been picturesque, but it inhibited physical growth.

Although Durham was a relatively small market town throughout the middle ages, it had nonetheless a significance and a uniqueness unrelated to economic factors. It was dominated by the clergy in a way comparable perhaps with medieval Canterbury, or even the Vatican City today; and it is the relationship between its inhabitants and its ecclesiastical overlords, the bishop and the cathedral priory, which is of perhaps the greatest interest. Also notable is an apparent absence of civil disturbances which marked, or marred, other medieval towns with church or lay overlords, such as York, Beverley or Bury St Edmunds. Although the church was a dominant and perhaps even a repressive force in the town, there are few signs of opposition to its rule or of unrest among its tenants. Finally, there is an obvious lack of sophisticated administrative or governmental development in Durham, common to many mesne boroughs such as Bury or Abingdon, where local initiatives were stifled by an ever-present overlord who was determined to maintain his rights unchanged and intact. All of these themes make a study of Durham more than simply a survey of yet another small medieval town and help to set it in a national context.

Of course, it cannot be claimed that the following study of medieval Durham is exhaustive; a number of topics of concern to historians of other medieval towns cannot be explored fully because of the limitations of the Durham evidence. It will quickly become apparent that the burden of the work rests upon the priory's archive. This is a natural result of the survival rate of the documents: the monks of Durham Priory and their successors were efficient archivists, but unfortunately the staff of the bishopric were less successful in preserving their muniments. At the outset of this project, it was intended to compare the estate management policy of the priory with that of the bishopric, but this has proved to be impossible. Even more seriously, few deeds or rental entries survive for what was the most prosperous and important part of the town, the central borough surrounding the market place, which was controlled by the bishop. Consequently a rather unnatural but, one hopes, understandable emphasis has been placed on the role of the priory in town life. Furthermore, any discussion of the religious life of the townsmen themselves, the parishes, town churches, chantries and religious fraternities which served the spiritual needs of the community is confined to the fringes of this survey. The apportionment of blame for this omission lies not with the deficiencies of the surviving evidence, but rather with the author and considerations of space; but it is at least one area of Durham's history where other historians have contributed through their work on the priory and the bishopric of Durham. Despite these shortcomings, the following account of Durham's urban community and its relationship with its ecclesiastical overlords between 1250 and 1540 is offered as a contribution to the continuing debate on the nature of urban life in the later middle ages.

Chapter 1

Urban origins: the growth and development of Durham to 1250

This city is famous throughout Britain, on its steep foundation, wondrously rising up about a rocky base. The Wear flows round it, a river with a strong current in whose waters live many kinds of fish... In the city, too, famous among men, lies Cuthbert the holy and blessed.[1]

Early local legend as well as successive generations of monks and their priors, such as John Wessington (1416–46), fostered the belief that St Cuthbert himself had chosen the site of Durham. In 995, or thereabouts, as the community of St Cuthbert, carrying the precious body of their saint, wandered through the northern counties trying to avoid the worst ravages of the Danish invaders, they happened to pass a wooded place called Dunholm or Dunhelm.[2] According to later accounts of the journey and to the tradition which grew around it, the bier of St Cuthbert suddenly became immovable, a clear sign from heaven that Dunholm was to be the saint's final resting place.[3] Some four centuries later, the monks were still asserting that there was not 'a church, a chapel or a house' built where the city and suburbs of Durham then lay before this almighty intervention.[4] But, churlish though it may seem to throw doubts on St Cuthbert's reputation as Durham's founding father, there are strong indications that he was not the first to recognise the great potential of the site. Other chronicle evidence suggests that there may have been a community of farmers settled in the area before St Cuthbert led his followers, spiritually at least, to the site. Some recent archaeological

---

[1] From *De Situ Dunelmi*, an Anglo-Saxon poem composed at Durham probably between *c*. 1050 and 1109, translated by V. E. Watts in *City of Durham, 1179–1979*, a brochure produced to celebrate the 800th anniversary of the granting of a charter by Bishop Puiset to Durham (Durham, 1979), p. 10. In its original form, it is printed in Symeon, *HistEcclesDun*, pp. 221–2.

[2] Doubts were raised by J. Cooper about the dating of this event. An alternative date of 992 has been suggested: see J. Cooper, 'The dates of the bishops of Durham in the first half of the eleventh century', *DUJ*, 60 (1968), 131–7.

[3] Symeon, *HistEcclesDun*, p. 79.   [4] Loc. XI, no. 5.

discoveries have shown traces of human activity on the peninsula antedating St Cuthbert's arrival. Moreover, contemporary historical references suggest that the choice of site was governed more by the political considerations of the day than by religious concerns.

None of this evidence, which will be examined later, can be accepted without question; but it has thrown some doubt on the late-medieval monks' claim that Durham was created by divine will. It does nothing, however, to belittle the impact St Cuthbert's presence made at Durham, whether or not the site was populated, even before the end of the tenth century. The fact that an important, indeed the most prestigious, northern saint was laid to rest at Durham brought fame to the area and generated urban growth; Durham was to become one of the most important centres of pilgrimage in medieval England. Furthermore, the small community of St Cuthbert was, by the later middle ages, transformed into a large and wealthy Benedictine priory, a landholder second only in importance to the bishops of Durham in the region. By then, Durham's bishops had become mighty secular princes, virtual rulers of their own lands and tenants in the north-east as well as spiritual leaders of the Durham bishopric. As the administrative centre of the bishopric, Durham housed all its offices, which were staffed by a small army of clerics. The town grew alongside this expanding clerical population and service industries developed to provision a great ecclesiastical centre. Durham was the principal market town for the region, while the large St Cuthbert fairs, held twice annually, attracted merchants from all over England. Such economic prosperity as there was can be linked directly with the coming of St Cuthbert to Durham; and it could be argued that Durham became a town of some size and significance only through the saint's intervention in its history.

The first part of this chapter attempts to elucidate the most obscure period of Durham's, and indeed of northern, history – the late tenth century, when the town was founded – and the reasons which lay behind the choice of such a seemingly unsuitable site. The second section traces the growth of military and religious buildings on the peninsula and the purely urban settlement around it from the late tenth to the early thirteenth centuries. A combination of archaeological and documentary sources have been used in this inquiry. Excavations in Saddler Street and Elvet provide what little information there is about the homes and occupations of Durham townsmen in this period, unrepresentative though it may be.[5] The chronicle *Historia Ecclesiae Dunhelmensis*, usually attributed to the monk Symeon, and its continuation, is perhaps the most important documentary source for the early history of Durham, but it shares all the common difficulties of this type of evidence. A considerable interval had elapsed between the events of the early eleventh century and the actual recording of them: Symeon, or whoever was the author, compiled his chronicle between 1104 and 1107.[6] Furthermore, he was not objective, for, as the 'official' historian of the monks of the newly founded Durham community, he wanted to show that the community had both 'a past of unbroken glory' and a continuity of tradition and landed possessions.[7] The bias of the monk's version of Durham's history is apparent in, for example, the account of the events following William Cumin's usurpation of, or intrusion into, a see to which he had no legal claim in the 1140s, an account which dwells, among other things, on the devastation of the town.[8] Symeon's chronicle, as well as those written later by the monks Laurence and Reginald, must be handled cautiously as historical sources, but each has value as a unique commentary on the topography of early medieval Durham. Reginald, in particular, gives a vivid contemporary description of the late-twelfth-century town in an apparently expansionist phase.[9] The only other supporting documentary evidence for this formative period of the town's history is contained in a few surviving twelfth-century charters. Their main contribution to this survey of pre-1250 Durham is to shed some light upon the still limited privileges of the burgesses of the city.

[5] M. O. H. Carver, 'Three Saxo-Norman tenements in Durham City', *MedArch*, 23 (1979), 1–80; M. O. H. Carver, 'Excavations in New Elvet, Durham City, 1961–73', *ArchAel*, 5th ser., 2 (1974), 91–148.

[6] Symeon, *HistEcclesDun*; H. S. Offler, *Medieval historians of Durham* (Durham, 1958), p. 7. On the problems of dates in this chronicle, see Cooper, 'Dates of the bishops of Durham', pp. 131–7.

[7] The very title of the work demonstrates this: *Libellus de exordio atque procursu istius, hoc est Dunelmensis Ecclesiae*. See A. Gransden, *Historical writing in England, c. 550–c. 1307* (London, 1974), pp. 115, 118–19; Offler, *Medieval historians*, pp. 7–8; B. Meehan, 'Outsiders, insiders and property at Durham around 1100', in D. Baker (ed.), *Church, society and politics*, Studies in Church History, vol. 12 (1975), pp. 45–6; A. Young, *William Cumin: border politics and the bishopric of Durham, 1141–1144*, Borthwick Papers, no. 54 (York, 1979).

[8] Symeon, *HistEcclesDun, Continuatio Prima*, p. 159.

[9] *Dialogi Laurentii Dunelmensis Monachi ac Prioris*, ed. J. Raine, Surtees Society, vol. 70 (1880); Reginald, *St Cuthbert*; Reginald, *St Godric*.

THE ORIGINS OF DURHAM

There is no substantial evidence, written or archaeological, to suggest that the town of Durham was anything other than a new foundation of the late tenth century. There are no signs of prehistoric activity on or around its peninsula, although the similarity of Durham's promontory site to that of Maiden Castle, a few miles to the south-east, invites comparisons. Excavations at Maiden Castle have revealed earthworks, and the suggestion is that it was probably a prehistoric defended manor or farm site.[10] Perhaps Durham's promontory was also fortified, a speculation which has not, as yet, been confirmed or rejected by any archaeological findings. Nor has the Roman presence in the north left any tangible remains in Durham. The closest evidence of Romano-British settlement in the area seems to be the farmstead with its own bath-house discovered at Old Durham, one mile to the south-east of the peninsula.[11] Yet it does appear that some kind of ecclesiastical centre had developed much nearer to the peninsula by the late eighth century, if the evidence of the *Anglo-Saxon Chronicle* can be accepted. The entry for the year 762 reads: 'Then Pehtwine was consecrated bishop of Whithorn at Elvet on 17 July.'[12] It has been suggested that 'Elvet' derives from the Old English *ælfet-ea*, meaning swan-stream or swan island, an appropriate name for part of Durham where, according to the account of the early-sixteenth-century traveller, John Leland, 'there [*sic*] Were is divided ynto two armes, and after shortely meating makith an isle'.[13] Slight as this identification may seem, it is given some weight because the entry only occurs in two versions of the *Chronicle* which have some claim to be northern-based and nowhere else.[14]

What the nature of this ecclesiastical centre at Elvet was and

[10] M. G. Jarrett, 'The Maiden Castle excavations', *TAASDN*, 11 (1958), 124–7; M. O. H. Carver and P. F. Gosling, 'The archaeology of Durham City', in P. A. G. Clack and P. F. Gosling (eds.), *Archaeology in the north: the report of the Northern Archaeological Survey* (HMSO, 1976), pp. 133–45.

[11] For its position, see appendix 1, map 3. I. A. Richmond and others, 'A civilian bath house of the Roman period at Old Durham', *ArchAel*, 4th ser., 22 (1944), 1–21; 29 (1951), 203–12; 31 (1953), 116–26.

[12] *The Anglo-Saxon Chronicle*, ed. D. Whitelock (London, 1961), p. 32.

[13] E. Ekwall, *The concise Oxford dictionary of English place-names* (Oxford, 1960); *Itinerary of John Leland*, ed. L. Toulmin Smith (London, 1906), vol. 1, pp. 74–5.

[14] See *Anglo-Saxon Chronicle*, ed. Whitelock, pp. xiv–xvii; *The Anglo-Saxon Chronicle*, ed. G. N. Garmonsway (London, 1953), pp. xxxvii–xli.

whether it was accompanied by a settlement of some kind remains a mystery, and a gap of some two centuries in the subsequent documentary evidence cannot be bridged. But with the next piece of evidence, we have the first clear identification of a place called Dunholm or Dunhelm from which the medieval town was to grow. We arrive at Symeon's chronicle of events, which, despite all its shortcomings, still has the best claim to be a record of the foundation of the town. The outline of the story has already been told, but was the site as truly virgin land as Symeon would like us to believe? Most telling is the chronicler's laconic remark that when the community of St Cuthbert arrived in this wooded area, they found a small plain which had been cleared and cultivated already.[15] Could there have been a settlement of sorts, perhaps a farming community, in the vicinity and was this 'plain' the peninsula which was to become the site for St Cuthbert's church? Support for this theory seemed to come from sample borings of soils taken from a site on the east side of the North Bailey.[16] The fourth layer of soil, christened the 'black bed' layer and composed of a fine quartz sand cemented by black carbonaceous mud, had been formed, Whitworth suggested, by a small, stagnant pond perched on the edge of the gorge of the River Wear. Mammal bones and traces of wheat and grass pollen which were found in this layer led him to deduce that agricultural clearance contemporary with the extensive development of grazing had taken place around this pond. Radio-carbon dating of fragments of wood gave him an estimated date of *c.* 900 to 950 and on the basis of all this evidence he came to the conclusion that there was a flourishing agricultural community established on the peninsula long before the arrival of St Cuthbert's followers.

Whitworth's theory has not gone unchallenged, however. Carver thought that the 'black bed' was more likely to be an occupation layer artificially terraced into the sand, and that the samples of pollen were merely food waste, foliage or wood brought together by the occupants of the site, rather than signs of cultivation or clearance.[17] He also disagreed with Whitworth's calibration of the date of his soil sample and gave a much wider

[15] Symeon, *HistEcclesDun*, pp. 80–1.
[16] T. Whitworth, 'Deposits beneath the North Bailey, Durham', *DUJ*, 61 (1968), 18–31.
[17] M. O. H. Carver, 'Early medieval Durham: the archaeological evidence', in *Medieval art and architecture at Durham Cathedral*, BAA conference transactions for 1977 (London, 1980), p. 15.

possible dating of between 750 and 1220, which is more frustrating for the historian of early medieval Durham. But these criticisms do not demolish the case for the early, pre-tenth-century settlement or cultivation of Durham's peninsula, and the revised dating may simply indicate a continuity of settlement on or around the site. The results of Carver's own excavation in 1974, on a site to the west of Saddler Street, provided exciting new evidence for the theory of pre-Cuthbertian origins for Durham. He has suggested that the earliest structures on the site were constructed in the middle of the tenth century. Clear evidence for the shape and alignment of these houses survives; they had a protective revetment of hazel woven on to oak and alder posts, which compares with one of the building techniques found in excavations at Pavement and Coppergate, York, for a similar period. Charred debris covered with patches of sand on the floor implied that these early houses were destroyed by fire. Judging by the tools and the offcuts from shoe-making leather found there, the earliest inhabitants of this site may have been leather workers, although the discovery of over 1,000 pottery sherds suggests the development of a pottery industry as well.[18]

The archaeological and documentary evidence, limited though it may be, supports the theory that St Cuthbert's followers came to an area which was already inhabited in the late tenth century. But there is no evidence to suggest that there was an urban community here, or even a rural settlement of any size. Indeed, the topography of the site militated against it, with a rugged peninsula surrounded on three sides by the narrow gorge of a fast-flowing river. Why then was this site chosen for the establishment of a town? First and foremost, it was easy to defend; the steep-sided craggy slopes of the peninsula descending to the River Wear were a natural deterrent to attackers. The narrow neck of land to the north which connected the peninsula to the surrounding countryside could be fortified easily by throwing across earth-works like those at Maiden Castle. The monk Laurence, writing in the middle of the twelfth century, commented that it was not easy for an enemy to break through these natural defences, and the security offered by such a site must have been its greatest

---

[18] Carver, 'Three Saxo-Norman tenements', 1–80; R. A. Hall, 'The topography of Anglo-Scandinavian York', in R. A. Hall (ed.), *Viking age York and the North*, CBA Research Report no. 27 (London, 1978), p. 36; A. MacGregor, 'Industry and commerce in Anglo-Scandinavian York', in Hall (ed.), *Viking age York*, pp. 53, 56.

attraction to St Cuthbert's community. They had, after all, been wandering through the north for many years in an attempt to find a secure home, and their long stay at Chester-le-Street, only six miles from Durham, makes it more than likely that they knew of the defensive potential of the peninsula site.[19] Several promontory sites were used throughout the Anglo-Saxon period primarily as fortified *burhs*, the most well-known, such as Malmesbury, Burpham and Shaftesbury, being those recorded in the Burghal Hidage. The strong natural fortifications of these sites made them more attractive to settlers because only a comparatively small amount of work was necessary to make them almost impregnable.[20]

Furthermore, Uchtred, the heir to the Northumbrian earldom and, as the son-in-law of Bishop Aldhun, the natural protector and patron of the community of St Cuthbert, had perhaps some influence over the choice of the site. The chronicler Symeon recounts how, under his guidance, the whole population from the River Coquet to the Tees rallied round and cleared trees so that dwellings could be erected and a church built.[21] This operation, reminiscent as it is of those levies raised by the earls of Northumbria to defend the north against Scottish invasions during the eleventh century, seems out of all proportion to the needs of a small religious community. Uchtred's eagerness to help the community to settle on the peninsula undoubtedly had some religious fervour and conviction behind it; but above all he probably wanted to establish an impregnable stronghold, a military headquarters to replace Bamburgh as the centre of Northumbrian resistance to the incursions of the Danes or the Scots. As K. C. Bayley puts it, 'Uchtred's activity and impressing of all the inhabitants suggests the foundation of Durham was due not to supernatural causes but to the military requirements of the Northumbrian earldom.' Perhaps, as Carver suggests, 'its origin could therefore be seen as much in the political strategy of the region as in the provision of a haven for its clergy'.[22]

[19] Laurence, p. 9; Symeon, *HistEcclesDun*, p. 70.

[20] M. Biddle and D. Hill, 'Late Saxon planned towns', *Antiquaries Journal*, 51 (1971), 70–85; J. M. Hassall and D. Hill, 'Pont de l'Arche: Frankish influences on the West Saxon burh?', *Archaeological Journal*, 127 (1970), 188–95; H. R. Loyn, *Anglo-Saxon England and the Norman Conquest* (London, 1962), p. 132.

[21] Symeon, *HistEcclesDun*, pp. 80–1.

[22] *VCH Durham*, vol. 2, p. 134; Dobson, *Durham Priory*, p. 23; Carver, 'Early medieval Durham', p. 16.

However, a town could not grow from fortifications alone, as the failure of the Alfredian fort of Pilton in Devon illustrates graphically. 'In the intervals between wars, a town could flourish only if there was a living to be made by craftsmen and traders', a flourishing local economy going further than 'relations with the castle garrison', as Beresford has demonstrated in his work on new town plantations.[23] Durham succeeded because it had more to offer its settlers than a good defensive site and a well-fortified enclosure. A network of small agricultural communities surrounding Durham provided enough surplus commodities to sell to both the castle garrison and the religious community; they in turn found a profitable local outlet for their goods. Some of the agricultural workers from the region would probably come to live in the place where they could see that their products would be in demand. Once Durham became the marketing centre for the region, its inhabitants would be able to diversify from purely agricultural production to more specialised manufacturing trades and service industries. They could live and trade, secure in the knowledge that they would find protection within the fortified *burh* should an attack come from Danes or Scots. Undoubtedly the presence of St Cuthbert's community and the shrine of the saint also gave a stimulus to economic growth. Both monasteries and castles attracted a steady stream of visitors, such as pilgrims, sanctuary-seekers, litigants, tenants or house servants. The Saxon town of Bury St Edmunds had to be enlarged to cope with the increased flow of pilgrims. Furthermore, monasteries actively encouraged urban growth and promoted trade outside their walls. At St Albans it was the tradition of the Benedictine abbey that Abbot Wulsig had established the market and provided building materials for settlers in the late tenth century. Pilgrim centres such as Canterbury were the goal of medieval tourists, who also required accommodation and, in particular, the services of the victualling trade; and from the pilgrim trade and the needs of the church, fairs could also develop.[24]

Nonetheless, a peninsula site did impose major restrictions on

[23] M. Biddle, 'Towns', in D. M. Wilson (ed.), *The archaeology of Anglo-Saxon England* (Cambridge, 1976), p. 137; S. Reynolds, *An introduction to the history of English medieval towns* (Oxford, 1977), p. 32; M. W. Beresford, *New towns of the middle ages* (London, 1967), p. 181; Loyn noted that only eight of Alfred's *burhs* reached municipal status in the middle ages: Loyn, *Anglo-Saxon England*, p. 132.

[24] Reynolds, *English medieval towns*, pp. 20, 41; Beresford, *New towns*, pp. 130, 326; H. C. Darby, *The Domesday geography of Eastern England* (Cambridge, 1971), pp. 197–9.

urban growth simply because of the limited amount of space
available for building; it also made communications with the
neighbouring countryside rather difficult. In an attempt to
overcome these handicaps, Durham's market place, and its
associated accommodation for traders, seems to have developed at
an early stage across the narrow neck of the peninsula; as such, it
was easily accessible from the north-eastern road into Durham,
the landward side of the peninsula.[25] The river formed an effective
barrier on all other sides and while it could be forded at some
points, there was no bridge across the river until Bishop Flambard
built the Old Bridge *c.* 1120. Nor was the river navigable to
Durham. It cannot have been easy transporting any bulky or
heavy goods to sell or to buy in Durham except by using the
north-eastern route. This limited communications system around
the peninsula probably indicates that the Durham market
depended almost exclusively on local trade rather than on long-
distance enterprise, at least in the eleventh century. Consequently,
Durham never developed into a large or wealthy commercial
centre as did its neighbours, York and Newcastle-upon-Tyne,
sited as they were with good inland communications and easy
access to the sea.

THE GROWTH AND DEVELOPMENT OF DURHAM TO *c.* 1250

The early growth of the town at Durham after the arrival of St
Cuthbert's community is most clearly seen in the building work
on the peninsula, a theme which dominates the Durham references
in the chronicle evidence. The fortification of the site demonstrates
the preoccupation of its bishops with military events in the north,
while the increasing number of religious buildings surrounding St
Cuthbert's great church shows the growing wealth and prestige
of the religious community. However, this comparative richness
of evidence for the peninsula should not blind us to developments
around it, although these are more poorly documented. Here a
genuine urban community was growing around the market place
and across the river, with its own churches and chapels, its
wooden houses, probably subject to frequent fire damage and
vulnerable to attack, and a complex street system. However, the
growth of any town should not be measured merely in terms of
its buildings, but also in the diversification of its trade, in its

[25] See appendix 1, map 3.

wealth and its status in relation to other medieval towns. These features are more difficult to quantify for Durham in the early medieval period, but an attempt will be made here to evaluate the available evidence for urban growth before 1250 and to analyse the reasons for Durham's success as a new town in a northern England which was, as yet, barely urbanised.

The fortification of Durham was obviously crucial to the growth of the town, for traders as much as clergy needed a guarantee of security and the promise of protection in this lawless border region. Much of the surviving documentary evidence for the events of the eleventh century revolves around the efforts made to turn Durham into an impregnable fortress capable of withstanding Scottish attacks. The main source of this information is the chronicle attributed to Symeon, which, as has been mentioned already, was written in the early years of the twelfth century. Its accuracy, particularly in the matter of dating events, is obviously open to question, but lack of any comparative material means that Symeon is used, perforce, as the basis of the study of the eleventh-century town. According to the chronicler, the first concern of Durham's founders was to improve the natural defences of the peninsula by ringing it with a defensive wall. Symeon's earliest reference to Durham's walls is dated 1006, when they were being severely tested by a Scottish siege. They passed with flying colours; the siege failed and, as the chronicler describes with relish, the heads of the slain, which had been washed by four women, were carried to Durham and placed on poles around the circuit of the walls (*per circuitum murorum*).[26] This last phrase suggests that these early walls were not simply thrown across the neck of the peninsula, its most vulnerable point, but that they were more extensive and formed a defensive enclosure. Excavations have not yet located the line of these fortifications, and they may have been little more than a timber palisade crowning an earthen rampart, as was usual at this period.[27] Later eleventh-century work seems to have concentrated on extending the circuit of the walls until they ringed the whole peninsula, with the probable replacement of any timber defences with stone.[28]

---

[26] Symeon, *De Obsessione Dunelmi*, in *Symeonis Monachi Opera Omnia*, vol. 1, Rolls Series (1882), pp. 215–6; Offler, *Medieval historians*, p. 10; Gransden, *Historical writing in England*, p. 120.

[27] H. L. Turner, *Town defences in England and Wales* (London, 1971), p. 52.

[28] Symeon, *HistEcclesDun, Continuatio Prima*, p. 140.

These walls, whether constructed of timber or by now of stonework, were apparently enough to enable Durham to withstand a second Scottish attack in 1040; but during the insurrection of 1069 after William I had sent his representative, Robert Cumin, to quell unrest in the north, the rebels did break through the defences.[29] Most significantly, the chronicler relates how the gates were breached in this rebellion. They were the weak points in the defences, and once they fell a massacre of the Durham garrison was inevitable: some 700 men were enclosed in the narrow peninsular area from which escape would be almost impossible. It is more than likely, however, that the events of 1069 were not just a reflection of the shortcomings of military design of this period; it is probable that the rebels had assistance from inside the fortified area, perhaps from townspeople employed there, because there was widespread opposition to Cumin, according to the chronicler.[30] This episode may have led to the strengthening of the gates in the walls, in particular the North Gate which guarded the main approach road to the peninsula. By the time the monk Laurence described it in the middle of the twelfth century, it seems to have had its own barbican; the approach to the gate from the north was steep, and the different land levels on each side of the gate made it more difficult to attack.[31]

Laurence's contemporary account of the walls illustrates how complex and sophisticated was the arrangement of internal and external defences. The external wall contained a south-west gate, an east gate with a steep path descending to the river, and the mighty North Gate.[32] Walls ran down from the south-east and south-west sides of the castle motte to connect the innermost defences with the circuit of the external walls. Internal walls protected the castle enclosure from the *placea*, the area between the castle and the cathedral, and another wall, probably the work of Bishop Flambard, ran along the east side of the *placea* from the castle to the apse of the church.[33] According to the late-twelfth-

---

[29] Symeon, *HistEcclesDun*, pp. 90–1, 98–9.

[30] For the background to this rebellion, which may not have been associated directly with Cumin himself, see B. Wilkinson, 'Northumbrian separatism in 1065 and 1066', *Bulletin of the John Rylands Library*, 23 (1939), 504–26; D. Whitelock, 'The dealings of the kings of England with Northumbria in the 10th and 11th centuries', in P. Clemoes (ed.), *The Anglo-Saxons* (London, 1959), pp. 70–88; Symeon, *HistEcclesDun*, pp. 98–9.

[31] Laurence, p. 10.   [32] See appendix 1, map 7.

[33] Laurence, pp. 9–10. According to the continuator of Symeon's chronicle, Flambard strengthened the walls *a cancello ecclesiae ad arcem usque castelli producta murum construxit*

century chronicler, Reginald, these walls dominated the view for
travellers who approached the peninsula. Wherever one wanted
to travel in the city, he said, one had to pass through the walls,
beneath battlements with their watching guards.[34] The sense of
being within a fortress town must have been very strong for
inhabitants and visitors alike in early medieval Durham.

The insurrection of 1069 and the fall of the town to rebel forces
brought about an important improvement in the fortifications,
and one which had a dramatic impact on the topography of the
town. It led directly to the planning and construction of a castle,
a castle built not only to deter Scottish attacks but also to
symbolise the re-establishment of royal authority in the north.
Building work began in *c.* 1072 and the castle was completed
about twenty-eight years later. The king delegated the supervision
of the project to Bishop Walcher and it was financed with
revenues appropriated from Waltham Abbey.[35] The castle was
built on a site overlooking the North Gate and the more
vulnerable land approaches to the peninsula, within the military
zone of the town. Consequently, no domestic buildings had to be
demolished to make room for the castle, as happened in Lincoln
or Norwich, for example.[36] The motte was probably raised first,
and excavation work has shown it may have been partly natural,
but it was supplemented with earth taken from the south ditch. It
is composed of yellow sand at the bottom and then layers of
tipped material, with brown sand alternating with brown earth
and topped with turf. It may have been crowned with a rampart
at first, and later with a wooden tower.[37]

Whatever the appearance of the castle was in the late eleventh
century, Laurence's mid-twelfth-century account describes the
motte as being surmounted by a round stone structure enclosing

longitudine: Symeon, *HistEcclesDun, Continuatio Prima*, p. 140. For the dates of the
bishops of Durham, see appendix 3.

[34] Reginald, *St Cuthbert*, pp. 211, 233; Reginald, *St Godric*, p. 334.

[35] Symeon, *HistEcclesDun.*, pp. 113–14; Symeon, *HistRegum*, pp. 199–200; *Regesta
Regum Anglo-Normannorum, 1100–1135*, ed. C. Johnson and H. A. Cronne (Oxford,
1956), p. 9.

[36] In Lincoln, 166 houses were demolished for the building of a castle and 98 were
demolished in Norwich: Reynolds, *English medieval towns*, p. 43; C. Platt, *The English
medieval town* (London, 1976), p. 37; H. C. Darby, 'Domesday England', in H. C.
Darby (ed.), *A new historical geography of England* (Cambridge, 1973), pp. 71–2.

[37] G. Simpson and V. Hartley, 'Excavation below Bishop Tunstal's Chapel, Durham
Castle', *Antiquaries Journal*, 33 (1953), 56–64; C. E. Whiting, 'The castle of Durham
in the middle ages', *ArchAel*, 4th ser., 10 (1933), 124, 128; D. C. Douglas, *William the
Conqueror* (London, 1966), p. 216.

a drum of wood, perhaps similar to the timber towers at Abinger
and South Mimms or the shell-keeps at Lewes and Farnham.[38] He
mentions that the castle had its own gateway and a drawbridge
over a ditch on its south side so that it could be completely
isolated from the rest of the *placea* and the outer bailey.[39] Within
the inner walls, the castle buildings, in a triangular layout, were
described by Laurence as two great palaces with porticoes, a
chapel supported on six columns, and the well. W. T. Jones,
writing in the *Victoria County History*, claimed that portions of
Laurence's palaces are to be found incorporated in the existing
ranges of the castle. The foundations of earlier buildings have
come to light from time to time in the castle courtyard, and the
position of the well was rediscovered in 1904, but no systematic
investigation of the domestic buildings of the early medieval
fortress has yet been undertaken.[40]

Any survey of military building on the Durham peninsula
shows clearly, despite the scarcity of the evidence, that the
pioneering work was complete by the end of the eleventh
century. The twelfth century seems to have been a period of
consolidation, when the existing defences were improved,
strengthened or repaired. During the twelfth and thirteenth
centuries, efforts were made to convert the castle from a purely
military stronghold into a comfortable residence and administrative headquarters for the bishop. This move compares with the
fashion in castle-building elsewhere in England. At Windsor, for
example, Henry II added halls and offices for the accommodation
of his court in *c.* 1175, and in both Dover and Orford castles the
keeps were made into more sophisticated accommodation suited
to royal visitors.[41] A fire which destroyed part of the north wing
of the castle during Bishop Puiset's episcopacy enabled him to
redesign and improve the castle buildings in the late twelfth
century, and the so-called Norman Gallery may date from this
period.[42] But this trend towards increasing domestic comfort
with only minor alterations to the defences may also reflect the

---

[38] Laurence, pp. 11–12; R. A. Brown, *English castles*, 3rd edn (London, 1976), pp. 32,
35–6; P. Johnson, *The National Trust book of British castles* (London, 1978), pp. 48–52.

[39] See appendix 1, map 8.   [40] *VCH Durham*, vol. 3, pp. 65, 69, 70.

[41] *VCH Durham*, vol. 3, p. 65; *Boldon Buke*, ed. W. Greenwell, Surtees Society, vol. 25
(1852), appendix, pp. xvii, xxi, xxii; Johnson, *British castles*, p. 50; C. Platt, *The castle
in medieval England and Wales* (London, 1982), pp. 36, 43.

[42] Reginald, *St Godric*, p. 182; *Scrip Tres*, p. 12; Whiting, 'The castle of Durham', p. 123.
For the dates of Puiset's episcopacy, see appendix 3.

very success of Durham's fortifications. Durham soon gained a reputation for invulnerability in the early medieval period. The castle and walls withstood a siege lasting four days in 1080. When William Cumin usurped the see of Durham between 1141 and 1148 he was able to hold the castle with a relatively small garrison against the forces of the incoming bishop and his supporters.[43] It was a tribute to the strength of the defences as much as anything that only an alliance between the earl of Northumbria, the bishop and many local gentry managed to unseat Cumin from Durham castle. Enemy forces always found it easier and safer to by-pass Durham castle, as the Scots did in 1136 and 1138. The battlegrounds of the north moved away from Durham and consequently the military significance of Durham's defences gradually diminished in the twelfth and early thirteenth centuries.

The effect of the fortification of Durham on urban development is more difficult to gauge from the sources. The fact that Durham was used as the base for military campaigns against the Scots in the eleventh century must have increased the risk of attack on the town and the possibility of an interruption of local trade. Frequent Scottish raids probably led to great feelings of insecurity as well as danger to life and limb from armies and fire damage. An influx of soldiers, such as in 1069 or in 1141, might bring in its wake welcome extra trade to the town, but it also brought destruction. According to the – admittedly biased – chronicle accounts, William Cumin's soldiers conducted house-to-house searches and fired many of the buildings in the town.[44] However, all was not gloom and doom for the inhabitants of the fortified town, for they were guaranteed protection within walls strong enough to withstand many punitive raids by the Scots in the twelfth century. Further, the extensive building operations on the fortifications would provide employment for many townsmen, and military activity probably gave an impetus to service industries. On balance, it seems that Durham's development into a military headquarters for the region was an encouragement to urban growth.

The impact made on the physical appearance of Durham by the growth of St Cuthbert's community was, like the military

---

[43] Symeon, *HistEcclesDun*, pp. 116–18; Laurence, p. 3; Symeon, *HistEcclesDun, Continuatio Prima*, p. 152; Young, *William Cumin*.

[44] Symeon, *HistEcclesDun, Continuatio Prima*, p. 159; Symeon, *HistEcclesDun, Continuatio Altera*, p. 164.

developments, confined to the peninsula area. The site which had been cleared by Uchtred's levies was to accommodate religious buildings as well as fortifications, and the construction of the two went hand-in-hand. The building of a church to the glory of God and to house the remains of their revered saint was of prime importance to the followers of St Cuthbert; a temporary church built of wattles or boughs was speedily replaced by the *Alba Ecclesia* and then by the *Ecclesia Major* which was dedicated in 998.[45] Symeon is again the only documentary source for these developments, but given that his main purpose in writing was to narrate the history of the church at Durham, perhaps fewer doubts should be raised over these references. The *Ecclesia Major* seems to have been the first and, for many years, the only stone building in Durham. However, it too was felt to be inadequate for the needs of the growing community; and shortly after the reorganisation of the community under the Benedictine rule in 1083, and before the castle had been completed, work began on the great cathedral which was to dominate Durham's skyline. The bishop and prior together laid its first stone in a ceremony witnessed by the monks and thus inaugurated work on a project which was to continue throughout the following century.[46]

The peninsula also contained accommodation for the religious. Before 1083, the members of St Cuthbert's community were secular clerks and each one had a house (*mansio*) in which he could live with his family.[47] It was probably in one of these houses, situated next to the west end of the church and called the bishop's house, that Robert Cumin was burnt alive in 1069.[48] After the founding of the Benedictine monastery by Bishop William de St Calais, an act which was by no means welcomed enthusiastically by the secular clerks, who were to be separated from their families and 'reformed' under vows of obedience to the rule of St Benedict,[49] this accommodation was reorganised. Land was set aside for an enclosed precinct to the south of the cathedral church

---

[45] Symeon, *HistEcclesDun*, pp. 79, 81–2. But Cooper thinks the date should be 995: Cooper, 'Dates of the bishops of Durham', p. 131.

[46] Symeon, *HistEcclesDun*, pp. 120–2, 128–9; Symeon, *HistEcclesDun, Continuatio Prima*, p. 139; Symeon, *HistRegum*, p. 260; *VCH Durham*, vol. 2, p. 7; H. H. E. Craster, 'The patrimony of St Cuthbert', *EHR*, 69 (1954), 177–99; W. Greenwell, 'Durham Cathedral', *TAASDN*, 2 (1869–79), 182–8.   [47] Symeon, *HistEcclesDun*, p. 81.

[48] Symeon, *HistEcclesDun*, pp. 98–9; Symeon, *HistRegum*, p. 187.

[49] The seculars were presented with an ultimatum to become monks or to leave the community. Most elected to leave: see Meehan, 'Outsiders, insiders and property', p. 45.

and communal facilities such as the refectory, built between 1088 and 1093, and the chapter house, built during the episcopacy of Bishop Geoffrey Rufus, were provided.[50]

These religious buildings were somewhat peripheral to the growth of Durham's urban area, as were the fortifications, but they had a direct effect on town life. The tomb of St Cuthbert attracted visitors from a wide area, such as the monks who travelled from New Minster and from Sherborne in the 1050s, attracted by stories of the saint's miraculous powers.[51] These pilgrims would need accommodation and feeding during their stay and this seems to have been provided by the inns or guest houses which emerged around the peninsula. Among the many miracles recounted by the early-twelfth-century chroniclers is one in which a Durham guest house, perhaps one of those catering for pilgrims, is mentioned. The story is in the long tradition of St Cuthbert's supposed antipathy towards women. A woman had attempted to enter St Cuthbert's church, but as soon as she set foot in the cemetery she was repelled by a violent wind and, gravely ill, she was taken *ad hospitium*.[52] The accommodation for pilgrims, including the hospital of St Giles at Kepier to the north of the town, is also described by the chronicler Reginald at the end of the twelfth century, along with the sights to be seen in and around the cathedral and the attractions offered to pilgrims in Durham.[53] This early form of tourist trade obviously brought great opportunities for Durham's shopkeepers, particularly the victuallers.

However, religious building work was not strictly limited to the peninsula, for the growing urban community was not served by the monks and their monastery church alone. There are references to parish churches and other religious buildings in Durham in the surviving twelfth-century charters as well as the chronicles. The best-documented example is the hospital and church dedicated to St Giles, the popular guest house for pilgrims. It was founded by Bishop Flambard in 1112, and it lay alongside the main road which led north-east from the peninsula. It may have been the original focus for the settlement called St Giles' Borough.[54] It was in this church that Bishop William de St

---

[50] Symeon, *HistEcclesDun*, p. 128; *VCH Durham*, vol. 2, p. 11. For the dates of the bishops of Durham, see appendix 3.   [51] Dobson, *Durham Priory*, p. 25.

[52] Symeon, *HistEcclesDun*, p. 95; *VCH Durham*, vol. 3, p. 8.

[53] Reginald, *St Cuthbert*, pp. 252, 271; Reginald, *St Godric*, p. 462.

[54] See chapter 2, pp. 44, 47. For its position, see appendix 1, map 3.

Barbara took refuge during William Cumin's forcible occupation of the see in the 1140s. According to the monastic chronicler's account of this incident, Cumin laid siege to the church, drove out the bishop and his supporters and, apparently in revenge, set fire to the hospital and its church, totally destroying them and the settlement nearby. The hospital was rebuilt after 1153 by Bishop Puiset, whose motives were nicely summarised by Dr Scammell as a combination of 'piety and some care for public health'. The new site chosen for Puiset's hospital was by the riverside, a little removed from the urban area, selected perhaps in an attempt to distance the hospital from any trouble which might in future embroil the town. It had its own chapel, a dormitory, infirmary, hall and *curia* where confessions were held. Of its thirteen brethren, six were chaplains, living the common life under a master and a prior appointed by the bishop. As part of its endowment, Puiset gave the borough of St Giles to the hospital. The parish church of St Giles was rebuilt during the same episcopacy, probably in its original position alongside the main road through the borough, to serve the growing urban community.[55]

The other Durham parish churches do not seem to have played such a dramatic role in the political history of the town and consequently they are not so well documented. The first surviving reference to St Nicholas' Church in the market place occurs in a copy of a charter, which Professor Offler has judged to be genuine in form, bearing the name of Bishop Geoffrey Rufus. The bishop granted his church of St Nicholas and Old Durham to Alverdus, the clerk, which indicates that the church was in existence by the early twelfth century at least and already it had an association with land in Old Durham which became its glebe.[56] In the late twelfth century, the chronicler Reginald refers to a church of St Mary within the town where boys were sent to learn their letters and to be well versed in psalms, hymns and prayers. This church could have been either of the two churches dedicated to St Mary which were situated in the Bailey, close to the priory itself, within the military zone of Durham.[57] Reginald describes a town which,

---

[55] *Durham Episcopal Charters*, pp. 64–5; Symeon, *HistEcclesDun, Continuatio Prima*, p. 159; *Memorials of St Giles, Durham*, ed. J. Barmby, Surtees Society, vol. 95 (1896), pp. 197–206; Scammell, *Hugh du Puiset*, p. 107; *VCH Durham*, vol. 2, pp. 11, 111.

[56] Reg.II, fol.184v; *Durham Episcopal Charters*, p. 126. See appendix 1, map 3 for the position of Old Durham relative to the town.

[57] Reginald, *St Godric*, pp. 59–60.

under successive bishops, had been converted into a centre of pilgrimage as well as the administrative and ecclesiastical headquarters for the bishopric. The magnificence of the cathedral with its many shrines attracted visitors to the city and thus increased its trade. There were churches catering for the growing parish communities and a hospital housing the poor and needy as well as the pilgrims. Bishops such as Flambard and Puiset, in particular, made Durham their capital city and seat of government, a small-scale Westminster worthy of the importance they felt their office held.

The growth of the town and its population probably complemented the ecclesiastical and military building on the peninsula, but it passes almost unrecorded in the surviving documentary evidence for the eleventh century. The market place is first mentioned in Symeon's account of the Scottish siege of 1040. The enemy, suffering great losses, was repelled by the inhabitants themselves and, it was said, the heads of the slain were raised up on stakes in the market place (*in forum*).[58] There is no clue in this chronicle evidence as to the position of the eleventh-century market place, but two possible sites can be advanced. Was the market held in the area between the church of St Cuthbert and the fortified enclosure on the peninsula, later called the *placea*? It is known that there were many houses here in the early twelfth century when Bishop Flambard cleared the site, but there is no mention of a market place alongside the domestic housing at this period.[59] Furthermore, it is unlikely that the bishops would have encouraged the growth of a market at the heart of what was the military zone of Durham, particularly when there was a threat of infiltration by the Scots. On the other hand, there are examples of market places being sited at the approaches to monastic churches and precincts in towns such as Bury St Edmunds, which raises at least the possibility that an early marketing area in Durham may have occupied part of the *placea* for a time in the eleventh century.

A second possibility, and perhaps the more likely one, was that Durham market place occupied roughly the same position it holds today, on the narrow neck of land joining the peninsula to the surrounding countryside, beneath the protecting walls of the castle. This position is comparable with the market places of other

[58] Symeon, *HistEcclesDun*, pp. 90–1.
[59] See p. 34; Symeon, *HistEcclesDun*, *Continuatio Prima*, p. 140; appendix 1, map 3.

towns in unsettled border areas, towns such as Alnwick or Ludlow, where trade flourished 'in the shadow of the castle' and received the protection and patronage of a garrison while being outside the fortified area.[60] Durham possessed only one *forum* throughout the middle ages, despite Prior Bertram's pious hope that he might acquire a licence to hold a market in Elvet Borough, and consequently the market place and the urban area immediately surrounding it was the centre of economic activity in the town.[61]

This trading monopoly is reflected in the prosperity of the Bishop's Borough by the early twelfth century. The borough's burgesses had to pay a fine of £5 to the king in 1130, which gives some indication of its estimated resources. Moreover, the borough was perhaps the first to receive a limited amount of written privileges from its overlord. A charter was obtained from Bishop Puiset in *c.* 1179, probably at no little cost to the burgesses, whereby they were awarded all the rights and customs of the inhabitants of Newcastle-upon-Tyne, customs which contained a range of mainly trading and judicial rights. Not all of these customs were relevant to the Durham situation; there were, for example, provisions concerning cargoes coming into the Tyne, but the Newcastle customs were the model to which local overlords looked for guidance when they decided to award a limited measure of independence to their urban tenants. Newcastle spawned a family of charters including those for Durham, Wearmouth and Gateshead, just as the York customs were used by towns further south.[62] Many of the trading privileges enumerated in the Newcastle customs, such as the exemptions from certain tolls and the trading monopolies bestowed on those who had a right to call themselves burgesses, would be of some economic advantage to the borough's inhabitants, as was the power to hold their own borough court to deal with cases concerning the burgess community. But the privileges of burgage tenure and burgess status outlined in the Newcastle customs did not confer complete political independence or the right to self-government on the borough's inhabitants. Nor was there

---

[60] Conzen, *Alnwick*, p. 29; Platt, *English medieval town*, pp. 27, 33.

[61] Cart.II, fol.251; see p. 29.

[62] Pipe Roll, 31 Hen.I (1130), printed in *Boldon Buke*, appendix, p. ii; Reg.I, part ii, fol.3; *VCH Durham*, vol. 3, pp. 54–5; *British borough charters, 1042–1216*, ed. A. Ballard (Cambridge, 1913), p. xlii; Reynolds, *English medieval towns*, pp. 98–9.

anything particularly startling or new about the content of the charter. The fact that the inhabitants of the borough had been described as 'burgesses' in 1130 suggests that it was merely a case of confirming in writing existing unwritten privileges.

The other Durham boroughs are first mentioned in twelfth-century documents. In a charter purporting to date from the episcopacy of Bishop William de St Calais, but which Professor Offler considers, for reasons of content and palaeography, could not have been drawn up before *c.* 1107, the bishop granted the convent 'Ælvet, so that the monks may have forty houses for merchants (*mercatorum domos*) for their own use'. Tenure of these houses was associated with the duty of contributing to the repair of Durham's wall.[63] Although this charter is not authentic, Offler's opinion is that it fairly represents what the monastery could claim to possess at the end of the eleventh century. It is most likely that the reference here is to the part of Durham later known as Old Elvet, the area surrounding the parish church of St Oswald. Apart from the somewhat vague and problematic reference to Elvet in the *Anglo-Saxon Chronicle* and the discovery of Anglo-Saxon stones in its church, this is the earliest documentary evidence of settlement to the east of the peninsula, settlement which had commercial possibilities.[64] Elvet may have been one of the parts of Durham which was fired by William Cumin's troops in the 1140s, although the chronicle account of the incident does not make it clear whether it was Elvet or the borough to the west of the river (the Old Borough) which was under attack.[65]

A new urban area adjoining Old Elvet, the borough later called New Elvet, was developed by Bishop Puiset, probably as a direct result of the construction of a bridge across the river to the east of the peninsula.[66] This expensive improvement in communications between the Bishop's Borough and the east bank of the River

---

[63] *qui prorsus ab omni episcopi servitio sint liberi nisi forte maceries civitatis sit reparanda, ad quam non maius quam de tot civitatis mercatoribus opus ab eis exigatur*: *Durham Episcopal Charters*, pp. 6–15; for the dates of the bishops of Durham, see appendix 3.

[64] R. J. Cramp, 'A cross from St Oswald's church, Durham, and its stylistic relationships', *DUJ*, 57 (1966), 119–24; R. J. Cramp, 'The pre-conquest sculptural tradition in Durham', in *Medieval art and architecture at Durham Cathedral*, BAA conference transactions for 1977 (London, 1980), pp. 1–9.

[65] *partem quoque burgi que ad monachorum jus pertinebat igni tradiderunt*: Symeon, *HistEcclesDun, Continuatio Prima*, p. 159.

[66] Puiset *fecit pontem de Elvete, et Burgum similiter*: *ScripTres*, p. 12.

Wear suggests that the bishop saw considerable trading potential in extending his authority over the eastern side of the bridge. In so doing, he did not hesitate to usurp any rights the priory had over this area, a situation he did not rectify until almost the end of his life. In his restoration charter, Puiset transferred all his authority over the borough in *Elvetehalge* to the priory, giving it undisputed lordship and the right to take all profits. Subsequently, Prior Bertram was able to issue two charters to his Elvet burgesses which delineated the boundaries of their borough and set the limits on their independence.[67] They were to be exempt from all customs, exactions and aids; and they were also granted one of the most important marks of burgage tenure, the right to dispose of their land without consulting the overlord. However, in return they were to pay an annual rent to the priory and to grind corn at the abbey's mill, two clear signs of the dominant lordship of the priory. Although the priory was unwilling to surrender any political power to its urban tenants, it was more than ready to encourage trade and economic growth, in the hopes of competing successfully with the Bishop's Borough. It was a measure of the buoyancy of trade in this borough that the prior tried, albeit unsuccessfully, to negotiate with the bishop for permission to hold a second market in Durham. 'If we, through the grace and authorisation of our lord the bishop, may obtain a market or market day in the borough, then all rights which pertain to them will be ours';[68] it was not just a matter of rights and privileges, of course, but also of financial profits.

The priory's borough to the west of the peninsula, the Old Borough, offered a complete contrast to the flourishing economies of the Bishop's Borough and the Elvet area. It seems to have provided no commercial competition at any stage, although there are some indications that it once supported a thriving agricultural community, perhaps comparable to Elvethall manor in Old Elvet. The surviving late-thirteenth- and early-fourteenth-century rent rolls and rentals of the almoner, one of Durham Priory's officers who was most active in the local land market, mention the sacrist's house or stable, the terrar's house built of stone, and hay

---

[67] The borough extended *a via quae jacet juxta domum Abbatis de Novo Monasterio ex aquilonali parte versus Scaltoc*: Symeon, *HistEcclesDun, Continuatio Prima*, p. 159; *ScripTres*, p. 12; 3.1.Pont.4; *Feodarium Dunelm*, pp. 198–99n; *VCH Durham*, vol. 3, pp. 13, 61; Cart.II, fol.251.   [68] Cart.II, fol.251.

barns and dovecots at the south end of South Street, all reminiscent of the Elvethall manor buildings.[69] The fact that the priory named this borough the 'Old Borough', clearly differentiating it from their 'New Borough' of Elvet, and indeed from the Bishop's Borough, which was occasionally referred to as the 'New Borough', implies an older settlement, but the surviving documentary references do not help to date its foundation with any degree of accuracy.[70] In a charter which has been dated to about 1128, Bishop Flambard restored *terram ultra pontem Dunelmi*, the land on the other side of Durham's bridge (the bridge he had built), to the monks. According to Henry I's confirmation of this charter in 1129, the land was valued at only £1.18s. per annum, a valuation which probably relates to the rental income the priory could expect from its tenants there.[71] This implies a community of little wealth in comparison with the burgesses of the Bishop's Borough, and the borough was certainly in decline by the late thirteenth century, when the almoner was administering it on behalf of the priory. There is no surviving evidence that the priory ever gave their Old Borough tenants any form of charter of privileges, but later-medieval sources show that the relationship between the priory and the Old Borough inhabitants resembled closely the situation in Elvet Borough.

Yet it was this less prosperous borough which, somewhat surprisingly, received the first direct link with the Bishop's Borough in the form of a bridge connecting the east end of Crossgate with Silver Street in c. 1120. The Old Bridge, an expensive and probably an impressive construction of stone, may have been one of the earliest stone bridges in England. London's wooden bridge over the Thames at Southwark, for example, was not replaced by a stone bridge until work which had been started in 1176 was completed in 1209: this may not be an altogether fair comparison, however, given the difference in scale of the London project.[72] The Old Bridge in Durham may have been built to

---

[69] See, for example, Alm. rent rolls. *c.* 1290/91, 1313/14, *c.* 1315. For a brief guide to the officers of Durham Priory and their duties, see appendix 4.

[70] See Cart.iv, fol.90; *Feodarium Dunelm*, pp. 191–5.

[71] 2.1.Pont.1; *Durham Episcopal Charters*, p. 107; 2.1.Reg.2; *Feodarium Dunelm*, p. 145n.

[72] *Diversas Wiri fluminis ripas continuavit structo de lapide magni operis ponte arcuato*: Symeon, *HistEcclesDun, Continuatio Prima*, p. 140; M. B. Honeybourne, 'The pre-Norman bridge of London', in A. E. J. Hollaender and W. Kellaway (eds.), *Studies in London history* (London, 1969), p. 17. The bridge was fortified: see W. T. Jones, 'The walls and towers of Durham', *DUJ*, 22–3 (1920–3), 6 parts; Whiting, 'The castle of Durham', p. 126; *VCH Durham*, vol. 3, p. 64.

encourage traders and local people from the surrounding area to come to the Durham market: a rise in their numbers would increase the tolls the bishop could take on goods entering and leaving the market. Possibly the building of this bridge a generation or so before Elvet Bridge reflects the dominance of the north-south route, running to the west of the peninsula, in the local network of roads. The construction of these bridges also seems to have led to the development of trade around the bridgeheads: shops and stalls were built on prime commercial sites on and around the bridges themselves while even the arches were later leased for storage space.[73]

These documentary references to Durham's boroughs, together with those concerning St Giles mentioned earlier, imply that by 1200 at least Durham was a sizeable urban community, composed of several independent and as yet physically separate units. It is likely that during the course of the twelfth and thirteenth centuries, years of what seems to have been rapid growth, these distinct entities grew together as the bridges provided a means of easy access between them and as the population increased. Settlement would spread gradually along the roads, blurring the borough boundaries. This gradual integration is marked by one important document, *le Convenit* of 1229, which standardised weights and measures in all boroughs and ensured that offenders would be treated equally wherever the offence had been committed.[74] This agreement reflected the recognition that there was a need for a jurisdictional framework which had a wider compass than that of the individual borough courts. It also confirmed the importance of trade in providing a stimulus to reform; the same imperative which had prompted the overlords to issue charters of privileges to towns led them to present a united front for the sake of good trading relations. Without this co-operation between the overlords, there was a danger that Durham would have fragmented into many small rival communities, each trying to survive without an adequate economic base and lacking any corporate identity.

One clear sign of a flourishing urban community at Durham is the number of buildings erected for communal use or for trading purposes by the early thirteenth century. Durham had a mint by the middle of the twelfth century which was Bishop Geoffrey

[73] *ScripTres*, p. 12; Beresford, *New towns*, pp. 112–19.
[74] *Feodarium Dunelm*, pp. 212–17; *ScripTres*, p. 37; *VCH Durham*, vol. 3, p. 13.

Rufus' reward for the political and military support he gave to King Stephen.[75] There were several mills, such as the bishop's mill behind the street of Clayport and the priory's Scaltok Mill in Elvet, to which tenants owed their suit.[76] The priory had its own bakehouse in Elvet which was destroyed by Bishop Philip in the course of a quarrel with the monks in the middle of the thirteenth century.[77] Industry during this period was probably very small scale and cottage based. The Saddler Street excavations revealed artifacts and rubbish associated with shoe making or leather working, although a small pottery industry may have antedated this activity.[78] No doubt industry and trade in the town were much enhanced by the institution of the great St Cuthbert fairs, which are first mentioned during Flambard's episcopacy and may have started as a result of the translation of St Cuthbert's body in 1104.[79] In all these ways, the town was showing evidence of commercial life and growth before 1200.

Despite such glimpses of expansion, however, the problem of reconstructing any accurate picture of the early-medieval town itself remains intractable. While the documentary and visual evidence for the military and ecclesiastical buildings on the peninsula is copious, the sources for domestic buildings are poor indeed. Rescue archaeology, ahead of redevelopment, has given some tantalising indications of the physical appearance of the town. The Saddler Street excavations, for example, show a development of building styles and techniques as well as a change in the layout of the tenements. The earliest surviving wattle-and-daub houses were replaced with more sophisticated timber structures placed end-on to the street within regular tenement boundaries which persisted until 1974.[80] A vennel, the local name for a lane passing between tenements, was made next to these

[75] It may have been the most northerly mint in the twelfth century: *VCH Durham*, vol. 2, p. 11; Reynolds, *English medieval towns*, p. 34. There may even have been a temporary mint in Durham in the late eleventh century: *VCH Durham*, vol. 1, p. 259; *Boldon Buke*, p. 11.

[76] *Boldon Buke*, p. 1; *Feodarium Dunelm*, p. 199; see chapter 2, pp. 54–5.

[77] *furnos in Elvete subvertit...*: *ScripTres*, pp. 17–27; see chapter 3, p. 101. For the dates of the bishops of Durham, see appendix 3.

[78] Carver, 'Three Saxo-Norman tenements', p. 1.

[79] *VCH Durham*, vol. 3, p. 10.

[80] Carver, 'Three Saxo-Norman tenements', pp. 1–71. This continuity of tenement boundaries compares with York, where the tenement boundaries in Skeldergate remained more or less the same from the Anglo-Scandinavian period to the eighteenth century: Hall, 'Topography of Anglo-Scandinavian York', p. 36.

tenements, probably in the late twelfth or the early thirteenth centuries, and it was paved with stone. There was a rubbish pit next to the vennel which showed signs of cleaning and maintenance. Excavations along the river-side in New Elvet revealed that town houses had been built end-on to the street. A tentative dating to the early thirteenth century suggests that they may have been constructed after a river wall was built to prevent flooding in this part of the town. These houses contained privies as integral parts of their structure and their foundations, at least, were stone-based, although the likelihood is that stone gave way to timber above ground level.[81] Whether any of these excavated remains can be considered typical of the standard of domestic housing in early medieval Durham is, of course, impossible to determine.

For an urban community living in houses which were mainly of wood, and thatched with straw or ling, the greatest danger lay not in the flooding of the River Wear but in the fires which swept through parts of the town during this period. The archaeological evidence of repeated fires in buildings on the Saddler Street site may be associated simply with the natural hazards of the pottery trade; a fire which started in the town below the north side of the castle and swept over the battlements, damaging the castle buildings early in Puiset's episcopacy, may also have had a purely local cause.[82] But there may be more serious explanations for such damage. At this time, Durham was in an area which was considered lawless border territory, open to Scottish incursions or other opportunist raiders. The town itself became part of the battlefield when, as the chronicler related, William Cumin burnt down the boroughs of St Giles and possibly Elvet or the Old Borough in the 1140s. The parts he spared were fired by his opponents, so no townsmen would be immune from the devastation.[83] When a fine of £5 was levied from the Bishop's Borough in 1130, only £2 went to the royal treasury. The rest was remitted on account of the burning of the burgesses' houses.[84] Despite this danger, which was, after all, exacerbated by the choice of building materials, there seems to have been no policy

[81] Carver, 'Excavations in New Elvet', pp. 91–148.

[82] *Dunelmum saevae tempestatis incendium conflagravit, omniaque aedificia episcoporum castellaria depopulando concremavit, et civitatis moenia plus quam aliquo prius tempore omnia exurendo consumpsit*: Reginald, *St Godric*, p. 182; Reginald, *St Cuthbert*, pp. 82–3.

[83] Symeon, *HistEcclesDun, Continuatio Prima*, pp. 152–3; *VCH Durham*, vol. 2, p. 138.

[84] Pipe Roll, 31 Hen.I (1130), printed in *Boldon Buke*, appendix, p. ii.

to restrict the thatching of roofs near important public buildings or to encourage building with stone as there was in other towns, notably London.[85]

There is one record of what amounts to the slum clearance of buildings in Durham during this early period, although not, apparently, to make room for rebuilding or redevelopment. According to the chronicler, Bishop Flambard razed to the ground the many buildings lying in the area between the church of St Cuthbert and the castle because of the danger of fire damage to the former and because of the health hazard. The chronicler's interpretation of Flambard's action may have been accurate; a fire which burnt the bishop's house next to the church in the insurrection of 1069 had, after all, set fire to the church's west tower. However, Flambard may have had additional motives. He may have wished to clear a civilian community away from an area which had become virtually a military sector; these houses were within the inner castle fortifications. Furthermore, in view of the increasing pilgrim trade, Flambard may have decided to improve the appearance of the approaches to the shrine of St Cuthbert. Perhaps it was no coincidence that one of the major ecclesiastical events of the century, the translation of St Cuthbert's body to its new position behind the high altar of the church, occurred during Flambard's episcopacy. However, the result was hardly very attractive: Reginald describes the area as being a sea of mud by the late twelfth century, a place where duels were fought or executions carried out.[86]

One theme which has recurred, somewhat plaintively, throughout this chapter is the lack of evidence, documentary or otherwise, for charting the growth of Durham accurately before the middle of the thirteenth century. It is only after about 1250 that records such as property deeds and rentals, for example, begin to survive in any quantity and make it possible to recreate, more completely and reliably, the growth of the town. It is paradoxical that what

---

[85] H. M. Colvin, 'Domestic architecture and town planning', in A. L. Poole (ed.), *Medieval England*, vol. 1 (Oxford, 1958), p. 69, n. 1 and n. 2; M. Wood, *The English medieval house* (London, 1965), p. 292.

[86] *Locum inter ecclesiam et castellum, quem multa occupaverant habitacula, in patentis campi redegit planitiem*: Symeon, *HistEcclesDun, Continuatio Prima*, p. 140; Symeon, *HistEcclesDun*, pp. 98–9; *VCH Durham*, vol. 2, p. 11; *VCH Durham*, vol. 3, p. 10; *quia modo apud Dunelmum in placea certaminis morti procubuit, et flatu effuso spiritum emisit*: Reginald, *St Godric*, pp. 189, 191.

appears to be the most formative and expansionist era of Durham, the eleventh and twelfth centuries, is the most poorly documented, as in so many English towns. It is possible, however, to speculate on the size and status of Durham in comparison with other medieval towns in the early thirteenth century. The overall layout of the town and its principal buildings were there before 1200; after this date there was some infilling of the street plan as the population of Durham grew, and the urban area may have encroached further on the surrounding countryside, but there were no significant changes to the urban landscape.

No reliable estimates of Durham's population during the period can be made because of the absence of the area from Domesday Book and from later poll-tax returns. J. C. Russell attempted to gauge the size of the town by comparing its importance as an ecclesiastical centre with other similar towns. His 'estimate of what such a place should have in population' was 2,000, which can hardly be taken as a trustworthy statistic.[87] Of greater value to urban historians are the attempts to evaluate Durham's place in a 'league table' of northern towns. It seems clear that by 1200 Durham had already been outstripped by its new neighbour, Newcastle-upon-Tyne. Newcastle grew rapidly, partly because it was a busy port with a thriving overseas as well as inland trade, but partly, perhaps, because it lacked the rather rigid control of ecclesiastical overlords. As a royal borough, it was allowed to develop more freely, and the creation of guilds, for example, showed a corporate spirit and independence which was always lacking in Durham.[88] In terms of other towns in the region, however, Durham, although of modest size, probably ranked alongside Gateshead and Carlisle in 1200 and ahead of Darlington or Stockton, while nationally it could perhaps be compared with Stamford or Nottingham, substantial market towns. But Durham did outstrip its near neighbours, including Newcastle, in one aspect; it had an 'honorific ascendancy', as Professor Dobson describes it, which resulted from its ecclesiastical importance in accommodating the shrine of St Cuthbert, the seat of the bishop with its fortified palace, and the site of a large and

[87] J. C. Russell, *British medieval population* (Albuquerque, 1948), p. 145; S. B. Holt, 'A note concerning Russell's estimate of the population of Durham City in the 14th century', *Durham County Local History Society Bulletin*, 22 (1978), 43–4.

[88] Beresford, *New towns*, p. 251; C. M. Fraser and K. Emsley, *Tyneside* (Newton Abbot, 1973), pp. 18–21.

wealthy monastery. This essential difference, which is one of status as much as anything else, is expressed in the late-twelfth-century survey called *Boldon Buke*. Durham is distinguished from other local communities of the bishopric by being called *civitas*.[89] It never became a royal or episcopal headquarters of the size of Canterbury, Winchester or York, but it had no rivals north of York; the repeated attempts by the Scottish king to annex Durham and its lands to his kingdom in the twelfth century show a recognition of the importance and prestige of the town in northern politics.

It is difficult for a modern writer to rival the vivid impression of late-twelfth-century Durham provided by the contemporary chronicler Reginald. His depiction of the town has two viewpoints, and in the first he speaks as an inmate of the Durham community, when he describes the ecclesiastical buildings, the muddy *placea* and the castle with its heavily guarded battlements. He looks down from the monastic precinct to the river below, with its dam, mills and water wheels. He sees the white houses of what was later called South Street on the opposite bank of the river.[90] But in a second *persona* Reginald visits Durham as if a pilgrim to offer candles in the cathedral. This pilgrim approaches Durham from the north along the main road (*via regia*) and passes one of the sanctuary crosses a mile from the city. He sees Kepier Hospital, St Giles' Church and the church of St Nicholas on his way to the peninsula. He mentions the shops in the market place with their fronts open to the street, the Saturday market day and the town crier. He passes lodging houses where pilgrims stay and proceeds up through the walls surrounding the peninsula. The journey ends when this pilgrim reaches his destination, the shrine of St Cuthbert within the great cathedral church.[91] These almost photographic impressions make a fitting place to bring to an end this survey of early medieval Durham, a town which attracted pilgrims and traders alike, which was a prize sought by Scottish kings and English usurpers. It is to the better-documented later-medieval fortunes of that town that this study must now turn.

[89] Dobson, *Durham Priory*, p. 36; *Boldon Buke*, p. 1.
[90] Reginald, *St Godric*, pp. 189, 191; Reginald, *St Cuthbert*, pp. 211, 233, 252.
[91] Reginald, *St Godric*, pp. 59, 334, 345, 388, 462; Reginald, *St Cuthbert*, pp. 206, 252, 266, 271.

Chapter 2

The urban landscape of Durham
1250–1540

The city of Durham is in a region which has as its natural boundaries the River Tyne and its valley to the north and the River Tees to the south. The landscape ranges from bleak moorland areas and the Pennine chain, rising to over 2,400 feet, on the west to a coastal plain on the east which lies at sea level. Although this region was described by medieval chroniclers as impoverished border country, it had many natural resources which could be exploited by its inhabitants. It was an area rich in mineral deposits such as lead, which was mined in Weardale in the middle ages. The bishop of Durham held some of the most valuable coal mines in medieval England at Gateshead and Whickham. The gently rolling countryside to the south-east of Durham was farmed by the monks of Durham Priory for its grain. There was cattle farming in the north of the region, with sheep grazing on the higher land to the west. Surplus agricultural produce was brought to the market towns of the area including Durham, Darlington and Stockton, and goods were shipped in and out of the region from the ports of Gateshead and Hartlepool. Furthermore, there was a network of small agricultural settlements, particularly in the east lowland areas of the county, like Boldon, Pittington, Easington and Billingham. Accordingly, Durham was surrounded by a relatively rich and varied hinterland.[1]

The town itself stands in a lowland area some fifteen miles from the coast, an area which is by no means lacking in visual and geological interest. The irregularities of the landscape are as characteristic of Durham today as they were in the medieval period. Local mythology has it that Durham is built on seven hills

[1] P. Beaumont, 'Geomorphology', in J. C. Dewdney (ed.), *Durham county and city with Teesside* (Durham, 1970), pp. 26–8; C. M. Fraser, 'The medieval period', in Dewdney, *Durham county*, pp. 207–8.

and in the late eighteenth century these hills were indeed very prominent. William Hutchinson commented :[2]

> Approaching the city from the north, it has the most romantic and uncommon appearance. It seems to be scattered over a multitude of irregular hills, (for the ground by which it is approached is thrown up into round mounts), and we discover various parts of the town, the castle, and churches, through several vallies [sic] in one point of view, so that they appear like so many distinct places.

The geology of the region accounts for this 'uncommon appearance', for Durham lies amongst thick glacial drift cover; and the so-called seven hills of Durham are rounded mounds of sand and gravel left after the retreat of glaciers. The general geological profile of the town is, at the lowest level, soft shales, overlaid by a coal seam now known as the 'low main seam', topped by carboniferous sandstone, the bedrock on which the west walls of the cathedral are founded. The coal seam outcrops all round the banks of the river, as does the sandstone, providing readily available materials for medieval builders. It is the glacial drift of sand, gravel and boulder clay deposited above this geological cross-section which accounts for the fertile land all around the peninsula.[3]

The glaciation of the region also affected the course of the local rivers. Today, Durham's peninsula is enclosed on three sides by the River Wear, which rises in the Pennines and falls gradually towards the north-east where it meanders out towards the sea at Sunderland. Originally, this river seems to have run to the east of Durham beneath the promontory called Maiden Castle, along what is now Team Valley, to enter the Tyne. A tributary river, the Browney, entered the Wear from Windy Hills (below the present railway station), joining it near the Sands; it ran across what became the neck of the present peninsula to the north of the market place. These ancient river valleys were buried beneath glacial drift when the ice retreated, although in the early modern period at least there were views on where the former course of the River Browney lay. John Leland noted in his *Itinerary* that[4]

---

[2] Hutchinson, *Durham* 2, p. 2.
[3] G. A. L. Johnson (ed.), *The Durham area*, Geologists' Association guides, no. 15 (1973), pp. 1–6; M. Johnson, 'The great North Gate of Durham Castle', *TAASDN*, new ser., 4 (1977), 114, n. 3; D. Pocock and R. Gazzard, *Durham: portrait of a cathedral city* (Durham, 1983), pp. 7–9. See appendix 1, map 9.
[4] *Itinerary of John Leland*, ed. L. Toulmin Smith, vol. 1 (London, 1906), p. 73.

Sum hold opinion, that of auncient tyme Were ran from the place wher now Elvet-bridge is, straite down by St. Nicolas now stonding on a hille, and that the [o]ther course, part for pollicy and part by digging of stones for building of the town and minstre, was made a valley, and so the watercourse was conveyid that way; but I approve not ful this conjecture.

As the ice retreated there was a readjustment of land and sea levels and both the River Wear and the River Browney had to re-excavate their valleys or cut out new ones as they headed towards the coast. The River Wear sliced through the glacial drift around Durham in a series of incised meanders; when the river encountered the hard sandstone bedrock, a deep, steep-sided gorge developed around what became the Durham peninsula. A naturally fortified neck of land, some 800 yards long, 250 yards from bank to bank at its narrowest point and containing about fifty-eight acres was left, surrounded on three sides by a fast-flowing river.[5]

Such an irregular landscape gave rise to a rather unorthodox town plan which has been described most graphically by the seventeenth-century writer, Robert Hegge: 'I may liken the form of this bishopric to the letter A and Durham to a crab; supposing the city for a belly and the suburbs for the claws'.[6] John Speed's plan of 1611 shows settlement spreading out along the road sides in all directions from the heart of the city.[7] The peninsula area appears to be congested, with a concentration of housing in narrow streets. Elsewhere, the buildings straggle out towards the countryside, until eventually buildings give way to gardens and orchards which merge into the common fields and pastures surrounding the town. Here and in the following chapter the components of this unusual urban landscape, such as the streets, the tenements and the river will be described in more detail over the broad sweep of 300 years of growth. More general themes of urban history will arise from this detailed survey: the study of Durham's so-called 'boroughs', for example, shows it is most unlikely that they were overflow areas but rather independent communities which gradually grew together. The close inter-relation of all the aspects of the town's plan, its street system,

---

[5] A. Holmes, 'The foundations of Durham Castle and the geology of the Wear gorge', *DUJ*, 25 (1928), 319–26.

[6] Robert Hegge, *The legend of St Cuthbert* (1626), ed. J. B. Taylor (Sunderland, 1816), p. 2; *VCH Durham*, vol. 3, p.1.   [7] See appendix 1, map 1.

tenement pattern and the physical features of its site, are also demonstrated. Above all, the limitations of a peninsula site for urban development are clearly revealed at Durham. The restricted settlement area and difficult communications prevented medieval Durham from becoming a dynamic industrial or trading centre.

The sources for a study of the landscape of medieval Durham are varied: the documentary material is drawn mainly from the cathedral priory rentals, account rolls, registers and title deeds which can be used to trace the history of particular tenements as well as buildings like mills and bridges. Unlike Symeon and his twelfth-century peers, no later chroniclers seem to have been interested in describing the contemporary city, but the great weakness, as far as documentary evidence goes, is that there are no municipal records. With the Durham boroughs firmly under the control of ecclesiastical overlords, there was little opportunity for townsmen to participate in the administration of their town. Archaeological evidence is also limited, as little work has been possible within the continuously occupied urban area, but the results of two major excavations, in Saddler Street and in New Elvet, are of value to the Durham historian.[8] There are no surviving contemporary maps or plans of the whole town, although there are two sketch plans of tenement boundaries in New Elvet and in the market place which date respectively from the fifteenth and the sixteenth centuries. The earliest known map of Durham is Matthew Patteson's map of 1595, which was engraved by Christof Schwytzer. John Speed's map of Durham, dating from 1611, is very similar in layout and the perspective representation of buildings, which leads to the suspicion that Speed based his plan on Schwytzer's work. Speed's map and John Wood's plan of 1820, the next detailed depiction of the city's tenements, can be used as the basis for a reconstruction of the appearance of the medieval city.[9] Although three centuries separate pre-Reformation Durham from Wood's town, it can be

---

[8] Carver, 'Three Saxo-Norman tenements', pp. 1–80; Carver, 'Excavations in New Elvet', pp. 91–148; P. A. G. Clack, 'Rescue excavations in County Durham, 1976–8', *TAASDN*, new ser., 5 (1980), 56–70.

[9] Misc.Ch.5828/12; Loc.xxxvii, no.113; R. A. Skelton and P. D. A. Harvey (eds.), *Local maps and plans from medieval England* (Oxford, 1986), no.15; P. M. Benedikz (ed.), *Durham topographical prints up to 1800* (Durham, 1968), pp. 1, 2, 86; R. M. Turner (ed.), *Maps of Durham, 1576–1872* (Durham, 1954), pp. 5, 29; R. A. Skelton, 'Tudor town plans in John Speed's *Theatre*', *Archaeological Journal*, 108 (1951), 113. See appendix 1, maps 5, 6, 1, 2.

shown from written sources that changes in the town's plan during this period were comparatively insubstantial.

SUBURBAN DEVELOPMENT: THE BOROUGHS

One of the most distinctive features of medieval Durham was its division into six separate parts. The peninsula with its fortifications was administered by the constable of the castle. There were four areas called 'boroughs': the Old Borough, the Bishop's Borough (otherwise known, somewhat confusingly, as the Borough of Durham), Elvet Borough (also called New Elvet) and St Giles' Borough. The sixth part was known as the Barony of Elvet, or Old Elvet. As a further complication, St Giles' Borough contained an area around St Mary Magdalen Chapel which was administered as a separate jurisdictional area by Durham Priory's almoner.[10] The first question to arise is just what was meant by the use of the term 'borough' in medieval Durham, a question which is difficult to answer precisely. The word occurs in some of the earliest documentary references to the urban area. In the later twelfth century, for example, Bishop Puiset restored *burgum factum in Elvetehalge* to the monks, and the same bishop granted the borough of St Giles to Kepier Hospital. In a charter of *c.* 1179, Bishop Puiset referred to the 'burgesses' of *his* 'borough', and the inhabitants of this area had been called 'burgesses' as early as 1130, when they were fined.[11]

Whatever the term meant in the Durham context, clearly a Durham borough cannot be compared with Alfredian fortified *burhs* such as Lydford, Malmesbury and Wallingford. The only part of early medieval Durham to be fortified was the peninsula area, and it was never called a borough.[12] Durham's boroughs did have a precise geographical significance, however. Each borough had a specific, delineated area which was understood and recognised by all of its inhabitants. The borough of New Elvet lay to the east of the peninsula within a loop of the River Wear. We know from the evidence of later property deeds and rentals that tenements in the street called New Elvet and on the north side

---

[10] Alm. rental, 1424.

[11] 3.1.Pont.4; *Feodarium Dunelm*, p. 198; *Memorials of St Giles*, pp. 195–6. For an account of the history of the Durham boroughs, see M. Hope Dodds, 'The bishops' boroughs', *ArchAel*, 3rd ser., 12 (1915), 81–185. See also chapter 1, pp. 25, 27–9.

[12] Loyn, *Anglo-Saxon England*, pp. 33–5; Reynolds, *English medieval towns*, pp. 31–2.

of Ratonrawe were in New Elvet Borough, whereas tenements on the south side of Ratonrawe, in Old Elvet Street and in Kirkgate, were in the Barony of Old Elvet.[13] St Giles' Borough was furthest from the castle or the cathedral to the north-east of the peninsula, and its southern boundary with the Bishop's Borough was marked by a lead cross in the road where Clayport became St Giles Street. This boundary followed the lanes later called Tinkler's Lane and Bakehouse Lane which ran from the main road to the river on the north and south sides of the borough.[14] The Old Borough lay to the west of the peninsula and its boundary with the Bishop's Borough on its north side was a clear geographical feature, the Milneburn. These borough boundaries seem to have been established from the earliest days of the urban settlement; certainly, by the middle of the thirteenth century, when the documentation becomes more prolific, there was a clear demarcation of tenements between the boroughs.

The so-called 'barony' of Elvet shared most of the characteristics of the other Durham boroughs. It too had a precise geographical area, a small community of traders or skilled craftsmen and a local court, all features of the other boroughs, as we shall see later. This court, called a free court or the court of the Barony of Elvet, regulated the lives of the tenants and maintained the rights of the overlord, in this case the hostillar of Durham Priory, who was also the overlord of New Elvet Borough. But the barony was never called a borough, nor is there any surviving evidence of the grant of a charter giving borough status to its inhabitants. Despite this, the hostillar's rentals of 1523 to 1534 refer to plots of land in the barony as burgages which were held in burgage tenure. The Barony of Old Elvet may have lacked true borough status, but it had many urban features, and by the later middle ages any differentiation between Old Elvet and the Durham boroughs implicit in the term 'barony' may have been illusory.[15] Hence in this chapter, Old Elvet will be considered as analogous to the other Durham boroughs.

Were Durham's boroughs, then, merely suburbs by another

[13] See, for example, Rec. Book 11; appendix 1, map 3.

[14] D. M. Meade, 'The medieval parish of St Giles', *TAASDN*, new ser., 2 (1970), 63; *VCH Durham*, vol. 3, p. 183.

[15] R. A. Lomas, 'A northern farm at the end of the middle ages: Elvethall Manor, Durham, 1443/44–1513/14', *Northern History*, 18 (1982), 27.

name? It could, perhaps, be speculated that these boroughs developed to relieve overcrowding in the central area of Durham, occupied as it was by the public buildings of the peninsula and the market place. However, such an interpretation is an over-simplification, based on topographical rather than genuinely historical evidence. Durham's walls, for example, cannot be regarded as significant in differentiating an urban 'core' from any extra-mural development. The castle wall enclosed the monastic precinct and houses for military retainers and ecclesiastical servants as well as the bishop's administrative buildings; but these did not form a self-supporting urban area. Indeed, it would be difficult to argue that the peninsula was, in any meaningful sense, 'urban'. A second wall around the market place, the town wall, was built as late as the early fourteenth century, long after the establishment of Durham's separate boroughs, and consequently its influence upon any 'suburban' development was non-existent.

The archaeological and documentary evidence for the origins of Durham's boroughs, vague and inconclusive as it may be, also casts doubt on any conventional theory of suburban development at Durham. The growth of a suburb should, by definition, follow the establishment of an urban 'core', yet there is an argument, based on documentary and archaeological evidence, for maintaining that there was a settlement at Old Elvet, probably centred around the parish church of St Oswald, before the peninsula was occupied by St Cuthbert's community. The Old Borough most probably antedated the development of the Bishop's Borough, an argument supported by the use of an alternative name for the latter in some title deeds, the 'New Borough'.[16] Although the Bishop's Borough was the geographical centre of the later-medieval urban area, it was not necessarily the first to be settled. The implication from the documentary evidence is that the Durham boroughs grew as independent communities at different times before and alongside the central borough of the town. They did not in fact develop as a result of overcrowding in the central area.

However, it is true to say that the boroughs of Durham share some features common to suburbs in other medieval towns such as Winchester, Lincoln and Bristol, with tenements spreading out along the main approach roads to the town beyond the limits of

[16] See, for example, Misc. Ch. 1872; chapter 1, pp. 28, 30.

the walled area.[17] Their characteristic shape, as in Winchester and Canterbury, was long, thin and linear, the result of the gradual spread of housing along the main routes into Durham.[18] The Old Borough extended to the south along South Street, to the west along Crossgate and Alvertongate, and to the north along Milneburngate. Old and New Elvet followed the lines of the main south and south-east roads running out of Durham. St Giles' Borough followed the line of the main road to the north-east. Even the Bishop's Borough, which at first sight has a nuclear shape deriving from its focus on the market place, grew outwards from it along the roads to the north-east (Clayport), to the south-east (Fleshewergate), and to the west (Silver Street). This borough had an extension on the west side of the river along the main road to the north (Framwelgate).

Another characteristic of suburban development is the large amount of space available for building and the greater width of roads, the results of a lower population density. The outer Durham boroughs consisted, broadly speaking, of one main, wide street with a tenement pattern which gave ample space to settlers. In contrast, the central borough contained a network of narrow streets leading into the market place with some back lanes and vennels. Tenements were smaller and irregular in shape, suggesting a greater concentration of population and a more restricted space for settlement around the market. Each borough, with the exception of New Elvet, also had its own church, as did the suburbs of Winchester or Hereford. The churches in Old Elvet, St Giles and the Old Borough may have acted as the focus of settlement for the boroughs as the tenement patterns around these churches seem to have been more congested and restricted and properties there were usually in occupation, suggesting a greater popularity than those in remoter parts of the boroughs. The inhabitants of the Old Borough fought long and hard for the independence of their chapel from its mother church in Old Elvet and this was finally achieved by 1431.[19] The limits of the urban area and perhaps of the boroughs themselves seem to have been

[17] D. J. Keene, 'Suburban growth', in M. W. Barley (ed.), *The plans and topography of medieval towns in England and Wales*, CBA research report no. 14 (London, 1976), p. 77; M. D. Lobel, 'Bristol', in M. D. Lobel (ed.), *The atlas of historic towns*, vol. 2 (London, 1975), p. 5.

[18] M. Biddle (ed.), *Winchester in the early middle ages* (Oxford, 1976), pp. 260–3; Urry, *Canterbury*, p. 186.

[19] 4.16.Spec.49; Surtees, *Durham* 4, p. 127; *VCH Durham*, vol. 3, p. 181.

marked by crosses in the roads leading out into the countryside, just as in Winchester the bars marked the boundaries of settlement.[20]

Some of Durham's boroughs show signs of decline by the later medieval period, the most obvious symptoms being an increase in the number of waste tenements, the lack of tenants to take up holdings and the amalgamation of tenements into larger units. The pattern seems to be that the boroughs furthest from the market place fared worst and, within them, the parts of their streets which lay on the fringe of the urban area were the first victims of this trend. The Old Borough seems to have suffered most, with many waste tenements, particularly in South Street, before the fifteenth century: by 1500 several tenements at the head of Crossgate and Alvertongate had been converted into closes. Framwelgate and St Giles Street were also affected by this decline and it seems that the urban area was shrinking in these parts of Durham. In contrast, the central Bishop's Borough appears prosperous and heavily populated throughout its existence, while in New Elvet, a river wall was built in the fourteenth century and land reclaimed for the building of new houses. The Elvet boroughs may indeed have gained in wealth from the decline of the Old Borough.[21]

Can the attempt to define the meaning of the term 'borough' in medieval Durham be taken any further, to include more than a purely topographical significance or a local identity? The documentary evidence indicates that the Durham boroughs had certain financial, legal and economic distinctions. Each borough had its own craftsmen or traders offering a range of services and products to the local community. In the Bishop's Borough, for example, there were trading quarters for butchers in Fleshewergate and for tanners in Framwelgate. But there were representatives of these and related trades in other boroughs as well. John Bacon, butcher, lived near the bridge in New Elvet Borough in 1374, and there was a small community of skinners in Crossgate within the Old Borough holding land above the Milneburn stream. In 1316, Roger de Ask, skinner, granted his burgage there to Richard de Bolum, skinner. The land to the west of this burgage was held by a barker in 1447 and the land to the east by

[20] Biddle, *Winchester*, pp. 264–5; Keene, 'Suburban growth', p. 78.
[21] Sac. rental, 1500; Carver, 'Excavations in New Elvet', pp. 125–6; Host. rentals, 1523–34.

a tanner in 1510.[22] The rentals show that these boroughs were not ghettoes for the poor or for the labouring classes, as seems to have been true of the Winchester suburbs.[23] Among the tenants in each street of each borough were representatives of the local country gentry, wealthy traders and craftsmen, as there were in Warwick and Canterbury, where it seems the attractions of larger tenements and nearby fields drew the richer townsmen to the suburbs. The Claxton family, who held valuable estates throughout the county and provided a sheriff of Durham in the early fifteenth century, had property in New Elvet Borough, as did Robert Danby, a member of the prior's council.[24]

Furthermore, some of the Durham boroughs possessed borough charters. The charter given to the Bishop's Borough by Bishop Puiset conveyed to its inhabitants the customs of Newcastle-upon-Tyne, presumably including the traditional attributes of burgage tenure as specified in those customs: 'a burgess can give or sell his land as he wishes, and go where he will, freely and quietly unless his claim to the land is challenged'.[25] Similarly, the prior's two charters to his burgesses of Elvet also granted the basic rights of burgage tenure, and the second of these charters mentioned the legal rights of the burgesses to have pleas heard within the borough.[26] Thus tenants who held land in a specific borough would have a close legal relationship to their borough and its court. It was where they were admitted to their tenements, making fealty to their overlord, and where they surrendered them; and they looked to the separate borough courts to settle their disputes. In a legal sense, as well as economically, Durham's boroughs had the means to operate as self-contained communities. Perhaps it should come as no surprise that there was, apparently, so little local appreciation of Durham as one single urban area, a town in its own right, through most of the medieval period. This emerges clearly in the deeds, where

---

[22] 4.2.Sac.3c; 1.16.Spec.15; W. Hylton Dyer Longstaffe (ed.), 'Local muniments from the vestry of St Margaret, Durham', *ArchAel*, new ser., 2 (1858), 29; Crossgate Court Book, fol. 121r.

[23] Biddle, *Winchester*, p. 260.

[24] Host, rentals, 1523–34; *VCH Warwickshire*, vol. 8 (London, 1969), p. 487; Platt, *English medieval town*, p. 38.

[25] *ut habeant omnes liberas consuetudines sicut burgenses de Novo Castello melius et honorabilius habent*: Reg. I, part ii, fol. 3; *VCH Durham*, vol. 3, pp. 54–5. For the Newcastle charter, see *English historical documents, 1042–1189*, ed. D. C. Douglas and G. W. Greenaway, 2nd edn (London, 1981), p. 1041; see chapter 1, pp. 27–8.

[26] Cart.II, fol. 251; 4.16.Spec.28; *Feodarium Dunelm*, p. 199.

the parties and sometimes the witnesses are commonly described as inhabitants of a particular Durham borough, not as townsmen of Durham itself. In a charter of 1418, for example, William Hakthorp granted land in Fleshewergate to Robert Elge of 'Elvet, next to Durham'.[27] However, it is clear that one of the Durham boroughs, the Bishop's Borough, was more important than all the others in the medieval period. Not only did it lie at the heart of the urban area, but also it contained the one Durham market place within its boundaries. This borough has some claim to pre-eminence and to be what contemporaries primarily thought of as 'Durham'.

What then were Durham's boroughs and what is the explanation for their growth? It seems that they were established as separate communities, each with their own focus of settlement, at a time before the building of Durham's two bridges enhanced the position of the central borough and its market. The attraction for settlers in Old Elvet and the Old Borough may have been the local church or it may have been the agricultural communities around Elvethall manor and a putative manor at the end of South Street. The foundation of a hospital at Kepier may have led to the development of St Giles' Borough, just as the siting of a religious house outside a town like Leicester seems to have encouraged suburban development.[28] A possible exception to this pattern may have been the development of New Elvet Borough which probably resulted from the construction of Elvet Bridge and the growing commercial importance of this bridgehead. Land may have been cheaper on the outer edges of the town: some of the rents derived from holdings in the Old Borough and Old Elvet were tiny, although the actual value of the property in economic terms may have been high. Certainly, tenements seem to have been larger in the outer boroughs than in the Bishop's Borough and this was no doubt an attraction to counterbalance the prestige and undoubted advantages of a frontage along the streets leading into the market place.

Another explanation for the growth of these boroughs and one which brings us to the crucial question of their status was the patronage of their overlords. The priory had the overlordship of three boroughs in Durham; the bishop originally held two until he transferred St Giles to Kepier Hospital. It is likely that the

---

[27] Misc. Ch. 2327.
[28] Keene, 'Suburban growth', p. 81; Platt, *English medieval town*, p. 37.

priory, in particular, would have made every effort to attract settlers or tenants to its boroughs because this would mean a higher income from rents and court payments, although there is no hard evidence to support this theory. Hence we see towards the end of the period the lowering of rents and the writing off of arrears by the priory in an attempt to fill tenancies and to prevent tenements becoming waste.[29] The charters of both the bishop and the prior to their Durham burgesses granted certain liberties and customs as an inducement to settlers and an encouragement to traders. However, the bishop always had the advantage in this competition for tenants because his borough possessed the only Durham marketing area. As in other medieval towns, such as King's Lynn, the administrative and legal partition of the urban area led to inequalities in opportunities for townsmen and to the emergence of one dominant borough by the later middle ages.[30]

It is then clearly misleading and restrictive to see Durham's boroughs as examples of traditional suburban growth. The surviving documentary evidence reveals no contemporary concept of 'suburban' status among the tenants of the boroughs. Deeds from the thirteenth and fourteenth centuries show that the inhabitants still often identified themselves with a particular borough, not with a suburb or the idea of a town called Durham.[31] To the townsmen, the borough with its court, its church and its customs was their home; they paid their customary rents to the overlord of their borough. The use of the term 'borough' rather than 'suburb' implies a certain legal or constitutional status; but this status should not be overestimated. The impracticalities of these subdivisions by the late medieval period were clear. It may have been possible for each borough to function independently in the early middle ages, and indeed before the market place developed in the Bishop's Borough and the bridges were built to improve communications it was necessary and inevitable that this happened. But in the longer term, these small boroughs could not remain insulated economically from each other. Any significant trading had to be done in the market of the Bishop's Borough. Weights and measures

[29] See, in particular, Sac. rental, 1500.
[30] V. Parker, *The making of King's Lynn* (London, 1971), p. 22.
[31] See, for example, PRO Durham Chancery Enrolments, 3/46, m. 20d, where land is described as lying 'in the borough of Elvet next to Durham' in 1446.

and legal processes and conventions were the same in all the boroughs; the prior's tenants caught offending in another overlord's borough would be returned to the prior's court for justice, and *vice versa*. By the late thirteenth century the boroughs were no longer even physically separate: they had grown together so that it was necessary to redefine the borough boundaries from time to time, especially when mortuary payments or services owed to a borough overlord were in dispute.[32] By the early sixteenth century, some documents refer to land being held, for example, in Crossgate, 'in the suburbs of Durham', implying a major shift in contemporary urban perceptions.[33] At the end of the medieval period, it is likely that the idea of separate and independent boroughs was theoretical rather than practical; it was maintained by the overlords out of financial considerations and legal convention.

RIVER, BRIDGES AND MILLS

It can be argued that one of the most important influences on the development of Durham was the course and nature of the River Wear. The peculiarities of the town's layout, its restricted site and its growth in a linear pattern along the routes leading from the centre, originated from the U-shaped course taken by the river around Durham's craggy peninsula.[34] The street plan was moulded to match the terrain, governed by the river's gorge and its most convenient crossing places, upon which routes converged. But this riverain influence was not limited to topography alone. It is unlikely that the independent development of Durham's boroughs would have reached such an advanced stage had the river not provided a formidable physical gap for over a century at least and so separated the inhabitants of different parts of the town in a way no man-made barrier could have done. Furthermore, the fact that the Wear was not navigable as far as Durham held back the town's commercial development. Although it did sponsor some water-based industries, such as tanning and dyeing, and it supported a series of mills, Durham never developed any kind of river trading links or boat-building

[32] See, for example, 4.16.Spec.56.
[33] See, for example, a lease of 1559: Loc.XXXIX, no. 60.
[34] This compares with the influence of the watercourses on the development of communications in King's Lynn: Parker, *King's Lynn*, p. 21. See appendix 1, map 10.

activities to compare with its neighbour, Newcastle, which had become one of the wealthiest ports in England by 1200.[35]

The relationship between Durham's inhabitants and their river was not always an easy one. Like any town sited beside a river, there was always a danger of flooding in Durham, made all the more acute by the constrictions of a narrow gorge. The powerful currents generated by flood water swept away the Old Bridge in *c.* 1400.[36] Any rapid rise in the water level led to the flooding of properties along the river banks in the lower parts of the town. Excavation work on properties beneath the west side of (modern) New Elvet revealed that these dwellings had been subject to repeated flooding during the late medieval period, and the building of a river wall at the end of the fifteenth century was an attempt to control and contain the river's course.[37] A *tempestas aquarum* raised the level of the Wear's tributary, the Milneburn stream, and destroyed its mill in 1402; and houses on the east side of Framwelgate and Milneburngate may also have been affected.[38] Mills and their dams were particularly vulnerable to flood damage. In 1492 the mill pond of the Milneburn mill had to be rebuilt because of inundation by a 'great river', but the mill which suffered most from the vagaries of the current was Scaltok Mill in Elvet. In 1420, for example, the mill pond was broken open by the overflowing of the River Wear. Finally, the difficulty of maintaining a steady flow of water to this mill and of keeping its dam in repair whenever the current was running strongly in the river seems to have resulted in its abandonment in the middle of the fifteenth century at the foot of a partially dried-up ox-bow lake.[39]

The River Wear was probably never used by the townsmen as their main source of drinking water. The people who lived by the river side, in Old Elvet and Milneburngate for example, may have drawn water straight from the river itself, but most inhabitants would use wells for their drinking supply. The river was most probably polluted by industry, the watering of animals brought

---

[35] Harbottle and Clack, 'Newcastle-upon-Tyne', p. 111.
[36] *VCH Durham*, vol. 3, p. 64. Repair work on the bridge was financed by the priory almoner in 1401 and 1402; Alm. accounts, 1401/02, 1402/03.
[37] Carver, 'Excavations in New Elvet', pp. 124–6.
[38] Alm. account, 1402/03, *Allocationes*.
[39] Alm. account, 1492/93, Repairs; the Scaltok Mill pond could not be repaired *causa superundacionis aque de Were … dirupti et confracti*: Burs. account, 1420/21, *Allocationes*; Misc.Ch.7100.

to market or to slaughter, and domestic waste, but the wells, taking water from some thirty to forty feet in depth, on the peninsula at least, would be relatively clean. The priory and the castle had their own wells and so did many of the houses in the Bailey. There were communal wells in St Giles Street (Hexham Well, named after the family near whose land it was situated), South Street (St Helen's Well), Alvertongate and Framwelgate. Durham had no elaborate system of watercourses to compare with Winchester or Exeter for example, but one significant late-medieval improvement in the water supply to the Bishop's Borough must have been the construction of a water course and pipe from the spring which rose in Thomas Billyngham's land in Sidegate ('le Paunthed') to the market place in 1450.[40] The monks had a further water supply brought from across the river to the precinct by aqueduct. It was, however, somewhat vulnerable to attack by an irate bishop. Bishop Philip de Poitou diverted the priory's piped water to the castle in the late twelfth century, and Bishop Bek broke the aqueduct in *c.* 1294.[41] The weather also affected this supply; in 1342 the bursar had to pay for water to be carried from the Wear because of a broken pipe, and in 1495 severe weather conditions blocked the aqueduct with ice.[42]

It is clear from the surviving local court records that most households used the river and Durham's streams for domestic purposes, such as washing clothes on stones in the Milneburn stream, a practice which was prohibited by the late fifteenth century, at least.[43] However, the lack of sophisticated sanitary arrangements either in the monastery or in the town led to other more unpleasant waterside activities. Many inhabitants of Crossgate were fined for having *latrina* in the Milneburn, or for throwing noxious effluent and rubbish into the stream. In 1510, it was ordered that no tenants were to throw manure or cadavers (presumably, let us hope, of animals!) into the Milneburn, or to wash cloth, water their horses or have latrines in the stream.[44] Clearly, attempts were made to keep the Milneburn, at least, clear

---

[40] Biddle, *Winchester*, pp. 282–5; PRO Durham Chancery Enrolments, 3/44, m.9.

[41] *aquam, quam a longe in planitiem castelli fratres conduxerant, in castellum transverti fecit*: *ScripTres*, p. 22; *VCH Durham*, vol. 3, p. 15.

[42] Burs. accounts, 1342, *Structura Domorum*; 1495/96, Repairs.

[43] A by-law of the Crossgate court ran: *tenentes comorant. et abuttant. super Milneburn et habent. latrinas et le Wesshyngstonez quod ea amoveant*: Crossgate Court Book, 13 January 1500 [1501].

[44] Crossgate Court Book, 10 April 1510, fol. 119r.

of pollution, just as in London the local courts attempted to restrict noxious practices in the Walbrook stream running through the city.[45] However, the River Wear itself, like the Thames, seems to have been regarded as an open sewer for the town and there is no surviving record of any attempt to control what went into it.

Two bridges were built across the River Wear to ease communications within the town. The Old Bridge, erected by Bishop Flambard in *c*. 1120, linked the Old Borough and Framwelgate street with the Bishop's Borough. After it had been swept away in the flood of *c*. 1400, it was rebuilt by Bishop Langley with towers and gates at both ends making it an integral part of the castle fortifications.[46] The New Bridge, or Elvet Bridge, was constructed during Bishop Puiset's episcopacy and it connected the Bishop's Borough with New Elvet Borough.[47] It had chantry chapels at both ends. These two bridges were the main crossing points of the river,[48] although there were also several ferries in operation and places where it was possible to ford the river. By the middle of the fifteenth century, there are references to another Durham bridge called Bow Bridge, which seems to have crossed the Wear some 300 yards south of Elvet Bridge to connect Kingsgate with the lane known in recent years as Water Lane in Old Elvet. This bridge remains a mysterious structure, because no documents refer directly to it; it is mentioned in the *c*. 1450 catalogue of the Durham muniments, the *Repertorium Magnum*, and also in a later hand on the dorse of some title deeds, where tenements were said to lie opposite 'Boubryge'.[49]

M. W. Beresford and others have illustrated graphically the influence of bridges and river crossings on a town's street plan and

[45] *London Assize of Nuisance*, ed. H. M. Chew and W. Kellaway, London Record Society, vol. 10 (1973), Introduction; *Memorials of London Life*, ed. H. T. Riley (London, 1868), pp. 23, 380, 478.

[46] *VCH Durham*, vol. 3, p. 64; Jones, 'The walls and towers of Durham'; Whiting, 'The castle of Durham', p. 126. Speed's plan of 1611 shows the tower at the eastern end of the bridge: see appendix 1, map 1.

[47] See chapter 1, pp. 28–9. For the dates of the bishops of Durham, see appendix 3.

[48] See appendix 1, map 10.

[49] *Rep. Mag.*, fol. 113; note on dorse of 4.16.Spec.70, 4.16.Spec.71 and 4.16.Spec.74; also referred to as *Pons Laurentii* in *Dobsons Drie Bobbes*, ed. E. A. Horsman (Durham, 1955), pp. xiii, 77. Carver suggests this bridge may have been the site of a ford: Carver, 'Excavations in New Elvet', p. 93.

also their tendency to attract trade and commerce.[50] Durham's roads were drawn to the crossing points of the river probably even before the bridges were built, and it is clear from the rentals and deeds that the bridges themselves and their land arches were the subject of intense commercial pressures. There were shops and booths clustering around the west end of the Old Bridge by 1375, and there were stalls and shops at the east end of the New Bridge by 1347. There were also shops on the New Bridge itself, yielding rent to the priory, and the land arches of the bridge were in demand as storage spaces. The chaplain of St James' Chapel at the east end of the bridge leased the area under two arches at the end of his chapel from the bishop in 1393; and in 1467 Bishop Booth leased an arch under Elvet Bridge to Richard Raket.[51] The building of two bridges by Durham's bishops was accordingly a good financial investment. The rents and tolls which could be taken on the bridges would produce a steady income and the improvement of communications with the market could only increase trade in the Bishop's Borough.

However, the costs of maintenance and repair work on the Durham bridges were probably high. When a bridge was swept away, as was the Old Bridge in *c.* 1400, or became so ruinous that major repair work or rebuilding was necessary, the bishop seems to have tried to share the costs with others. The issuing of indulgences, common throughout the country, was one method tried at Durham. During Richard Fox's episcopacy, the bishop issued indulgences to those contributing to the repair of the Old Bridge.[52] The tolls charged for crossing the bridges probably went towards such work. The cost of smaller repairs seems to have been shared by the users, including the priory, and all the priory officers made contributions towards paving work on both bridges from time to time.[53] Another source of money for bridge repair work took the form of rents from certain properties in the town called 'briglands', land donated by the pious specifically for maintaining the Durham bridges. Isolda de Aplingdene assigned

[50] Beresford, *New towns*, pp. 115–16. For the importance of the bridge at Newark in the development of Stamford, see A. Rogers, 'Medieval Stamford', in A. Rogers (ed.), *The making of Stamford* (Leicester, 1965), p. 38.
[51] Surtees, *Durham* 4, p. 56; PRO Durham Chancery Enrolments, 3/48, m.7.
[52] Hutchinson, *Durham* 2, p. 375; *Public Works in Medieval Law*, vol. 2, ed. C. T. Flower, Selden Society, vol. 40 (1923), pp. xix–xxiii. For dates of the bishops of Durham, see appendix 3. [53] See below, pp. 64–7.

three rents of 1*s*. each from her house on (*super*) the Old Bridge to maintain three bridges (the Old Bridge, the New Bridge and Shincliffe Bridge) in the late thirteenth century. Thomas Gernum left half an acre of oats per annum as a contribution to the upkeep of Elvet Bridge in his will dated 1248.[54] Some of the land granted to the chantries at either end of the New Bridge may have had an additional rent charge for bridge work. Perhaps the chaplains of these chantries, which were built above the land arches of the bridge itself, also had to make some contribution to the work, but there is no surviving evidence of such payments.

The most important industrial use of the river was to power the eight water mills which, at one time or another, were sited along its banks. Durham Priory operated six of these mills, though not all at the same time. Scaltok Mill in Elvet must have been one of the first public buildings to be erected in Durham: in Prior Bertram's charter to his burgesses of the 'new borough' (dating from before 1198), one of the borough boundaries was described as the road leading to 'Scaltoc'. Its exact position is marked on a plan of *c*. 1440–5.[55] The mill was in use until about 1462, when it was abandoned in favour of the South Street mill; both the name and the milling were transferred to South Street.[56] Although the South Street mill is first mentioned in the bursar's account roll of 1426, when it seems to have been acquired by the priory, it may have been in existence long before this date. By 1517 there were two mills here called 'Scaltokemylnes', described in 1542 as two water mills under one roof.[57] The priory's own mill, called *molendinum domus*, lay on the opposite bank of the river below the cathedral and dated from at least the time of Bishop Philip de Poitou. This bishop, in the course of his argument with the monks, obstructed the road to the mill with stones.[58] A second mill was built next to it in *c*. 1416 and these mills were known as the Lead Mill and the Jesus Mill by the sixteenth century.[59]

---

54 1.2.Sac.37; 3.15.Spec.6.
55 Cart.II, fol. 251; Misc.Ch.6794(b); Misc.Ch.7100; see appendix 1, map 11.
56 See Burs. accounts, 1458/59, 1462/63, Receipts; M. Snape, 'Durham 1440 × *c*. 1445', in Skelton and Harvey, *Local maps and plans*, no. 17.
57 Burs. rental, 1517; Rec. Book II, 1542. In a lease of 1551, these mills are described as 'water corne mylnes' called 'Scaltokmylnes': Loc.XXXIX, no. 13.
58 *itaque, qui ad molendinum dicebat, ne quid ad sustentacionem inferretur, lapidibus obstruxit*: *ScripTres*, p. 22.
59 These two mills were erroneously identified as the bishop's property by K. C. Bayley on the basis of a history of the church of Durham which has been attributed to William de Chambre: *ScripTres*, pp. 153–4; *VCH Durham*, vol. 3, p. 64.

Finally, the priory held the Clock Mill on the Milneburn which had been, in the time of Bishop Flambard, part of the endowment of Kepier Hospital. It was in the possession of the almoner by the late thirteenth century and it remained in use throughout the medieval period.[60] The bishop's mill, mentioned in *Boldon Buke* (*c.* 1183), was downstream from the Old Bridge, on the east side of the river behind the Clayport tenements; and Kepier Hospital had its own mill to the north of Durham, also on the east bank of the river.[61]

Mill buildings are some of the few extant medieval properties in modern Durham: both the South Street mill and the priory's fulling mill below the cathedral survive, albeit in a restored form. Documentary sources reveal some details about the medieval appearance of these buildings. A small lane led down to the mill at the south end of South Street and, according to the priory sacrist's rentals, the miller had a house and held the land surrounding this mill. There were buildings and land for the miller alongside the Clock Mill on the west side of Milneburngate.[62] A simple drawing of Scaltok Mill in Elvet survives in a plan from the middle of the fifteenth century, showing it to be a single-storied building with a pitched roof. This roof was thatched by 1428. There was a house next to the mill, presumably for the use of the miller.[63]

Why did a relatively small town like Durham need so many mills?[64] Part of the answer lies in the use to which the mills were put. Two of these eight mills were fulling mills, where locally produced cloth was cleaned and thickened, if only for a short period of their history; the South Street mill was a fulling mill when it was acquired by the priory, probably in the early fifteenth century, although by 1462 it was described as a water mill for grinding corn.[65] One of the two abbey mills below the cathedral was reconstructed as a fulling mill at a cost of £15. 0s. 9d. in *c.* 1416 but it was in disuse for much of the fifteenth century.[66] It is

---

[60] Reg.III, fo. ix–xi; PRO Durham Chancery Enrolments, 3/43, m.6.
[61] *Boldon Buke*, p. 1; *Memorial of St Giles*, pp. 202–3; PRO Durham Chancery Enrolments, 3/43, m.7. For the dates of bishops of Durham, see appendix 3.
[62] Sac. rental, 1500; Rec.Book II, 1542; Burs. account, 1446/47.
[63] See appendix 1, map 11 (Misc.Ch.7100); Burs. accounts, 1428/29, 1432, Repairs.
[64] Another relatively small town, Winchester, had a comparatively high number of mills. There were eleven in total, five within the walls and six outside: Biddle, *Winchester*, pp. 282–3.   [65] Burs. accounts, 1446/47; 1457/58; 1462/63, Receipts.
[66] See, for example, Burs. accounts, 1427, 1434 and 1437, Receipts. A lease of 1551 describes both abbey mills as corn mills, which may indicate that the fulling mill had

interesting that the priory was prepared to experiment with this new economic venture at a time when its revenue from Durham property was falling,[67] and when the experiment was found to be ill-judged, it was put into reverse. The other Durham mills were corn mills throughout their history, grinding local corn for domestic use. An equally important reason for the number of mills in the town comes back once more to the pattern of lordship; each overlord was obliged to provide and maintain at least one mill to serve his tenants in the Durham boroughs, since among the conditions of their tenure he demanded that they grind their corn at his mill. The multiplicity of overlordship in Durham spawned buildings, such as mills and bakehouses, and institutions like the borough courts, which were as much a reflection of the obligations of tenure as of the requirements of late-medieval townsmen.

Not only did the Durham overlords have to make provision for their tenants; they also had to ensure that their own needs were met. The mode of operation of a Durham mill reveals which group it was intended to serve, the landlords or the tenants. Some mills were kept in hand by the overlords for their own domestic needs, like the priory's corn mill below the cathedral. Those mills which were farmed out for a fixed annual sum were the ones used by the tenants for grinding their own corn, such as Scaltok Mill in Elvet. This second category was a consistent and relatively reliable source of revenue for the overlord; Scaltok Mill rendered £12 per annum by 1419, a sum which seems to have become a fixed amount in the fifteenth century. The annual farm of the South Street mill rose after its conversion from a fulling mill from £6. 13s. 4d. in 1462 to £13. 6s. 8d. in 1507.[68] But much of this revenue could be lost if, for example, the mill had to be repaired during the year and it was thus stopped for several months. In 1379, Nicholas Harpour and John Cok were allowed £6. 13s. 5d. of their farm for a twenty-week stoppage at Scaltok, and in 1420 Roger Milner was allowed £10. 6s. of his farm of £12 on account of damage caused by the flooding of the river.[69] However, the income of the farmer was not secure because it

been converted to a corn mill before the end of the medieval period: Loc.xxix, no. 13.   [67] See chapter 4, pp. 121, 130.

[68] Burs. accounts, 1419/20, Receipts; 1462/63, Receipts; Burs. rental, 1507. When the name 'Scaltok' was transferred to the South Street mill, so was this old farm: Burs. account, 1473/74, Receipts.

[69] Burs. accounts, 1379/80; 1420/21, *Allocationes*.

relied on the extraction of suit of mill from tenants. If his mill was at a standstill, he could not demand this tenurial obligation from them and thus he had no income. It was in his interest to see that all tenants who owed suit to his mill actually rendered it and he had the responsibility for bringing offenders to court. In 1333, John de Castro Bernardi, the farmer of Scaltok Mill in Elvet, met two women in Crossgate carrying flour which had been milled at another mill. He took the flour from them and brought them to court where it was ruled that 'all tenants of the Old Borough are obliged to mill their grain at Scaltok Mill'.[70] This obligation would be particularly resented since it meant a long journey for those holding property on the west of the peninsula to the priory mill beyond the south-east edge of the urban area. It is hardly surprising that the prior's court rolls reveal a succession of such cases involving suit of mill throughout the fourteenth century. The farmers of the mills were not necessarily the same men as the millers: in 1360 the farmers of Scaltok were Thomas Harpour and Robert de Elyngeham, but a man called William Milner seems to have done the milling for them and to have kept the mill in repair. On the other hand, John Potter, who held the Clock Mill from 1492 to 1501, is described as 'farmer and miller'. Edward Milner, alias Noteman, who leased the bishop's mill in 1513, may have been the miller as well as the farmer; but John Gower 'gentleman' who leased it in 1517 and William Richardson, mercer, who leased it in 1500, would have employed a professional miller to operate the mill.[71]

Even when a mill was farmed out, the responsibility for the upkeep of its buildings and the associated weir and pond rested with its owner, not with the farmer. In the case of the priory mills, the bursar accounted for repairs to the mills below the cathedral and to the South Street mill, while the almoner supervised the repair of the Clock Mill. These repairs could be very expensive for a priory officer, especially when a mill had to be completely rebuilt. In 1394, the Milneburn mill had to be reconstructed at a cost of £7. 11s. 5d., but in 1402 the good work was undone when the mill was destroyed *per tempestatum aquarum*. The two abbey mills below the cathedral were rebuilt in 1509 at

[70] Loc.IV, no. 197.
[71] Loc.IV, no. 75; Burs. account, 1360/61, Repairs; Alm. account, 1492/93, Repairs; Alm. rental, 1501; PRO Entry Book of Leases, Durham 8/78, fols. 5, 10: PRO Book of Leases, Durham 3/10, fol. 47(23).

a cost of £8. 0s. 2d.[72] Each year, small amounts had to be spent on replacing mill wheels or other mechanical parts such as the 'trindells, milnyrens, 2 spindels and 2 ryndes' bought for Scaltok Mill in 1342.[73] Equally expensive were repairs to mill ponds and dams. The priory, represented by the bursar, seems to have maintained the whole weir or dam which ran across the River Wear between the mills below the cathedral and the South Street mill. Expenditure was particularly heavy in 1338, 1353 and 1374 (£7. 10s., £11. 6s. 11d., and £40. 11s. 6d. respectively) when large timbers were carried to the mill pond. The sides of the pond seem to have been constructed from wood and stone, but each year small payments were made to women for fetching moss to plug the gaps as the sides were breached.[74]

Durham's river was thus the source and support for much of what little industrial activity Durham sustained in the medieval period. It drove the mill wheels to grind corn for domestic use and, albeit briefly, to full cloth probably for a small local market. It provided a stream of water necessary to a local tanning industry, an industry about which nothing more is known than the names of its workers and its location mainly in the Framwelgate area, downstream from the town.[75] Unfortunately, the shallows in the river and the weirs built to improve the flow of water to the mills impeded the development of any river traffic; and even inland trade was hampered by restricted communications between Durham's market and the country beyond the River Wear. For these reasons perhaps more than any others, Durham was relegated to the status of a small town by the later medieval period, a status which probably would not have changed greatly even had any of the eighteenth-century schemes to make the Wear navigable succeeded.[76]

THE STREETS

The streets of a town contribute in no small measure to its characteristic layout and provide a framework into which the tenements and their buildings are set. The influence of the river on

[72] Alm. accounts, 1394/95, Repairs; 1402/03, Allowances; Burs. account, 1509/10, Repairs.   [73] Burs. account, 1342/43, *Structura Domorum.*
[74] Burs. accounts, 1338/39, 1353/54, 1374/75, Repairs.
[75] See chapter 5, pp. 153, 164–5.
[76] E. Hughes, *North country life in the eighteenth century* (Oxford, 1969), pp. 13, 77, 293–8.

the crab-like plan of medieval Durham has already been recorded, but equally it determined to a large extent the road system in and around the town. The steep-sided, craggy peninsula had been by-passed by the main north–south route on its western side; but the east–west route running through the Durham market place across the neck of this peninsula had to cross the river twice. The narrow streets were focussed on these crossing points, probably even before the two bridges eased communications through the town. Another major route led north-east from the market place, following the ridge which was the continuation of the spine of the peninsula.[77] The physical features of this site restricted the further development of subsidiary streets, and once the street plan was established, man-made features of the landscape, such as the building of a castle, town walls and gates, made little impact. Durham's street plan was one of the most enduring and idiosyncratic features of the urban landscape.

Durham's medieval street plan had four main elements. First, there were three primary routes which converged on the market place: these were Clayport, from the north-east; Fleshewergate, from the south-east; and Silver Street from the south-west. Second, there were the outward extensions of these streets as they fanned out away from the constricted centre of the town and the bridges themselves which connected the boroughs to the east and west of the peninsula with the market place. Clayport ran north-east, becoming St Giles Street which led directly to Sherburn and hence to villages such as Pittington to the north-east of Durham. Fleshewergate divided into Sadlergate, running due south up to the castle gate, and Souterpeth leading to Elvet Bridge. Once across the bridge, the road further divided between New Elvet, proceeding towards Scaltok Mill, and Old Elvet, heading out south-east towards Shincliffe and Houghall. Silver Street dropped down to the Old Bridge and so into the Old Borough where it divided into three streets. South Street ran due south from the bridge towards Stockton; Crossgate was the main route to Brancepeth, and Milneburngate, later becoming Framwelgate, was the road to Chester-le-Street and Newcastle-upon-Tyne. All of the streets in these first two categories were called *via regia*, *via alta* or *vicus* in the deeds, indicating that they were of major importance in the street plan. Third, there were some subsidiary

---

[77] Compare with Alnwick, where the pattern of roads around the town could be identified with geological features: Conzen, *Alnwick*, pp. 13–16.

streets which connected different parts of each borough, such as Ratonrawe in New Elvet Borough and Walkergate in the Bishop's Borough. These streets (called simply *via* in the deeds) were of purely local significance, since they were not through-routes. Finally, there were a few narrow lanes or 'vennels' (*venella*) between neighbouring tenements. These gave access to the river, to wells, to the backs of tenements, to orchards or to a building lying behind the street line.

It is difficult to date the establishment of Durham's street plan or indeed of any of the individual streets with any certainty. It is probable that the streets were in existence from the earliest days of the town, particularly if, as argued earlier in this chapter, the boroughs developed as an independent network of communities around the peninsula. Some of the streets may have taken their names from these communities, in which case perhaps the evidence for the founding of the boroughs can be used to date the streets. Bishop Puiset's charter, for example, in which he restored the borough of Elvetehalge to the monks, may be the earliest documentary reference to the street of Elvet Borough as well as to the borough itself.[78] However, in the case of one borough at least it is clear that it was named after its principal street. Bishop Puiset granted Kepier Hospital a borough in the street of St Giles in the early twelfth century.[79] Here, the street took the name of the parish church by which it passed. From this admittedly scanty evidence, it appears that Durham's street plan and many street names were settled by the twelfth century. In comparison, Keene and Biddle estimate that the High Street in Winchester and its side streets were in existence by the tenth century and that all the principal streets of the medieval and modern plan were there by 1148. The Canterbury rentals show that the modern street plan can be carried back into the twelfth century and it is thought that most of the main streets were in existence by the tenth century. In contrast, Bristol's main street plan was fixed only by the relatively late date of 1300.[80]

Durham's street names seem to have remained unchanged throughout the medieval period, a stability which compares with

[78] 3.1.Pont.4; *Feodarium Dunelm*, pp. 198–9n.
[79] *Memorials of St Giles*, p. 195; *VCH Durham*, vol. 2, p. 111.
[80] Biddle, *Winchester*, pp. 279–82; Urry, *Canterbury*, p. 185; T. Tatton-Brown, 'Canterbury's urban topography: some recent work', in Riden (ed.), *The medieval town in Britain*, p. 91; Lobel, 'Bristol', p. 8.

Winchester, where there were only three changes in street names before the sixteenth century, but contrasts with Canterbury where it seems to have been more usual to refer to a street by its destination rather than a fixed name.[81] There are some minor variations of spelling in the Durham names: Crossgate was 'Crossegath' in 1306, 'Crossegate' in 1292 and 'Crosgate' in 1294 while Milneburngate appears as 'Milnburngate' (1309) and 'Milbornegaite' (1542), but these names are easily recognisable as variations on the same theme.[82] More confusing are the cases of streets which had several names in use at a given time. Fleshewergate (*Vicus Carnificorum*) was also known as the *Bucheria* as early as 1281 and occasionally as 'Cookrow' in the fourteenth century, names which refer to the predominant trades in the streets. Sadlergate or *Vicus Sellarii* was occasionally referred to as 'the street of the North Gate' (*vicus porte borialis Dunelm.*) in early-fourteenth-century deeds.[83] Here the clerks, if not the inhabitants, seem to have been torn between using an occupational street name or a locational name referring to the most striking monument in the street, the North Gate. Apart from these variant or alternative names, no Durham street changed its name in the medieval period.

Many of the street names of medieval Durham have a common ending in -gate (earlier, in -gath), such as Crossgate, Alvertongate, Framwelgate, or Fleshewergate, which is derived from the Old Norse *geata* meaning 'street'. Other elements of Durham's street names are derived from geographical features; most obviously, South Street is the main road to the south. Framwelgate and Milneburngate take their names from a well and a stream near the street.[84] Clayport may refer to the soil consistency near this street, or perhaps to the condition of the road surface in the early middle ages! Some names refer to buildings in the street, such as St Giles, near the church of that name, and the Baileys, within the castle fortifications. Another group of names originates from trades or occupations which may have predominated at one time in the street. Fleshewergate was where the butchers lived; Sadlergate, the leather workers, Souterpeth, the shoemakers, and Walkergate, the cloth workers. Other street names fall into no category;

[81] Keene, *Winchester*, vol. 1, part 1, p. 55; Urry, *Canterbury*, p. 202.
[82] See, for Crossgate variants, 4.18.Spec.1; Misc.Ch.1961; Misc.Ch.2372; for Milne-burngate, Misc.Ch.1966; Misc.Ch.2375; Rec. Book II.
[83] See, for example, 6.1.Elem.5″.
[84] Ekwall suggested that Framwelgate may mean 'strong spring' street: Ekwall, *Dictionary of English place-names.*

Alvertongate may have meant the street leading to Alverton or it may have referred to the name of a family living in the street. The Elvet and Old Elvet names remain mysterious in origin, with no particularly convincing derivation.

Durham's street plan, like its street names, has always been resistant to change, as a comparison between Speed's plan of 1611 and Wood's plan of 1820 shows.[85] Rental and other evidence leaves us in little doubt that Speed's plan reflects the primary and secondary routes of medieval Durham fairly closely. Most of these medieval streets are still in existence today, although the building of North Road in the middle of the nineteenth century and the ring road of the 1960s with its new bridge (Leazes Bridge) has on the one hand extended the town plan in a different direction (towards the north-west) and on the other amputated the borough of St Giles and part of Clayport from the rest of the settlement.[86] Nothing so drastic occurred in medieval Durham. There may have been encroachments on the street-line in popular streets such as Fleshewergate and Sadlergate, where there were booths in front of the tenements; however, these cannot have posed any major traffic problems because no cases of illegal encroachments seem to have come to court. Whereas in Winchester or Norwich, castle-building led to the blocking or diverting of streets, in Durham it had no effect on the streets because the main part of the peninsula had been allocated to military requirements from an early stage.[87]

The small lanes or vennels were less stable, not surprisingly, as they were narrow pedestrian ways rather than well-used streets and many were in private hands. Some of these vennels were moved relatively easily in the medieval period; the vennel which led between the tenements on the south side of Crossgate to the cellarer's orchard behind them was moved two tenements further up the street sometime during the fifteenth century. The old vennel had become part of the renovated burgage of St Cuthbert's Guild and so a new vennel had to be created to the west of the old. This vennel was in private hands; it was part of the property belonging to this guild, and as such it could be moved to suit the guild's requirements.[88] Another example of the relative im-

---

[85] See appendix 1, maps 1 and 2.   [86] Pocock and Gazzard, *Durham*, pp. 18–22.
[87] Biddle, *Winchester*, p. 303; J. Campbell, 'Norwich', in M. D. Lobel (ed.), *The atlas of historic towns*, vol. 2 (London, 1975), p. 8.
[88] See Longstaffe, 'Local muniments', p. 28; Alm. rental, 1501.

permanence of vennels can be seen in St Giles' Borough. William
Hexham was summoned to appear before the borough court in
1340, accused by the inhabitants of St Giles Street of obstructing
a right of way across his land from the main street to a common
well behind the tenements. During the hearing it emerged that
the path had come into existence only after the buildings on
Hexham's tenement were destroyed in the Scottish raids of the
early fourteenth century. When Hexham came to rebuild his
tenement, he blocked this illegal path.[89]

The instability of some of these 'private' vennels is balanced by
the stability of other vennels which seem to have been public
property. These public vennels, such as the vennel leading from
South Street to St Helen's Well, were kept open by court order, as
the Crossgate Court Book shows. Public vennels had a tendency
to become blocked with rubbish from the surrounding tenements
and the court issued repeated orders to the borough inhabitants in
the late fifteenth century and early sixteenth century to clear
them.[90] Those lanes which gave access to the castle walls were to
be kept open at all times, even if they were in private hands, for
military reasons. In 1450, the priory tried to block a lane from the
North Bailey to the walls by closing the gate beneath the tower
of St Mary's Church. The bishop objected on the grounds that the
gate had to be open to give access to the fortifications in wartime
and also to the monastic cemetery.[91]

Although the main purpose of the majority of Durham's streets
was to provide good communications between the town and the
countryside and between different parts of the town itself, in
addition, each street contained a mixture of residential and
commercial functions. Very few streets were primarily residential
although there were some like South Street, Alvertongate, the
Baileys and Ratonrawe in New Elvet which seem to have
contained very few workshops, booths or even brewing
equipment in gardens behind the buildings. Most workshops and
commercial premises were to be found in the streets of the
Bishop's Borough. There were tanneries and goldsmiths in
Sadlergate and butchers' stalls in Fleshewergate. Many tenements
in Framwelgate contained 'barkhouses' (that is, tanning houses)
and brewing equipment, and there were kilns within tenements in

[89] 6.4.Elem.11.
[90] See, for example, Crossgate Court Book, 11 January 1502 [1503].
[91] 2.16.Spec.37.

63

Clayport and across the boundary into St Giles' Borough.[92] But the market place was the focus of most commercial activity in Durham. Mercers leased shops around the market place and there were stalls under and around the tolbooth in its south-western corner. According to Speed's plan, it was a large, rectangular area, presumably filled with temporary stalls on market days. Its monopoly of trade in the town seems complete, for there is no surviving evidence of any other street markets in Durham, although a post-medieval horse fair held in St Giles Street may have had medieval antecedents.[93]

The responsibility for repairing and maintaining Durham's main roads and streets seems to have been borne by the overlords of individual boroughs. Thus the priory's obedientiaries, in particular, the hostillar, the almoner and the bursar, organised the work on roads in priory boroughs and provided the finance. However, it appears that the priory was expected to contribute to paving in the Bishop's Borough as well, on the bridges and in the Bailey, presumably because of the expense of bridge work and, in the case of the Bailey, because it gave access to the monastic precinct. There is no surviving evidence to suggest that the bishop contributed to road repairs outside his own borough. More minor streets and public vennels were probably repaired by those inhabitants living near them. The vennel leading to St Helen's Well from South Street was supposed to be repaired by the inhabitants of South Street, although the frequent presentations before the Crossgate court suggest that it was a duty often shirked.[94]

The priory account rolls reveal that the money needed for road repairs was considerable, which in itself is indirect evidence for the popularity of this small medieval town in the region. The number of carts coming to the market, as well as the pilgrim traffic and those summoned to attend courts and meetings within the castle would all exert considerable wear and tear on the main routes into the town. There was a variety of fund-raising methods employed for road repairs. First, there were the irregular and very occasional large grants of pavage made by the bishop to his

---

[92] See, for example, John Yowdale's tenement in Framwelgate: 1.18.Spec.25; for kilns in Clayport, see 5.2.Elem.14 and 5.2.Elem.16.
[93] Surtees, *Durham* 4, p. 55, and note e; appendix 1, map 1.
[94] See, for example, Crossgate Court Book, 11 January 1503.

burgesses, for resurfacing the streets in his own borough.[95] This money was to be raised, like murage, from the collection of tolls on specified goods coming to the market which were then assigned to roadworks. Pavage was administered by two or three collectors, elected by the borough inhabitants, and again, like murage, it was open to corruption by collectors who could divert funds to line their own pockets.[96] Presumably there were fluctuations in the amount raised depending on the type and quantities of goods brought into the market, and the collectors might have to wait for many months before enough money was gathered to start the work. However, pavage grants usually had a strict time limit imposed on them of perhaps three or five years.

The priory officers relied on a different method of fund-raising. Lacking sufficient resources in their own individual accounts to undertake any major roadwork, they collected contributions from other obedientiaries which were allocated to specific building projects in a given year. For the major repair work, a man, often a cleric in minor orders, was appointed to be the overseer *ex precepto Prioris*; he hired his labourers, paid for the necessary materials and then presented his account to a priory officer for settlement. No detailed road-repair accounts survive for the medieval period, but the entries in the priory account rolls, such as the hostillar's contribution of £1. 3s. 4d. in 1421 to Master William Doncastre for the repair of the road in Elvet and the almoner's contribution of 2s. for the same year, show the system at work.[97] Doncastre, the vicar of St Oswald's Church, supervised much of this type of work between 1421 and 1430 in Crossgate as well as in Elvet. It is also notable that he was employed by the priory to act as a trustee for the purchase of property on their behalf at the same period.[98] Other supervisors mentioned in the account rolls were the chaplains Thomas Kay, in 1431, and John Fyscheburn, in 1422, who were both involved in repair work on the Old Bridge.[99] Routine maintenance work on streets required

95 Bishop Hatfield granted pavage and murage to his Durham burgesses in March 1379: PRO Durham Chancery Enrolments, 3/31, m.13. Bishop Langley granted the same in January 1409: PRO Durham Chancery Enrolments, 3/34, m.2.

96 See the case recorded in PRO Durham Chancery Enrolments, 3/32, m.8.

97 Host. account, 1421/22, *Dona*; Alm. account, 1421/22, *Dona*. There is one surviving building account dating from 1545 in which the supervisor of building work in the Bailey was Thomas Hunter: Misc.Ch.2869.

98 See, for example, Alm. accounts 1421/22; 1422/23; 1423/24; 1430/31, *Dona*.

99 Alm. account, 1431/32; Burs. account, 1422/23, *Dona*.

a less elaborate system of financial control and oversight. Under the 'necessary expenses' section of the account rolls, priory officers made small individual payments direct to workmen for road repairs. In 1347, for example, the hostillar paid 1s. 8d. for repairs to the pavement next to the North Gate and in Souterpeth. In 1383 the sacrist paid for the repair of the North Bailey (2s. 6d.) and the almoner paid John Pavitor for paving the street in front of the doorway to his exchequer in 1456.[100]

In some cases, the account rolls reveal the type of materials bought for road repairs and hence the nature of road surfaces in late-medieval Durham. The main streets such as St Giles, Old and New Elvet, Framwelgate, Crossgate and the bridges were paved with 'shaped stones', but paving probably did not continue beyond the edge of settlement. The secondary roads and vennels may have consisted of beaten earth. When a road near Scaltok Mill was flooded, one of the complaints made against the priory in the 1440s was that the flooding was the result of earth being taken from the road to shore up the mill dam.[101] Most of the money spent by the priory's obedientiaries on road repairs would not be used on these dirt tracks but would be devoted to the maintenance of the paved streets which carried most of the traffic to Durham's market or to the castle and the monastic precinct.

Certain roads in Durham needed constant rebuilding, as the account rolls emphasise, presumably as much because of the volume of traffic they carried as through any faults of construction. The roads in Elvet, for example, were repaired at some cost in 1412, 1418, 1419, 1421 and 1422. Elvet Bridge was repaired in 1378, 1381, 1397 and 1418. Framwelgate Bridge was repaired in 1401, 1402, 1414, 1419, 1422 and 1421.[102] The Bailey was also expensive to maintain. The sums of money concerned varied from a few pence to many shillings. The hostillar contributed large sums almost every year between 1383 and 1426 for work all over the town, rising to £2. 12s. 8d. for paving the Bailey in 1413.[103] The almoner contributed regularly to road

---

[100] Host. account, 1347/48; Sac. account, 1384/85, Expenses; Alm. account, 1456/57, Repairs.
[101] Misc.Ch.5828/9.
[102] For repairs to Elvet roads, see Alm. accounts, 1412/13, *Expense Varie*; 1418/19, 1419/20, 1421/22, 1422/23, *Dona*. For repairs to Elvet Bridge, see Alm. account, 1378/79, *Dona*; Burs. accounts, 1381/82, 1397/98, *Expense Necessarie*; Host. account, 1418/19. For repairs to Framwelgate Bridge, see Alm. accounts, 1401/02, 1402/03, 1414/15, 1419/20, 1431/32, *Dona*; Burs. account, 1422/23. *Dona*.
[103] Host. account, 1413/14.

repairs between 1397 and 1432, but the sums were smaller than those given by the hostillar. The bursar contributed less than the almoner overall, with expenditure being highest between 1397 and 1423. The last years of the fourteenth century and the early years of the fifteenth century seem to have marked the peak of contributions and support by the priory to road repairs in Durham, a period when, as will be demonstrated in a later chapter, its income from its urban property was falling.[104] The fact that the priory diverted considerable sums of money to roadworks and that elaborate arrangements were made for financing the work indicates the importance which the overlords of Durham attached to keeping them in good repair. The paving of the streets would have improved both the access to Durham and the appearance of the town and it may have accompanied a period of commercial expansion.

TENEMENTS, MESSUAGES AND BURGAGES

The last ingredient which goes to make up the characteristic appearance of a town's plan is the pattern, or lack of it, of tenements along the streets. As with every other aspect of Durham's topography, the layout of tenements at the centre reflects the constraints of the peninsula site. The congestion of irregular plots of land around the market place demonstrates graphically the popularity of the Bishop's Borough for settlement and the relative prestige of a street frontage near the market place. The outer boroughs, separated as they were from the central trading area by the river, had a much more regular and generous tenement layout because there were fewer physical restrictions and the land market was perhaps not so competitive. Indeed, on the fringes of the urban area, it is possible to see that the medieval town was retreating as tenements amalgamated or were converted from domestic accommodation into closes and orchards. Tenement boundaries, which in other parts of the town were one of the most durable features of the urban landscape, were becoming blurred in those parts of Durham which seem to have been in recession in the later middle ages. The countryside was beginning to advance into streets which, like South Street, had once possessed all the characteristics of an urban community.

Before the tenement patterns of medieval Durham can

[104] See chapter 4, pp. 121, 130.

be analysed, some attempt must be made to grapple with the almost bewildering variety of terms used by contemporaries to describe plots of land. The three words most commonly found in the Durham documents are *tenementum*, *messuagium* and *burgagium*. *Tenementum*, the term which will be used in this chapter, seems to have meant no more than a distinct unit of land with precise boundaries, usually fronting or 'abutting' a street. It might have contained buildings, but it is dangerous to infer this from a medieval document without other supporting evidence. A tenement which had buildings within its boundaries was usually said to be *tenementum edificatum* or *tenementum de novo constructum*, as in the case of the almoner's tenements at the end of Elvet Bridge (1424).[105] The legal title to a tenement was the main concern of a tenant, for it gave him both status in town society and a valuable asset which he could leave to his heirs or realise for a substantial sum of money. The importance to his landlord was not the land or what was on it, but rather the rent owed by that tenement as well as certain additional services. The terms *messuagium* and *burgagium* may have had some special meaning in the early medieval period, but by the later middle ages they seem to have been used interchangeably and somewhat loosely. In 1479, John Richardson resigned to Robert Patson any claim he had to 'one tenement or burgage with its appurtenances' in Framwelgate.[106] It is probable that what was understood by the terms tenement, messuage or burgage changed and blurred over the years, becoming no more than legal jargon. This impression is strengthened by the observation that certain groups of documents such as final concords always contain the same term, messuage, to describe land holdings, whether or not there was a building on the plot.

In some medieval towns the terminology was much more precise, however. In Alnwick, for example, a burgage was a land holding in the town while a tenement was a holding in Bailiffgate, a street occupied by castle retainers.[107] *Burgagium* was, perhaps, used more cautiously by medieval conveyancers because it implied burgage tenure and all its accompanying privileges. It is clear that the concept of burgage tenure itself was well established in Durham: in 1500, William Waynman was said to be a burgess by virtue of his tenure of a certain burgage on the south side of

---

[105] Alm. rental, 1424. [106] 1.18.Spec.39.
[107] Conzen, *Alnwick*, p. 22.

Crossgate.[108] However, burgage tenure was not only attached to burgages in Durham; it was associated with land called tenements and messuages. This is clear from the almoner's rental of 1424 where several tenements in South Street, for example, are said to be held *in liberum burgagium* and to owe a money rent called a freehold rent. So what we seem to have in late-medieval Durham is a flexible terminology which probably disguises a conventional legal relationship between landlord and tenant.

The general pattern of tenements along Durham's streets is difficult to assess with certainty from medieval sources because of the lack of contemporary plans for the whole town and the rarity of deeds which give any exact dimensions of tenements. Apart from the mid-fifteenth-century plan of a few tenements in New Elvet and the possibly mid-sixteenth-century plan of a corner of the market place, which can hardly be called representative of tenement patterns in Durham, Wood's plan of 1820 is the earliest surviving guide to tenement shapes.[109] It shows that most tenements were long, strip plots lying short side to the street frontage at a right angle to the street line in a typical 'high street' or 'herringbone' pattern which has been found in medieval towns such as Market Harborough and Alnwick.[110] The exceptions to this pattern occurred at street corners, where the tenements interlocked in complex patterns, or where the dictates of the site led to tenements lying long side to the street. The slim medieval documentary evidence suggests that Wood's plan reflects the medieval layout fairly closely; fourteenth-century deeds describe property in Crossgate, for example, as lying 'in length from the roadway as far as the Milneburn'. Reginald Sesse's holding in Sadlergate was seven feet in breadth along the roadside and seventeen feet in length from the road to the castle motte.[111]

The conclusions to emerge from this somewhat ambiguous evidence are that the layout of Durham's tenements produced a mixture of long, narrow 'herringbone' plots along the streets in the outer boroughs and small irregular plots near the commercial

---

[108] Sac. rental, 1500.

[109] Loc. XXXVII, no. 113; Misc.Ch.5828/12; see appendix 1, maps 5, 6, 2.

[110] H. Carter, 'The geographical approach', in M. W. Barley (ed.), *The plans and topography of medieval towns*, CBA Research Report no. 14 (London, 1976), pp. 15–16; Platt, *English medieval town*, pp. 30, 51; Parker, *King's Lynn*, p. 33.

[111] For Crossgate, see, for example, undated deed (possibly late thirteenth century), Misc.Ch.2049; charter of 1320, 1.16.Spec.30. For Sadlergate, see, for example, undated deed (? late thirteenth century), 6.1.Elem.1**.

centre, particularly around the market place and the bridgeheads. The reasons for this mixture can be deduced from geographical and economic factors. Beyond the peninsula, without the restrictions imposed by the uneven terrain and the river's gorge, a regular, almost planned layout of tenements could develop. As the edge of the urban area was reached, the plots became larger and less well-defined and they merged with the common fields of the boroughs. In the central borough and the Bailey, severe limitations were imposed not only by the physical features of the site, but also by the occupation of most of the available land on the peninsula by the monastic precinct, the castle and fortifications. The Bailey tenements and plots on the west side of Sadlergate and Fleshewergate were attenuated by the line of the walls and the castle motte. Such physical constraints restricted the depth of individual tenements and led to some peculiarities of shape. Thomas de Asgarby's tenement in Sadlergate was one of the best examples of such eccentricities; his plot of land was thirty-eight feet long, five feet wide on the east side and two feet wide on the west side.[112]

Furthermore, the average size of tenements in the central area of Durham seems to have been much smaller than those in the outer boroughs. Robert Cocus held land in the Bailey which was forty-eight feet in length but only eight feet wide.[113] Roger Sesse's holding in Sadlergate is perhaps an extreme example, but a holding in Fleshewergate measured only twenty feet in length and twelve feet in width and it was called, appropriately enough, 'le Colhole'.[114] Such small units of land probably reflect the intense competition for a market frontage in the commercial centre of Durham: booths were often built out into the street as an additional source of rent for the landlord and to provide extra trading premises. There may have been a relationship between the value of a frontage and the width of a tenement in Durham, as M. R. G. Conzen found in Alnwick, but this is hard to prove, given the lack of dimensions in the deeds.[115] Around the market and at the bridgeheads, where opportunities for trading were greatest, tenements seem to have had narrower street frontages.

[112] 2.11.Spec.33.
[113] Undated deed (possibly late thirteenth century), Misc.Ch.2398.
[114] 6.1.Elem.1**; undated deed, 3.18.Spec.2.
[115] Conzen, *Alnwick*, p. 28.

Even within one borough, there were variations in tenement sizes which probably related to the popularity of the street. In the Old Borough, the tenement pattern was more regular in Crossgate and Alvertongate, and frontages seem to have been narrow in contrast with, for example, South Street: there, some larger tenements were interspersed with orchards and closes. Rental and account-roll evidence shows that South Street was an economic backwater as early as the fourteenth century with many waste tenements, unpaid rents and the amalgamation of tenements into larger units.[116] Crossgate was more prosperous, with no shortage of tenants ready to take up holdings in the street, several trades operating there and the borough court house generating activity. The tenement pattern may reflect the relative popularity as well as the prosperity of Durham streets.

There is a striking continuity of tenement boundaries in Durham, as in many medieval towns such as York, for example, where, in Skeldergate, the tenement boundaries of the eighteenth century have been carried back to the Anglo-Scandinavian period. In Canterbury, William Urry was able to trace the origins of the modern ground plan back into the twelfth century.[117] The results of excavations in Saddler Street, Durham, were equally dramatic. The late-eleventh-century fenced tenements lying end-on to the street beneath the castle survived as the property boundaries until 1974.[118] Several reasons for this fossilisation of tenement boundaries can be suggested. Such boundaries are usually conditioned by the street framework and once a street line is set it rarely changes. In these circumstances, it is difficult for new property boundaries to emerge. The concentration of population in at least the centre of a town and the steady demand for sites means it is unlikely that tenements would change greatly, except to be subdivided to increase the number of tenant holdings. Lastly, it was not in the interests of the overlords that boundaries should shift constantly, so producing difficulties in assessing and levying rents. The rarity of boundary changes is emphasised by the existence of only two examples in the surviving Durham sources. One concerned the tenements at the top of Sadlergate which were

116 Sac. rental, 1500; Alm. rental, 1424; Wood's plan, 1820 (see appendix 1, map 2); see chapter 4, pp. 125, 128, 140.
117 Hall, 'Topography of Anglo-Scandinavian York', p. 36; Urry, *Canterbury*, p. 185.
118 Carver, 'Three Saxo-Norman tenements', p. 9.

swept away when the North Gate was rebuilt and extended
c. 1313 : the original tenement boundaries were lost.[119] In the second
example, from Crossgate, a vennel was moved further up the
south side of the street during the fifteenth century as a result of
the rebuilding of houses on two tenements held by the guild of St
Cuthbert.[120] Boundary changes such as these were so unusual that
they merited special reference in the rentals and deeds.

However, within individual tenement boundaries, there was
constant change as tenements were subdivided or amalgamated
with neighbouring plots. Often a tenement was halved or
quartered and four buildings erected on it, each owing a separate
rent. Sometimes the back part of the tenement was portioned off,
to be amalgamated later with the neighbouring tenement. The
permutations were endless. Richard Undermaistre's tenement on
the south side of Crossgate was divided into two and each part
owed the almoner a rent of 4½*d.* per annum in 1344.[121] In Elvet,
a tenement was divided and each part called a 'moiety' in the
rentals; the division had been accurate and fair and presumably
longitudinal, for each part measured twenty-two feet in front
(1396).[122] When the almoner rebuilt his tenement at the east end
of Elvet Bridge, he divided it into three separate units. A special
inquiry was held in 1404 in which the boundaries of this tenement
were enumerated with great care to forestall any possibility of a
future claim against the priory by the tenants.[123] Amalgamations
of tenements, though not of rents, usually took place on the outer
edges of the town and in those streets which, like South Street,
seem to have gone into decline in the later medieval period. It was
carefully recorded in the sacrist's rental of 1500 that John Claxton
held eight burgages amalgamated into a close at the top of
Crossgate. Yet the original tenement boundaries and the rents
were not forgotten, because the sacrist's rental of 1500 recorded
that four of the eight burgages owed rent of 4*d.* each, a fifth of 8*d.*,
the sixth of 5*d.* and the other two of 4½*d.* each.

In the medieval rentals it is interesting to observe that some
tenements in Durham were identified by their own names rather

---

[119] In May 1313, William de Denum and Adam de Boghes were ordered to 'enquire
diligently' into the value of the messuages of John de Pollowe and William, rector
of St Mary's Church in the North Bailey, and of any others near the North Gate *quae
amoveri debent pro muro Barbecan portae faciendo: RegPalDun* I, p. 338.

[120] See Longstaffe, 'Local muniments', p. 28; Alm. rental, 1501.

[121] Alm. rent roll, 1344/45.

[122] Burs. rentals, 1396, 1397, Elvet.   [123] 1.6.Elem.5★; Alm. rental, 1424.

than by the name of a tenant. Such names can be divided into three categories. The first category contains names derived from a family which held the tenement for many years. Some of these tenements seem to have been substantial holdings belonging to the burgess-class of prosperous townsmen or of local small landholders. In Alvertongate, for example, the almoner held four burgages which were amalgamated into a close by 1424, called Forsterhouse. Among the names of previous tenants who had held this land was Gilbert Forester who had, presumably, given his name to these tenements.[124] The burgage called Bedforthplace in Old Elvet may have been held by the Bedford family in the early medieval period, as Hagthorpplace on the *placea* was held by members of the Hagthorp family in the middle of the fourteenth century.[125] A second category is taken from the occupation of those who once lived there. This category includes names like 'le Barkhousyarde', a garden in Sadlergate; Copperplace, a tenement in North Bailey; 'le Byre' and 'le Haverbarn', two waste tenements at the end of South Street; 'Mevhanthouse' in South Street; and those tenements which took their names from some religious or municipal organisation which met there, like 'le Tolbothe', a burgage in Crossgate; or 'le Gildhall', a great hall of stone in the market, for example.[126] A third, and the smallest, category of names seems to have related to the shape, size or position of the tenement. Into this category comes 'le Colhole', a strip of land in Fleshewergate, and 'le Cornerbothe', which was, as its name suggests, the tenement on the corner of the market place and Fleshewergate.[127]

The names of tenements, like their boundaries, seem to have been remarkably resilient; many appear in the first surviving rent roll of the almoner, dating from *c.* 1290, and they were still in use in the rentals of the fifteenth century. Of course, the rentals themselves were very conservative documents; the fact that a name was recorded there may not mean it was in current usage unless there is other corroborative evidence, for example, from deeds. There is only one surviving instance of a name of a tenement changing during the medieval period. Four tenements known as 'Lithfothall' in the early medieval period became 'le

---

[124] Alm. rental, 1424.
[125] PRO Durham Chancery Enrolments, 3/62, m.1d; Misc.Ch.1707; Misc.Ch.1703.
[126] See 3.2.Sac.3; PRO Durham Chancery Enrolments, 3/71, m.12; Alm. rental, 1424; Sac. rental, 1500.   [127] 3.18.Spec.2; Misc.Ch.2009.

Shyrefhous' by the middle of the fourteenth century. It may be significant that this property was acquired in the early fourteenth century by the de la Pole family of Hull merchants, who were involved in shipping wine, among other goods, from Hull to Newcastle and so to Durham. They may have used this house as their commercial base when involved in transactions with the bishop and Durham Priory.[128]

Although few of the surviving medieval sources give much accurate or precise information about the shape and size of tenements, it is suggested that tenement boundaries in Durham were one of the most stable elements of the urban landscape. The street plan and the tenement pattern, in particular, remained remarkably resistant to change, a resistance which was, it can be argued, a result of the physical limitations of the site as well as the lack of industrial development of the town. One of the main conclusions to emerge from the study of Durham's urban landscape is that it changed very little in the period between *c.* 1250 and 1540. Consequently, it is also possible to gain some impression of the medieval city from more modern sources, such as John Wood's plan of 1820, and even by observations of property boundaries in Durham today in those streets near the city centre where changes have been minimal and where there has been a continuity of ownership from the medieval priory to the modern dean and chapter of Durham.

[128] 2.2.Elem.16; Alm. rental, 1424; *VCH Yorkshire, East Riding*, vol. 1, p. 81.

Chapter 3

Durham's medieval buildings

Although it is the buildings on the peninsula which give Durham its distinctive appearance today, as they did in the medieval period, they were entirely untypical of the character of the medieval town which lay beyond the castle and cathedral walls. The greatest feats of medieval architecture and engineering were devoted to improving Durham's defences against the Scots and to glorifying God in the magnificence of the cathedral. However, the majority of Durham's inhabitants lived and worked in a less elevated sphere in the small and undistinguished market town huddling below the castle walls which is the subject of this study. There were few houses or public buildings of any character in medieval Durham. Most were single-storied, small, wooden and thatched.[1] They were places of work as well as family homes, overcrowded and completely lacking in privacy, a prey to fire damage or flooding. It is these buildings which are surveyed in this chapter.

Such a general survey of Durham's domestic buildings reveals graphically the parts of the urban area which were most popular with tenants and thus heavily populated. Some streets – for example, Crossgate, Clayport, Fleshewergate, Sadlergate and New Elvet – seem to have had a continuous line of housing along both sides of the road throughout the medieval period. These streets, it can be argued, were those where frontages were most valuable and where, on commercial grounds, those with trading or manufacturing interests wanted to live. For similar reasons, there was also a concentration of buildings, public as well as domestic, around the market place. By contrast, in the parts of Durham which lay furthest from the market, in Framwelgate,

---

[1] As in medieval Colchester, where apart from the castle, the monastic buildings and the town walls there was 'no grand architecture' and little difference between the town and the neighbouring village streets: R. H. Britnell, *Growth and decline in Colchester, 1300–1525* (Cambridge, 1986), pp. 10–11.

South Street and St Giles, buildings had fallen into decay by the late fourteenth century. They were not always repaired and consequently significant gaps had appeared in the street line by 1500.[2] This evidence supports the view, gained from other sources, of decline – or at least some contraction – of the urban area which was advanced in the previous chapter. This trend may have been the result of a conscious policy followed by the priory. There are indications in the priory account rolls that more money was directed towards housing repairs in the central, profitable streets in the boroughs while property on the outskirts of the town was allowed to decline. It was here that the countryside impinged most clearly on the urban area, as gradually these waste tenements returned to agricultural land and barns or dovecots replaced domestic buildings.

This survey of Durham's buildings is equally important for the evidence it provides, however tangential or negative, of the town's status and wealth in comparison with other urban centres; in other words, the buildings can be used as a 'measure of urbanism'.[3] If found, the presence of a large number of stone-built houses with halls in the town would have implied a relatively high standard of wealth, at least among a few prosperous families or traders. In contrast, rows of small, uniform cottages would suggest a predominantly artisan or labouring community. Furthermore, the quality and scale of domestic building in the town could test any theories of urban or population decline in the late-medieval city.[4] In reality, there were few stone-built houses to be seen anywhere in medieval Durham, but there is ample documentary – and some archaeological – evidence for many simple wooden houses, evidence which implies that the majority of the town's inhabitants were never very wealthy and did not enjoy a particularly high standard of living. Although there were obviously improvements in building techniques, such as the introduction of timber-framed houses by the end of the fourteenth century, the fact that simple wattle-and-daub houses were still being constructed or renovated in Durham as late as the end of the fifteenth century shows that the level of wealth in the town did not keep pace with progress in building technology.

[2] Sac. rental, 1500.

[3] J. Munby, 'Medieval domestic buildings', in J. Schofield and R. Leech (eds.), *Urban archaeology in Britain*, CBA Research Report no. 61 (London, 1987), p. 156.

[4] D. M. Palliser, 'The medieval period', in Schofield and Leech, *Urban archaeology*, p. 58.

Durham's medieval buildings

The number of public buildings, such as guild halls and court houses, which are found in a medieval town obviously has some bearing on the degree of corporate life or of municipal independence enjoyed by its inhabitants. There were no 'municipal' funds as such in Durham, a position directly comparable with medieval Westminster, for example, and so there were no communal works, like a town hall, undertaken by the whole community.[5] The building of a town wall in the early fourteenth century may seem the exception to this assertion, because it arose as a result of corporate action organised by the Durham townsmen, but the initiative for this work and the financial arrangements originated with the bishop. He simply delegated the responsibility for collecting the tolls assigned to financing it (murage) and the oversight of its construction to leading burgesses in his borough.[6] This lack of communal activity or even the impetus towards it on the part of the inhabitants is hardly surprising, given the fragmented lordship and administration of the town outlined in the previous chapter. But the result was that, as in Westminster, the smaller units of administration – the borough and the parish – assumed a greater importance which is reflected in their public buildings.[7] Nearly every part of the town had its own court house, a church or chapel and a guild hall. The number of these guild halls seems to have increased by the fifteenth century as a result of the founding of new religious guilds, perhaps indicating both a growth in popular piety and the wish of Durham's inhabitants to have a greater share in parish affairs. However, only one such hall was of any architectural distinction, the hall of St Nicholas' Guild in the market place, and many of the others seem to have fallen into disuse by the end of the medieval period, a state probably more reflective of the limited amount of money available for maintaining ventures of this kind rather than any decline in religious belief. The multiplicity of court houses was unusual for a town of Durham's size, but these court buildings were by no means a measure of the town's independence or of the townsmen's privileges. The courts were not run by townsmen but by the borough overlords, and as

[5] A. G. Rosser, 'The essence of medieval urban communities: the vill of Westminster, 1200–1540', *TRHS*, 5th ser., 34 (1984), 91–112.

[6] See, for example, Bishop Kellaw's grant of murage of 13 May 1315: *RegPalDun* 2, p. 1071.

[7] Rosser, 'Essence of medieval urban communities', p. 101.

such they indicate the very close legal and financial control exercised within the separate jurisdictional areas.

This chapter is divided into two sections, the first containing a description of domestic buildings, the houses, cottages and workshops in which Durham's medieval inhabitants lived. Public buildings like court houses, guild halls and bakehouses are described in the second section.[8] Most of the documentary sources for this chapter are drawn from the priory archives. The title deeds are a prime source, especially leases which, in several cases, specify the dimensions of a building or enumerate the individual rooms within a house. Many leases, particularly those issued by the sacrist, include detailed conditions for the tenant, such as undertaking repair work and maintenance to certain specifications. The priory account rolls provide information about the organisation of the building trade and the materials used in construction work. Where the responsibility for the upkeep of a public building fell to a priory officer, as in the case of bakehouses, their appearance and construction is detailed in the accounts. The records of the borough courts contain a mass of references to buildings in cases concerning, for example, a tenant's responsibility to maintain the frontage of his property, to avoid damage to neighbouring properties by repairing faulty gutters or sewers and to prevent the sub-letting of outbuildings to undesirable characters. More serious criminal cases heard in the prior's court, such as alleged burglaries, give incidental references to the contents and furnishings of houses. But the evidence for Durham's buildings is not confined to documentary sources alone. Two excavations in the urban area, in modern Saddler Street and New Elvet, revealed the dimensions and internal plans of some medieval town houses as well as the materials used in their construction.[9]

DOMESTIC BUILDINGS

Undoubtedly the periphery of the market place with the streets leading into it, all contained within the Bishop's Borough, was the part of medieval Durham which contained the greatest number of domestic buildings. Speed's plan of 1611 shows a

---

[8] Mills, which were also public buildings in this sense, are discussed in chapter 2, pp. 54–8.

[9] Carver, 'Three Saxon-Norman tenements', pp. 1–80; Carver, 'Excavations in New Elvet', pp. 91–148.

continuous line of housing along these streets, and the title deeds reveal a keen competition among tenants for valuable property here, which is marked by the subdivision of tenements and the construction of booths in front of existing workshops.[10] Outside this congested 'inner-city' area, commercial pressures on land seem to lessen in direct relationship to the distance from the market place and the plans of houses built on the larger tenements there may have been more spacious. Unfortunately, no complete medieval domestic buildings stand in Durham today to support the documentary evidence. Some partial survivors are to be seen, for example, in Silver Street, Owengate and in the restored Jewellery Centre in Millburngate, while several houses in or around the peninsula have medieval cellars.[11] It is difficult to reconstruct any visual image of the medieval town from these remnants. However, the documentary evidence does provide detailed information about the materials, the construction and, in a few cases, the dimensions of these buildings.

The Durham documents contain a wide variety of terms to describe a building erected on a landholding. The word most commonly used to describe any category of domestic building from the smallest workshop to the largest hall-house is *domus*. *Cotagium* appears in the late fifteenth century, particularly in Elvet, to describe simple, small and uniform dwellings probably built to accommodate labourers.[12] *Mansio* is rarely found and seems to indicate a more substantial dwelling, such as the one held by Robert Rodes next to the South Gate in the South Bailey in 1449.[13] *Camera* denotes a room within a building, and *solarium* and *celarium* are terms which describe rooms in a house lying above or below the workshop of a domestic property. *Shopa*, *celda*, *seuda* or *botha* are used to describe the working area which had direct access to the street frontage. William Vaginator, for example, leased a stall with a solar built above it and a small cellar (*ceuda cum solario supraessenter...et parvum celarium*) in Fleshewergate in 1309, a description which succinctly explains the relationship between the principal rooms of his house.[14] Occasionally the type of workshop is specified by the use of a term such as *tanneria*.[15]

---

[10] See appendix 1, map 1; there was a similar situation in medieval Bristol: Lobel, 'Bristol', p. 13.
[11] Pocock and Gazzard, *Durham*, p. 53. Millburngate is the modern spelling for the street called Milneburngate in the medieval period.
[12] Alm. rental, 1424, Elvet.   [13] 2.18.Spec.20; 2.18.Spec.29.
[14] Misc.Ch.2006.   [15] See, for example, Loc. IV, no. 52.

A survey of building types and materials in medieval Durham quickly shows that there were few imposing stone-built houses in the town. There were some on the peninsula at the end of the thirteenth century; several county families had their town houses in the Bailey and its associated streets. These houses were held from the bishop by various forms of military service, on condition that, for example, adequate accommodation was provided for armed men and stabling for specified numbers of horses in times of war. Ralph de Amundevill's 'capital' messuage in the South Bailey contained stabling facilities for eight horses in 1244.[16] Consequently, such houses were designed to cope with military contingencies or with large numbers of guests, whether armed retainers or family relatives from the country attracted to Durham by a social event such as the holding of the assizes, and they contained many rooms.[17] Another part of Durham where stone houses were to be found was around the market place. Here, it seems, lived the merchant class, if such a grand title can be attributed to the small group of men whose opportunities to make a profit from trade in Durham were somewhat more restricted than, for example, their Newcastle counterparts.[18] Reginald Mercator probably built his 'great hall of stone' (*magnum hospicium* with *aula lapidis*) in the market place in the late thirteenth century from the proceeds of trade with the priory.[19] But there were a few stone houses in other parts of Durham as well, although these seem to have been a rarity. Thomas Blagrise had a house in Alvertongate in 1296 which contained a stone cellar (*unum celarium lapideum*) and access to the solar was by external stone steps.[20] Tenants removed stone from the ruined house of the terrar in South Street, probably to repair their own houses, in the early fourteenth century.[21] Excavations have produced evidence of stone houses in Milneburngate, which have been dated provisionally to the late twelfth century, and in Elvet, where a series of houses built between the thirteenth century and the late fourteenth century had walls of ashlar or of coarse sandstone rubble bonded with clay.[22] If it can be argued that these stone houses represent the homes of the rich, then it appears that

[16] 3.2.Sac.9b.
[17] See, for example, Jordan de Claxton's house in the Bailey: 1.1.Finch.13*; below, p. 86.
[18] See chapter 5, pp. 157–8, 166–7, 182.   [19] 6.1.Elem.6; Alm, rental, 1424.
[20] 1.2.Sac.32.   [21] Loc.IV, no. 1.
[22] Report in *Durham Advertiser*, July 1983; Carver, 'Excavations in New Elvet', p. 109.

a scattering of wealthy Durham inhabitants extended to all the boroughs. As in other medieval towns such as Bristol and Winchester, the wealthier Durham townsmen appear to have lived side by side with the poor in conditions which we might term slums today. But the greater number of references to stone-built properties in the Bishop's Borough and on the peninsula suggests that these were the parts of Durham which were more fashionable for the rich.[23]

Durham masons and house-builders did not have far to go for their building materials; they had to look no further than the sandstone which outcropped all around the banks of the gorge of the River Wear. Both the sacrist and the almoner had quarries at the south end of South Street, and there are references to a quarry of the 'community' nearby. These quarries may have supplied stone for the construction of Thomas Blagrise's house. Walling stone for house-building in the North Bailey was brought from the almoner's quarry in Elvet by his Shincliffe tenants in 1456. The sacrist's South Street quarry provided stone to repair a tenement in Souterpeth in 1480 and for building in Clayport in 1474.[24] However, the expense both of working and of carrying the stone to houses in Durham even over these short distances must have been considerable: no doubt this helps to account for the rarity of stone houses in Durham, a position which compares with other larger medieval towns like Winchester or Bristol but contrasts with, for example, early medieval Canterbury.[25]

However, there is an abundance of documentary references to wooden houses in medieval Durham. Timber was by far the most common building material, presumably because it was cheaper to obtain and it was in plentiful local supply. The cathedral priory, for example, drew on its extensive holdings of forest-land near the town for wood and timber. In 1372, timber for a house called 'Lythfothouses' in the North Bailey came from Bearpark, Coddisley and Elvetwood and spars came from Muggleswick.[26] When the priory commoner rebuilt a tenement in Clayport in

[23] Lobel, 'Bristol', p. 13; Biddle, *Winchester*, p. 347.
[24] Alm. rental, 1424; Alm. accounts, 1456/57; 1480/81, Repairs; Comm. account, 1474/75, Carriage.
[25] Biddle, *Winchester*, pp. 346–7; Lobel, 'Bristol', pp. 4–5. In contrast, thirty stone houses are mentioned in the Canterbury rentals: Urry, *Canterbury*, p. 193. Salzman estimated that the carriage of stone over twelve miles cost as much as the stone itself: L. F. Salzman, *Building in England*, 2nd edn (Oxford, 1967), p. 119.
[26] Alm. account, 1372/73, Repairs.

1474, he acquired timber from Hett wood. The bursar paid Ralph Joulyn for 'spers' which Ralph had fashioned at Muggleswick in 1368 to be used in houses in Crossgate and Elvet.[27] Alternatively, unfinished wood was transported to the building site by priory tenants, to be worked and shaped ready for construction by carpenters there. In 1404 the carpenters building tenements in Souterpeth acquired and worked on timber which had been carried to the site by the tenants of Witton and Shincliffe. When new houses were built in the South Bailey in 1348, the bursar paid the workmen £1. 19s. for carpentry work which included the cutting and sawing of large timbers.[28]

Two methods of construction of wooden houses can be elicited from the Durham sources. One was the full-scale timber-framed house, where a basic framework of large timbers supported the external walls which were then filled in with planks or plaster covering wattlework. This structure could become quite complex, incorporating two storeys with many subsidiary rooms. Practically the only evidence for this type of construction in medieval Durham survives in leases. In 1410, for example, the sacrist leased a tenement in Framwelgate to Robert de Merington, a barker, on condition that he built a new house in the tenement 'two pairs of sills' ('Syles') in length.[29] The house which Richard Smyth was to build in his Framwelgate tenement in 1392 was larger than this; it was to contain 'three pairs of sills newly built along the front of the burgage'.[30] The lack of standing buildings means that it is difficult to estimate what these measurements meant in Durham terms; but M. R. G. Conzen estimated, on the basis of the Alnwick evidence, that the distance between the average 'couple' or pairs of sills was eighteen feet. He calculated that the standard frontage of a house of two structural bays was twenty-eight to thirty-two feet, with a depth of eighteen to twenty feet.[31] Such houses were clearly sizeable, solid architectural constructions.

The base of these timber-framed houses was formed by a rectangle of massive pieces of timber called ground sills, upon which the principal posts were morticed in at the corners. These posts in turn carried the horizontal wall plates which supported the roof timbers. Usually the landlord undertook to provide the

---

[27] Comm. account, 1474/75, Carriage; Burs. account, 1368/69, Repairs.
[28] Alm. account, 1404/05, Repairs; Burs. account, 1348/49, *Structura Domorum*.
[29] 2.2.Sac.3a.
[30] Misc.Ch.6777. [31] Conzen, *Alnwick*, pp. 32–4.

largest pieces of timber for the house and the stonework for the foundations, and the tenant did the rest. Merington's lease is a case in point, for it was specified there that the sacrist would provide the timber (*meremium*) for the house and quarried stone for the foundations. A firm foundation was essential for the stability of the timber-framed house and there are many references in the account rolls to work on the base of these houses. In 1468, for example, Robert Litster and John Clerk were working on the clearance of foundations (*le riddyng fundi*) for a new property in Elvet and in 1470 the foundations of a house in 'Gelygate' were being excavated.[32] What happened when the foundations were not secure is revealed dramatically in a Crossgate court case of 1502. John Wodemous was accused of trespass because he had demolished William Richardson's house by throwing down *lez propoz et silez*.[33] Once the framework of this timber house was erected, the walls were filled in, probably with solid pieces of wood in the earliest houses. By the middle of the fifteenth century, however, most houses had cheaper wooden planks between the framework or wattle and plasterwork, known as 'beam-filling', probably as a result of the increasing scarcity of timber. In 1468, for example, William Androwson worked on *le bemefelyng* of a tenement in the South Bailey at a rate of 6½d. for two-and-a-half days.[34]

A much simpler and cheaper method of constructing wooden houses was revealed in the Saddler Street excavations. The earliest structures on that site, dating from the tenth and eleventh centuries, were of oak and alder posts or stakes set at close intervals with hazel wattles or branches woven between.[35] The walls of these houses would have been infilled with daub, and a small, one-room house plan was the result. This seems to have been the earliest method of building timber houses in Durham, as it was in Southampton, Winchester and Anglo-Scandinavian York, but it continued at Durham throughout the later middle ages.[36] In 1423, for example, when a tenement in New Elvet was repaired, the infirmarer paid for *spritt, wattill et dalbyng* – *spritt*

[32] Burs. accounts, 1468/69; 1470/71, Repairs.
[33] Crossgate Court Book, 12 Jan. 1502.
[34] Burs. account, 1468/69, Repairs; Salzman, *Building in England*, p. 192.
[35] Salzman, *Building in England*, pp. 187, 195; Carver, 'Three Saxo-Norman tenements', p. 9.
[36] Platt, *English medieval town*, p. 57; Biddle, *Winchester*, pp. 345–6; Hall, 'Topography of Anglo-Scandinavian York', p. 36.

presumably being an upright stake between which the wattles were woven.[37] Although the sophisticated timber-framed house would provide more comfortable as well as more fashionable accommodation, the cost of its construction was probably beyond the means of many Durham townsmen, whereas the simple, wattle-work house could be constructed cheaply for the poorer inhabitants.

Roofing materials for houses in late-medieval Durham were of two types, straw or thatch, and stone called 'slatestone'. An oak shingle, found during the Saddler Street excavations, suggests that this may have been the earliest roofing material in Durham, but it is unsupported by any other evidence so far. The one example of lead being used for roofing was on the abbey's mill below the cathedral in the sixteenth century.[38] The account rolls show that straw or thatch was most commonly used, presumably because it was cheaper to transport and it was more readily available. A tenement in Old Elvet was roofed with 'lyng' in 1450, while the bursar bought straw called 'rede' for roofing houses in St Giles in 1415. The bursar also bought brushwood for roofing houses in 1357 and 1362.[39] Ralph Dove was paid 15s. 6d. for roofing three houses with straw in the South Bailey in 1377 and William Androwson was paid 3s. 6d. for the straw roofing on a tenement in Elvet in 1462.[40] Small payments were made to women for carrying straw, 'lyng' and thatch to building sites in Durham on many occasions as, for example, in 1388, when the bursar paid 16s. 6d. to women carrying 'straw called ling' and 'watling' for houses in St Giles.[41] The popularity of this roofing material continued unabated into the sixteenth century in spite of the undoubted fire risk. Other medieval towns such as Canterbury and London had begun to legislate against the use of thatch by the early thirteenth century, but there is no evidence of any such regulation in medieval Durham.[42]

Slatestone, being more expensive both to quarry and shape, was, on the evidence of the account rolls at least, infrequently used as a roofing material in Durham, although there were some very

---

[37] Infirm. account, 1423/24, Expenses.
[38] Carver, 'Three Saxo-Norman tenements', p. 16; see chapter 2, p. 54.
[39] Alm. account, 1450; Burs. accounts, 1415/16, 1357/58, 1362/63, Repairs.
[40] Burs. accounts, 1377/78, 1462/63, Repairs.
[41] Burs. account, 1388/89, Repairs.
[42] Urry, *Canterbury*, p. 194; Colvin, 'Domestic architecture', p. 69, nn. 1, 2; Wood, *English medieval house*, p. 292.

local sources of supply. It was worked in 'Welpdalequarrell', South Street, by John Sclatter in 1329; and in 1469 William Waynman and John Robynson carried two fothers (cart-loads) of slate from Harom quarry to John Milner's tenement in the North Bailey.[43] There is no perceivable geographical pattern within the town to those houses which had slatestone roofs, nor do they seem to have been invariably associated with the houses of richer tenants, as the priory account rolls indicate. In 1447, the almoner's tenement at the end of Elvet Bridge had a stone roof, as did the house called 'Halfetyn' in the North Bailey and a tenement next to the North Gate. The almoner's principal tenement in St Mary Magdalen Street had a new stone roof in 1455 and when the bursar repaired two tenements in New Elvet in 1423, he provided roofing stone (*lapides tegulati*) for the work.[44] Four cart-loads of 'Sclatestanes' were carried to the house of Richard Arnald in the North Bailey in 1420, and John Peirson, slater, put three roods of stone roofing on the tenement next to Clayportgate in 1432.[45] But such examples are rarely found in the documents.

Stone may have been used for the chimneys and gables of houses, although clay or plasterwork were perhaps more common; a gable of plaster (*gabulum luteum*) was built on the almoner's tenement in Old Elvet in 1449. John Hedley worked for fifteen days with unspecified materials on the gables (*le gavillez*) of a new tenement in St Giles Street for 5s. in 1462.[46] Chimneys were an important and integral part of all domestic buildings in Durham. When the priory commoner erected three houses within one tenement in Clayport in 1474, he had a chimney made for each. Thomas Bicheburn repaired and made one chimney in the Bailey for 5s. in 1407 and William Androwson repaired one plasterwork or daubed chimney (*caminum luteum*) in a tenement in Framwelgate for 1s. 2d. in 1469.[47] Lead was used for the guttering between houses. In 1464 William Plomer made a lead gutter in the tenement next to Clayportgate for 1s. while Thomas Plummer mended 'lez Goters' in this tenement in 1432 for 4s. 10d.[48] Blocked gutters were a source of contention

[43] Burs. accounts, 1329/30, *Structura*; 1469/70, Repairs.
[44] Alm. account, 1447/48, *Tectura lapidea*; Alm. account, 1455/56; Burs. account, 1423/24, Repairs.
[45] Burs. accounts, 1420/21, 1432/33, Repairs.
[46] Alm. account, 1449/50, *Laborarii*; Burs. account, 1462/63, Repairs.
[47] Comm. account, 1474/75, *Laborarii*; Burs. accounts, 1407/08, 1469/70, Repairs.
[48] Burs. accounts, 1464/65, 1432/33, Repairs.

between neighbours in medieval Durham. In 1503, Thomas Ferrour of Bicheburn was ordered by the Crossgate court to mend a faulty gutter in Edward Forster's tenement which had caused damage to one of the priory cellarer's burgages. The bursar paid 3s. 4d. to have a gutter next to Thomas Thornburgh's tenement unblocked in 1432. Meanwhile, it was the 'evesdroppes' of William Lomley's house in St Giles Street which had to be repaired in 1338 because rain falling from them had damaged William Shurveton's neighbouring tenement.[49]

No contemporary plans of any domestic buildings in Durham survive and only the occasional title deed gives any details of the internal layout of houses. One such example is that of Thomas Blagrise's house in Alvertongate in 1296. It was a two-storey dwelling with a cellar, presumably a vaulted store room, on the ground floor, and a solar, the living quarters, above. Access to the cellar was presumably from the street frontage, but external stone steps led up to the solar.[50] One of the more spacious houses in Elvet Borough, which was held by the Danby family, had its own private chapel by the early sixteenth century.[51] Several larger Durham houses contained halls: Reginald Mercator's late-thirteenth-century stone house in the market had a great hall, as did the house of Peter de Vallibus, knight, in South Street (probably of a similar date) and John Hakthorp's tenement in Souterpeth which was called 'Herthall' (1387).[52] Jordan de Claxton's 'great house' in the Bailey contained a 'great hall with a chamber', probably built of stone (1284), and many additional rooms. There was a hen house (*domum pultar.*) called 'insethus' and a great chamber, one privy (*cloaca*), one solar and a cellar. This was surely one of the largest houses in Durham.[53]

More typical than the large hall-house was the smaller building which had a solar as living quarters above a shop or store room on street level. In 1334, John de Botelesfeld held a burgage with a cellar and solar at the west end of Elvet Bridge.[54] In the late thirteenth century, Roger Neuton granted Reginald Mercator a tenement in the market place and the rent from two cellars beneath the solar of this tenement.[55] In one case, a solar was built

[49] Crossgate Court Book, 26 April 1503; Burs. account, 1432, Repairs; 4.14.Spec.36.
[50] 1.2.Sac.32.
[51] Host. rentals, 1523–34.
[52] 6.1.Elem.6; Alm. rental, 1424; 6.5.Elem.2; Misc.Ch.2218.
[53] 1.1.Finch.13*.   [54] 3.2.Sac.39.   [55] 6.1.Elem.8.

above or over the Milneburn stream.[56] These so-called cellars were not necessarily below street level, as, for example, in the case of the Blagrise house in Alvertongate. But in some cases, as for example beneath the arches of the bridges, they were probably cellars in the modern sense. In 1490, Sir Nicholas Rawlyng, the priest of St James' Chantry in St Nicholas' Church, came to an agreement with William Stokdale over the rent from cellars at the west end of Framwelgate Bridge 'now wastid and ruinous'.[57]

The documents show that many tenants lived over or behind their shops, workshops or storerooms, as they did in other medieval towns such as Oxford or Winchester, for example.[58] Furthermore, one property was often subdivided along the street frontage into a number of shops. In 1375, Gilbert de Clyfton granted Peter Dryng a tenement with four shops on the corner of Milneburngate and the Old Bridge. A shop in the market place next to the Cornerbooth with a house built over it was leased to Thomas Burton, a merchant, in 1438.[59] Both these shops and the stalls, called *cende* or *sende*, could be leased separately from the living quarters behind them. Some of these stalls may have been temporary lean-to structures, as they were in other medieval towns such as Winchester, where they were associated particularly with butchers, but many seem to have been an integral part of the building. In the late thirteenth century, Reginald Sesse held a *celda* some seven feet broad and seventeen feet long with the interior of a house in Sadlergate. Possibly his stall was built in front of the house, and there was a solar above it. The late-fourteenth-century stalls under the tolbooth in the market place were probably built into its undercroft, although they may have started life as temporary, portable benches for selling goods. The difference in terminology between the stall and the booth ('bothys') may imply a more transitory trading post. Booths were erected not only at the front of houses but also on the bridges: Ralph, son of Alice de Wyntonia, held three 'bothys' on the Old Bridge at the end of the thirteenth century, for example.[60]

[56] *fuit solarium supra aquam*: Alm. rent rolls, 1333/34.
[57] 3.18.Spec.31.
[58] W. A. Pantin, 'Medieval English town house plans', *MedArch*, 6–7 (1962–3), 205–6; Keene, *Winchester*, vol. 1, part 1, p. 157; Wood, *English medieval house*, p. 81.
[59] Misc.Ch.2334; Misc.Ch.1700; Pantin, 'Medieval English town house plans', p. 205.
[60] Biddle, *Winchester*, pp. 338–9; Sesse's charter is undated: 6.1.Elem.1**; *Bishop Hatfield's Survey*, ed. W. Greenwell, Surtees Society, vol. 32 (1857), p. 163; for the booths on the Old Bridge, see undated charter, Loc. xxxvii, no. 74.

Several tenements contained workshops or outbuildings which by their names or the implements associated with them indicated the trade of the occupier. In 1336, John Tunnock was accused of breaking into two tanneries (*tannarie*) in Sadlergate and South Street and stealing hides. John Yowdale's lease of two burgages in Framwelgate in 1467 itemised several outbuildings which contained sixteen lead vessels (*plumba*) associated with tanning or brewing. These included a brewhouse (*pandoxatria*), a malt kiln (*thorale*) and a tanning house (*domus tannator.*). Alice Cronkley had a malt kiln (*ustrina*) and a 'brewlede' in her tenement in Framwelgate in 1466, and William Couper held a tenement called a 'barkehouse' in 1427.[61] Many domestic buildings contained equipment for brewing, such as that of Walter de Esche in Crossgate with its *plumbo, cuba, taptraw et rahente* (1310), all names for lead vessels and implements which may have been placed in the gardens behind the houses.[62] Also to the rear of the houses were the 'bakdwellyngs' or 'bakhouses' referred to in the Crossgate Court Book. Tenants were instructed regularly to remove these shacks altogether or to prevent vagabonds living in them, as in 1509 when all tenants were enjoined to remove *le Bakdwellys in domibus* or pay a fine of 1s.[63] This evidence suggests that there may have been serious overcrowding in certain boroughs in Durham and that one solution, albeit illegal, was to house a floating population of vagrants and the poor in temporary and probably primitive shacks well behind the street frontage.

The surviving documents divulge little about the furnishings or the decoration of these domestic buildings, or indeed about the standard of domestic comfort enjoyed by Durham's townsmen. Much has to be gleaned from stray incidental references in the account rolls. Some properties probably had stone fireplaces linked to their chimneys, like the one constructed by Richard Hogeson in a house in Crossgate in 1421. Others, like Richard Walker's tenement in Old Elvet, had merely a hearth (*le harthe*) and the smoke would have to make its escape through a hole in the roof or through the windows.[64] Excavations have shown that the floors of the earliest structures in Sadlergate were of rammed

---

[61] Loc. IV, no. 52; 1.18.Spec.25; Burs. account, 1466/67, Repairs; Burs. rental, 1427.
[62] Misc.Ch.2533.
[63] Crossgate Court Book, 10 Jan. 1509, fol. 108v.
[64] Alm. accounts, 1421/22, Repairs; 1447/48, *Laborarii*. The Saddler Street excavation revealed an open hearth in the earliest house on the site: Carver, 'Three Saxo-Norman tenements', p. 9.

sand which was later replaced with trodden clay. Progress is marked by the flagged floors of the houses built in Elvet in the thirteenth and fourteenth centuries which suggest a raising of living standards.[65] Parts of two window frames were excavated in the west wall of a house in Elvet. There are references in the bursar's accounts to supplies of nails and 'band crokes' for windows and doors in his properties.[66] Although these houses were basically one- or two-room structures, accommodation could be supplemented by using partitions called 'intercloswalls' or 'entercloswalls'. In 1458, William Johnson, a carpenter, made 'del entercloswallez' in two tenements for 3s. and John Lyle and William Androwson were paid for le *dalbyng* of the 'entre-closewallez'.[67] The implication of these references is that the partitions had a timber frame infilled with plaster work. Other walls within the houses may have been lined with thin planks of wood called 'waynscot'. In 1372, the almoner bought in sixty 'waynscot' for use in his houses throughout Durham.[68] However, the scarcity of references to 'waynscot' in the documents suggests that it was rarely used in the average Durham home. It may have graced only the houses of the richer inhabitants.

Cases of alleged theft heard before the prior's court furnish somewhat melancholy evidence of the standard of domestic comfort enjoyed, or once enjoyed, by some Durham inhabitants. William Stanhop's house in Elvet seems to have been quite richly furnished: in 1338 he accused John Horne of stealing a hanging and a linen sheet (*tapetum* and *lintheamen*) from it. Julia del Comunhous was accused of breaking into a chest in John Ferur's house in the Bailey and stealing twenty marks of silver, thirty florins, one gold brooch (*firmaculum deaurum*) and other goods to the value of £40 in 1327. However, many inhabitants seem to have had little in the way of household furnishings. A 1516 inventory of goods belonging to a house in Crossgate revealed only one 'Brassepot' worth 10d., three 'Dublerrs' worth 2s., six 'Desches' (1s. 6d.) and thirteen 'Saussers' (1s. 6d.). Furniture and possessions in the average small wooden house in Durham were probably rudimentary and few in number.[69]

[65] Carver, 'Three Saxo-Norman tenements', pp. 68, 70, 74–5; Carver, 'Excavations in New Elvet', pp. 109, 111.
[66] Carver, 'Excavations in New Elvet', pp. 101–2; Burs. account, 1348/49, *Structura*.
[67] Burs. account, 1458/59, Repairs.   [68] Alm. account, 1372/73, Repairs.
[69] Loc. IV, no. 2 (16 June 1338); Loc. IV, no. 15; Crossgate Court Book, 18 Nov. 1516, interleaf fol. 169r.

The maintenance, repair and rebuilding of houses in Durham occupied a large proportion of the town's craftsmen and labourers, and as such the building trade was of some importance in Durham's economy. Building workers were organised in groups according to their particular skill. One group comprised the men who worked with stone. Few skilled masons seem to have been involved in the domestic market, a reflection, perhaps, of their more elevated craft status and their preoccupation with large-scale building projects for the priory or the bishop; rather, it was craftsmen described as layers, setters and wallers who were employed for small building operations in the town. These were men such as John and William Kay, who made walls in the bursar's houses in Elvet in 1368 and 1376; John Belle, stone-cutter (*latamus*), who repaired a house in Framwelgate in 1416; and Richard Farne, who made stone walls and daubed gable ends and the chimneys in a tenement in North Bailey in 1472.[70] A second important group of building workers were the carpenters, men such as Ellis Harpour and John de Martindale, employed by the bursar to work on his houses in Elvet and on the abbey mill and Scaltok Mill in 1376. Richard Thekyston, carpenter, worked on the bursar's houses in Framwelgate and Elvet in 1416. William Johnson, carpenter, made a loft in the tenement next to St Giles' cemetery and built 'entercloswallez' in the bursar's tenements in 1458.[71]

Roofers, the *cooperatores* or 'thekers', formed another group of building craftsmen. Donald Scot, 'theker', roofed both the *Meysondieu* in the Bailey and houses in South Street with brushwood in 1357 and 1358. John Peirson, 'sclater', roofed the tenement next to Clayportgate and tenements in St Giles Street with stone in 1432.[72] Other workmen involved in domestic building were the plumbers who made gutters for the houses, such as William Plomer who worked in Clayport (1464) and in Silver Street (1471). It is interesting to observe here the retention of an occupational surname which reflects accurately the trade of its holder; such examples are rare after the fourteenth century.[73] Plasterers such as Richard Hogeson (*lutarius*) made a chimney in Crossgate in 1421; smiths such as John Scot of Elvet made

---

[70] Burs. accounts, 1368/69, 1376/77, 1416/17, Repairs; Alm. account, 1472/73.
[71] Burs. accounts, 1376/77, Repairs; 1416/17, Repairs; 1458/59, Repairs.
[72] Burs. accounts, 1357/58, 1358/59, *Structura Domorum*; 1432/33, Repairs.
[73] Burs. accounts, 1464/65, 1471/72. On occupational surnames, see chapter 5, pp. 146–7.

ironwork for repairing the bursar's houses in 1339; and locksmiths such as John Loksmyth made three locks with keys for a tenement in St Giles Street in 1466.[74] The priory seems to have employed the same band of men drawn from these different building trade groupings to work regularly on priory buildings throughout the town, as the names recur in successive years. These skilled men, in turn, employed labourers and men known as *famuli*, probably those in apprenticeship, to help them in their work.

The priory account rolls demonstrate several different methods of organisation of domestic building and repair work which can be compared with the work on roads and mills already described.[75] In some cases the bursar, or the priory officer whose properties were involved, seems to have recruited and paid building craftsmen directly and to have bought in materials for the work himself. In 1458, for example, the bursar paid Henry Wrake 6s. 4d. to thatch a house in St Giles Street and he paid the hostillar 6s. 8d. for 100 thraves (or stooks) of straw for that roof.[76] It was more common, however, for the bursar to delegate the purchase of the materials as well as the direction of the work to the craftsmen he employed. When Robert Bryan built the walls of three tenements in St Giles Street in 1454, he was paid an extra 6d. for acquiring 'le dalebyng stowres' and 'wandez' for the tenement.[77] John Barker's house in Framwelgate was repaired in 1416, and stipends were paid to John Belle, a stone-cutter (*latamus*), Richard Thekyston, carpenter, and Thomas Curwen and Gilbert Huest, labourers, who seem to have been responsible for the organisation of the work.[78] The bursar paid Richard Colier and two members of his household (*famuli in mercede*) when they repaired the walls of a house in Elvet in 1419, and the construction of a new tenement in the Bishop's Borough, including an itemised payment (*mercedem...in parcell.*) to William Kempe and William Sawer, cost the bursar £4. 18s. 2d. in 1425.[79] It is clear that in such cases the skilled workmen recruited any additional labour needed and bought their own materials in return for a lump sum from a priory officer. A third method of organisation was to leave the repair work to the tenant of the house, and to pay him for the materials he used or to offset the

---

[74] Alm. account, 1421/22; Burs. accounts, 1339/40, 1466/67, Repairs.

[75] See chapter 2, pp. 57–8, 64–7.

[76] Burs. account, 1458/59, Repairs.　　[77] Burs. account, 1454/55, Repairs.

[78] Burs. account, 1416/17, Repairs.　　[79] Burs. accounts, 1419/20, 1425/26, Repairs.

cost of repair work by making him an allowance on part of his annual rent. Richard Walker made a gutter and a hearth in his own tenement in Old Elvet in 1447 for which he was paid by the almoner.[80] However, much repair work probably never entered the account rolls at all, because, as we have already seen, one of the conditions attached to many priory leases was that the tenant was to be responsible for the upkeep of his own property at his own expense.

Where there was an agreement between building workers and a priory officer to undertake a particular job, an arrangement was made for the payment of their wages. This could be in the form of a contract of employment where the money was paid on completion of the work, or, more informally, on an hourly or daily basis as the work progressed. In the case of a formal contract or agreement with a particular craftsman, wages were described as being paid in the form of stipends (as with the payment to John Belle and Richard Thekyston in 1416) or by agreement inclusively (*in grosso* as with Robert Litster and John Clerk for work on the foundations of a tenement in Elvet in 1468). In contrast, when Robert Bryan worked on the walls and roof of tenements in New Elvet, Silver Street and St Giles in 1449, he was paid on a daily basis, 5*d.* per day for himself and 4*d.* for his servant (*famulus*). Robert Androwson was paid 4*d.* per day for thatching a tenement in South Bailey and his servant, 3*d.* per day, in 1454. That year, Robert Bryan was also paid 4*d.* per day for walling and roofing work.[81]

All the evidence indicates a fairly high annual level of building work within the priory's Durham estate, although this is not necessarily reflected in the total amount of money spent annually on repairs to *domestic* property. Expenditure fluctuated greatly depending on the nature of the work; in some years it was fairly low, probably because it covered only small-scale repair or maintenance work. In other years, when several properties were being reconstructed, there had to be major outgoings, as in 1348, when the bursar paid out £6. 10*s.* 9½*d.* to rebuild houses in the South Bailey, or in 1423 and 1424 when houses in Elvet were rebuilt (£4. 0*s.* 2*d.* and £4. 10*s.* 6½*d.*), and in 1443 when two

---

[80] Alm. account, 1447/48, *Laborarii.*
[81] Burs. accounts, 1416/17, 1468/69, 1449/50, 1454/55, Repairs.

tenements in St Giles were rebuilt (£6. 4s.).[82] Furthermore, in some years a priory officer had major outgoings on the public buildings in his care, such as the reconstruction of churches and chapels. In such years the building craftsmen would be fully employed on these projects, and domestic property repairs would have to take second place because the priory's financial resources were stretched in other directions. Despite the efforts to keep the priory's tenements in Durham in good repair, it is clear that by 1500 many houses on the outskirts of the Old Borough and some in Old Elvet had fallen into disrepair; it was difficult to find tenants to take up properties and many of the sacrist's rents, for example, were not paid.[83] By the later middle ages, the priory obviously found difficulty in maintaining the whole urban estate, and it may have concentrated its resources on those houses near the centre of the town, especially around the market place, which were most valuable and could command the highest rents.

However, such problems of financial management within the priory's urban estate were irrelevant to those craftsmen who were fortunate enough to be recruited into the priory's building workforce. They had the security of knowing that their skills would always find employment in Durham, if not on domestic properties, then on the many public buildings for which the priory was responsible. The organisation of the building trade cut across borough boundaries; skilled craftsmen were drawn from each part of the town and they worked on any priory properties which were in need of repair in all boroughs. The building trade was one of the most important service industries in the town. Further research is necessary to reveal the network of connections between members of the trade, their places of origin as well as their Durham homes, and the work they performed, not just for the priory but also for the bishop. Were the same men employed to maintain the urban estates of the bishop and of other Durham overlords, such as the master of Kepier Hospital, or was there perhaps a separate workforce recruited by each significant landlord? Was the Durham building trade even larger than the priory records would lead us to believe? More detailed investigation of the wages and stipends paid to these men and of the prices of building materials would tell us more about this important segment of the urban economy, one which grew with

---

[82] Burs. accounts, 1348/49, 1423/24, 1424/25, 1443/44, Repairs.
[83] Sac. rental, 1500; see chapter 4, pp. 114–15, 125.

the expansion of the priory's urban estate in the fourteenth century and maintained its high level of activity in the later middle ages.

PUBLIC BUILDINGS: GUILD HALLS, BOROUGH COURT HOUSES AND BAKEHOUSES

Within Durham, as in all medieval towns, there were several buildings which had a more than purely residential or commercial significance. These places have some claim to be called 'public' buildings since they were not built exclusively for one family or landlord but were used by a large proportion of Durham's inhabitants on a daily or weekly basis. Broadly speaking, there were three categories of such public buildings in Durham. First, there were halls or houses which, while they may not have been erected by a religious guild, were certainly rented, maintained and used by the guild for business or social activities. Second, there were court houses, built by the overlords of each borough for use as judicial as well as administrative centres of the area. Third, there were buildings erected by the overlords to satisfy the requirements of urban tenure, such as the mills and the bakehouses where tenants were obliged to grind corn and bake bread. Each category of public buildings will be surveyed in more detail below, except the mills which have been discussed earlier. Churches and chapels, which also have a claim to be considered public buildings, are excluded from this survey.[84]

In many medieval towns such as Alnwick or Canterbury, for example, public buildings were erected in main thoroughfares or around the market place, at the centre of town life and commercial activity.[85] It is one of the peculiarities of Durham's topography, however, that public buildings were to be found in every part of the town. There were guild halls or guild houses, for example, in Framwelgate, Elvet, Clayport, the Bailey and the market place. This dispersal of public buildings seems to have been a direct result of Durham's division into distinct boroughs, each with its own judicial and tenurial administration requiring separate court houses and its own communal identity which needed shared facilities at a very local level. However, it is clear that the majority of guild halls or houses, if not the other public buildings of this

---

[84] See chapter 2, pp. 54–8.
[85] Conzen, *Alnwick*, p. 36; Urry, *Canterbury*, pp. 129–30.

survey, were sited in the Bishop's Borough at the centre of the urban area. The guild of St Nicholas had a hall on the north-west side of the market place, and there was another guild house nearby in Walkergate, one in Clayport and another in the Bailey ('le Mawdeleyngyldehouse'). No doubt the prestige attached to having a hall or house in such valuable commercial locations was matched by the convenience of a central location so near to the one market place of the town.

There are references to six separate guild properties in Durham in the medieval period, all associated with religious rather than craft guilds. These were 'le Gildhall' in the market place, belonging to the guild of St Nicholas; 'le Gildhous' in Walkergate, which may have been a meeting place for the guild of Corpus Christi; the house of St Cuthbert's Guild in Clayport; 'le Gildehouse' in Framwelgate, probably used by the guild of St Margaret; the 'Mawdeleyngyldehouse' in the North Bailey; and the house of the Holy Trinity Guild in New Elvet. The origins of these guild properties are, like those of the guilds themselves, very obscure, but some were in the holding and occupation of their respective guilds by the late thirteenth century at least, according to the surviving title deeds. The history of the guild hall in the market place is more fully documented than most. It originally belonged to a merchant, Reginald, who in a charter of *c.* 1271 conveyed it to the almoner's chantry in St Nicholas' Church. It was then leased to the brothers of the guild of St Nicholas for their guild hall at a rent of £1 per annum. Here, a domestic building, probably one of the most imposing in Durham, had been converted into a public building before the end of the thirteenth century.[86] The guild house in Clayport is mentioned in a possibly late-thirteenth-century charter in which representatives of the guild of St Cuthbert, Richard de Sireburne, William de Witewell, William *presbiter*, Richard *diaconus*, William de Redinges and Robert, son of Hervicus, 'with the consent of the whole fraternity of the guild of St Cuthbert', conveyed the guild's house to John, son of Hugh Tiwe. Subsequently, the same John, with his surname spelt 'Tywe', referred to as a 'burgess' of Durham, granted a rent from the 'house of the guild' in Clayport to St Cuthbert and the fabric fund of the cathedral.[87] The guild house, or houses, in Framwelgate acquired this name before St James'

---

[86] 6.1.Elem.6★★; Alm. rental, 1424.   [87] 4.2.Sac.1; 4.2.Sac.2.

Chantry Chapel was founded on Elvet Bridge in the late thirteenth century. Thomas, son of Lewyn, allocated the rent he drew from the houses of 'le Gilde' to supplement the endowments of his new chantry foundation.[88]

The other Durham guild houses or halls may have been of later foundation. There are no surviving documentary references to the presumed hall of the Corpus Christi Guild in Walkergate before the sixteenth century. In a copy of a deed of 1526 which was enrolled in the bishop's chancery, John Mathowe granted Thomas Blakden, goldsmith, three gardens and a tenement next to 'le gildhous', lying between the city wall and the road in Walkergate.[89] This relatively late reference may simply be a reflection of the scarcity of surviving evidence for the Bishop's Borough, for it seems unlikely that such a prestigious and wealthy guild would lack a meeting place after 1437 at least, when the Corpus Christi Guild was reorganised. The property may have been acquired for the use of the guild shortly after this date. There is one clue in the remaining title deeds to the location of an earlier home for this guild. In 1397, John Hagthorp granted a chamber within his capital tenement called 'Herthall' at the head of Souterpeth to a number of men (who probably acted as trustees), on condition that it and an entry to the chamber alongside the tenement be assigned to the chaplain of the Corpus Christi Guild. This chamber may have been no more than private accommodation for the guild's chaplain; or it may have been a meeting place for the guild before it acquired land in Walkergate.[90] The guild of the Holy Trinity in St Oswald's Church had to wait until 1472 before they found a site for their guild house. In that year, the prior leased to John Tonge, alderman, burgages on the west side of New Elvet so that the guild could build its own house on the land.[91] Of course, the guild may have rented accommodation previously for its meetings but this lease indicates that the guild had by now sufficient funds to pay an annual rent for land and to afford the expense of construction work.

Only one of these six guild properties was called a 'hall'. The guild of St Nicholas held a building which is described as a large hospice or stone hall (*magnum hospicium* or *aula lapidis*) in the deeds and rentals. Excepting the churches and chapels, it may have been

---

[88] Undated charter, 2.11.Spec.52.
[89] PRO Durham Chancery Enrolments, 3/74, m.4d.
[90] PRO Durham Chancery Enrolments, 3/36, m.11. [91] 4.17.Spec.35.

the one public building of any great size beyond the confines of the peninsula in late-medieval Durham and it was probably the only guild property to be built of stone. The other guilds had buildings described as guild 'houses' which may have been converted from domestic properties for use by the guild organisations. Some were occupied by tenants, perhaps acting as caretakers, who paid rent to the guild. In 1316, the burgage in Framwelgate called 'le Gildehouse' was held by Alice de Hornby and Christine, daughter and heiress of Marjory Haunte. John Tywe held St Cuthbert's guild house in Clayport in the late thirteenth century, but he seems to have sub-let it to Benedict Carpenter.[92]

It is clear from the later history of some guild houses or halls that they ceased to be used by guild members or for guild functions by the later medieval period. Even the imposing guild hall in the market place was converted into an inn, perhaps when the guild had fallen on hard times. After its dissolution, when the guild's possessions were valued at only £1. 3s., the tenement called 'le Crowne', which had once belonged to the guild of St Nicholas, was granted to John Wright and Thomas Holmes of London (1553).[93] The decline of the 'Mawdeleyngyldehouse' was even more marked. It was probably ruinous by 1427 at least when a charter describing a tenement in the North Bailey mentioned that 'Mawdeleyngyldehous' was once built there but the land had been incorporated into John Dyghton's tenement. In 1448, Richard Raket held a piece of land in the North Bailey on which, it was said, was once built that house called 'Mawedelyngildhous'. However, the original significance of the building in the lives of the townsmen was not lost altogether; its name was retained long after it had disappeared.[94]

There is no surviving evidence for the existence of any halls or houses used by craft guilds in medieval Durham, a situation which reflects both the relative insignificance of trading organisations in the town and their late development.[95] They may, of course, have used the religious guild houses as meeting places, but in the absence of any firm documentary evidence, we should pass to the next category of public buildings in Durham, borough court houses. Each borough (including for this discussion, as others, Old Elvet Barony) had its own court house which was built in a

---

[92] Misc.Ch.1934; 4.2. Sac.2.   [93] *CPR 1547–53*, p. 244.
[94] Misc.Ch. 1823, 1837, 1839, 1844.   [95] See below, chapter 5, pp. 183–4, 188–9.

central position within the borough. The court house for the Bishop's Borough was called 'le Tollebooth' and it was situated in the market place, a position which compares, for example, with the tolbooth in Darlington's medieval market place.[96] Although it is not marked on either the mid-sixteenth-century plan of this area or on Speed's plan of 1611, it can be located fairly accurately by reference to the endorsement of a deed of 1434. This document concerned the conveyance of the Cornerbooth, a tenement lying on the south-east corner of the market place at the junction with Fleshewergate, and the endorsement stated that the property lay *iuxta le Tollebooth*.[97] The court building for the priory's Old Borough was also called a tolbooth. It had a prime site on the north side of Crossgate opposite St Margaret's Chapel and just to the west of the junction of all the main roads in this borough.[98] The hostillar's tenants in Old Elvet owed service to and appeared before his court held in the hall of the manor of Elvethall, while the Elvet Borough court was held in the guild house of the Holy Trinity Guild on the west side of New Elvet after 1472. This interesting conjunction of communal functions in the one building was brought about in the prior's lease to the guild, which laid down the condition that the hostillar and his servants should have access to this guild house whenever it was necessary to hold the borough court. However, the court may have met in Elvethall manor hall before this date.[99] This lease is a unique example in the Durham records of medieval timesharing; a public building would not be occupied continuously by whatever organisation was attached to it, and such an arrangement was a sensible attempt to maximise the use of the building. Finally among these borough court houses, Kepier Hospital's 'Curthous' for its tenants in St Giles' Borough was situated in the main street of that borough in the late fourteenth century.[100]

It is to be expected that court buildings would be some of the earliest public buildings in any medieval town, since they had a great financial as well as a legal significance in urban life. They were places where an overlord could collect fines, tolls and rents from his tenants and enforce the obligations of the tenurial relationship. They were equally important in a symbolic sense as

[96] Clack, 'Origins and growth of Darlington', p. 76.
[97] Misc.Ch.2040. [98] Sac. rental, 1500.
[99] 4.17.Spec.35; *VCH Durham*, vol. 3, p. 62.
[100] *Memorials of St Giles*, pp. 162–3; Meade, 'The medieval parish of St Giles', p. 65.

98

the visible evidence of an overlord's control over his tenants and his borough. However, there are no surviving early-medieval documentary references to tolbooths or court houses in Durham. The tolbooth in the market place is mentioned in Bishop Hatfield's survey of *c.* 1380, although clearly it must have been in existence long before this date.[101] The property called 'le Tolbooth' in Crossgate was acquired by the priory as late as *c.* 1442; before then it was in private hands and it was never described as a court house. Previously, the court may have been held in South Street, perhaps in the terrar's house at the south end of the street, although that house was already ruinous by 1339, but more probably in the stone house described in the almoner's rental of 1424 as the place where the moot-hall of the prior (*pretorium prioris*) used to be.[102] The earliest reference to a specific court house for Elvet Borough dates, as we have seen, from 1472. The court of St Giles' Borough may have met within Kepier Hospital itself, the headquarters of the overlord, in the early medieval period, for it was in easy access of the urban area of the borough. However, after the hospital was rebuilt by the riverside, away from the houses of St Giles Street, it is likely that the court house was relocated within a house in the street itself.[103]

The name given to two of the Durham borough court houses, 'tolbooths', may be of some topographical significance, and contrasts with names like 'burwarmot' in Lincoln, 'portman moot' in Bury St Edmunds and 'husting' in London, names which were descriptive both of legal processes and of those participating in them.[104] The Old Borough and the Bishop's Borough courts were held in 'tolbooths', a word which suggests a rather temporary structure. Other booths mentioned in Durham title deeds were, as we have already observed, one-roomed shops or lean-to structures erected in front of a tenement for trading purposes.[105] Perhaps the earliest Durham court buildings were indeed of a rudimentary design and it was only in the later medieval period that these structures became more permanent. The surviving medieval sources reveal little about the appearance

---

[101] *Bishop Hatfield's Survey*, p. 163.
[102] For the Crossgate tolbooth, see, for example, 1.2.Sac.8; Sac. account, 1442/43. The terrar and the steward held a court in South Street in 1312: see Loc. IV, no. 229; Alm. rental, 1424. [103] See chapter 1, pp. 24–5.
[104] J. W. F. Hill, *Medieval Lincoln* (Cambridge, 1948), pp. 186–7; Urry, *Canterbury*, pp. 88–9; M. D. Lobel, *Bury St Edmunds* (Oxford, 1935), p. 15.
[105] See above, p. 87.

of any of the Durham court houses, but such evidence as there is strongly suggests that the tolbooth in the market place had been a development among simple market stalls. By the late fourteenth century, it was a first-floor room with stalls beneath it, as was its Darlington counterpart. John Custson held nine stalls *sub le Tolleboth* and John Bowman held a stall (*selda*) beneath it in *c.* 1380, according to Bishop Hatfield's survey.[106] Originally, the court itself may have met in one such stall or booth to take market tolls and to receive the obligations of burgage tenure from the inhabitants of the Bishop's Borough. As both the work-load of the court and trade in the market place increased, a more permanent structure could have been built to house the stallholders and the court could have moved upstairs. Robert Surtees, writing in the nineteenth century, states that the medieval tolbooth was a wooden building which was replaced by Bishop Tunstall with a stone building surmounted by a large cupola. This more grandiose design no doubt befitted its enhanced status.[107]

Nothing can be discovered about the appearance of other court buildings in medieval Durham. The financial responsibility for the repair or maintenance of the tolbooth in the Old Borough and the court house in New Elvet does not seem to have been borne by any priory obedientiaries and consequently these structures do not feature in the building works section of their account rolls. The hall at Elvethall manor where the Old Elvet court met, along with the other manorial buildings there, was maintained by the hostillar, but few details of the construction of the hall survive in his or the manor's account rolls. In the case of the Elvet court house built *c.* 1472, it is likely that the costs of building repairs were borne entirely by the guild of the Holy Trinity in St Oswald's Church, which leased the tenement from the priory and used it for guild meetings.[108]

Two of the main tenurial obligations of the priory's urban tenants in Durham were the duty to grind corn at the overlord's mills and the duty to bake bread at his bakehouses. In turn, the priory was required to provide mills and bakehouses to serve its tenants and to keep them in good running order throughout the year by regular maintenance and repair work. The problems and

---

[106] *Bishop Hatfield's Survey*, p. 163.
[107] Surtees, *Durham* 4, pp. 46–7; see also Bishop Langley's *Valor* printed in *VCH Durham*, vol. 3, pp. 23–4; the original in PRO Durham Ministers' Accounts, C.C.220196.
[108] 4.17.Spec.35.

expense this caused have already been explored in the discussion on mills in the previous chapter. Bakehouses were no less important to the Durham tenants, and they comprise the last category of public buildings to be considered here. The priory provided two communal bakehouses for its tenants, one on each side of the peninsula in Elvet Borough and in the Old Borough. Both of these priory bakehouses were located near important route centres in the boroughs, close to the bridges and the riverside, just behind the street frontage in convenient access positions for the tenants. The Elvet bakehouse, which was sited among other properties near Elvet Bridge, was in use from the middle of the thirteenth century at least; when the priory was in dispute with Bishop Philip de Poitou, the bishop overthrew the ovens in Elvet (*furnos in Elvete subvertit*), presumably in an attempt to reduce the priory's income.[109] As there is no surviving evidence for a separate bakehouse in Old Elvet, priory tenants living there may have baked their bread in the Elvet Borough bakehouse, or they may have had some baking facilities within Elvethall manor buildings. A second priory bakehouse for its Old Borough tenants was built near the Old Bridge, on the south side of the street leading up towards Crossgate. It had come into the priory almoner's Durham estate by a grant from William, son of Richard, son of Wydon of the Old Borough, in an early, possibly late-thirteenth-century charter.[110]

The other Durham overlords exacted similar tenurial obligations from their tenants and they too provided communal bakehouses in their boroughs. The bakehouse for St Giles' Borough was situated on the north-west side of the street, a position located by reference to title deeds concerning properties in St Mary Magdalen Street. Tenements in that street, such as the land held by Agnes Hextildesham in 1330, were said to lie behind the bakehouse (*retro pistrinam*) of St Giles Street.[111] No surviving documentary evidence reveals the position of the bishop's bakehouse, but we know that it was in operation by the late twelfth century because *Boldon Buke* recounts that it rendered ten marks in *c.* 1183.[112]

A good deal of information survives about the construction of the priory's bakehouses in the obedientiaries' account rolls, as it does for mills, because both 'public' buildings were assigned to

---

[109] *ScripTres*, p. 22; for the dates of the bishops of Durham, see appendix 3.
[110] 6.1.Elem.3*; 6.1.Elem.4*.   [111] 6.4.Elem.3.   [112] *Boldon Buke*, p. 1.

the endowment of individual obedientiaries who were held financially responsible for their repair and maintenance. In return, it was anticipated that the suit of bakehouse payments owed by *all* the borough inhabitants would more than cover any outgoings for building work, or indeed, the stipend given to a baker employed by the obedientiary. The Elvet bakehouse was part of the bursar's estate; it had stone walls and a slate roof, presumably to lessen the fire risk to the surrounding properties. John Peirson roofed the bakehouse with slatestone in 1432, and its stone walls were repaired in 1453. Fundamental rebuilding took place from time to time, as in 1347, when a small oven was constructed at a cost of £1. 16s. 2d.; in 1469, when masons made new foundations; and in 1499 when it was rebuilt.[113] Between these years of relatively heavy expenditure, however, the bursar's bakehouse seems to have run reasonably cheaply, at least in comparison with the mills. The bakehouse in the Old Borough was in the almoner's endowment, and he leased it out with a solar, cellar and garden, presumably for the accommodation of the baker. The foundations and vault (*volta*) of the bakehouse were made from local stone which was brought from the 'Aumenerbarn' in South Street in 1469 and special 'Thilstone' from the sacrist's quarry there in 1478. The internal walls of the bakehouse, the gables and the chimney may have all been of wood and plasterwork; Thomas Bowet was employed for four days in daubing and rough-casting the gables (*lez pergynging et dalbura*) in 1494 and there is no reference to this bakehouse having a stone roof.[114] Despite the undoubted fire hazard of this bakehouse, sited as it was in the midst of congested wooden domestic properties, there is no surviving evidence of any accidental damage to neighbouring houses.

This survey has demonstrated that medieval Durham contained a wide variety of public buildings in all parts of the urban area, some of which, like the guild hall of St Nicholas and perhaps the tolbooth in the market place, were substantial, stone-built structures. Examples of larger, stone-built, two-storey domestic buildings can also be given, again from each part of the town. But these were not typical of the standard of domestic architecture in

---

[113] Burs. accounts, 1432/33, 1453/54, Repairs. For particularly heavy expenditure on this bakehouse, see Burs. accounts, 1347/48, 1469/70, 1499/1500, Repairs.

[114] Sac. rental, 1500; 6.1.Elem.3*; Alm. accounts, 1469/70, 1478/79, 1494/95, Repairs.

Durham, any more than the impressive monuments to episcopal and conventual power on the peninsula were representative of the town. The balance of the evidence, poor though it may be, confronts us with the inescapable conclusion that medieval Durham was not a particularly wealthy or fashionable place in which to live. It was equipped with all the public buildings necessary to a town of its ranking and importance in the region, but its relative poverty in industry and trade was reflected in the lack of spacious or complex stone or even timber-framed houses of a wealthy merchant group and the absence of halls for craft organisations. Even the abundance of public buildings like court houses and bakehouses, which is striking in relation to the size of the town, should not mislead us into thinking that Durham had a flourishing communal identity. Rather, it was a mark of the dominance of those in authority, the overlords of Durham, who required such buildings for administrative purposes. Of all the buildings discussed in this chapter, perhaps the guild houses alone can be viewed as expressions of the townsmen's aspirations, being the one category of public buildings erected or bought at the instigation of the inhabitants. A visitor to Durham in the later middle ages would be left with a strong visual impression of the might of the church and the dominance of lordship in the town. Beneath the symbols of power on the peninsula lay a subservient urban community which lacked any powerful symbols of its own.

Chapter 4

Landlord and tenants: the economic relationship between Durham Priory and its urban tenants in the later middle ages

Durham Cathedral Priory had a dominant interest both as landlord and landowner in the town which surrounded the peninsula. No less than three of Durham's five boroughs were under the direct overlordship of its obedientiaries: Old and New Elvet were managed by the hostillar and the Old Borough was administered by the sacrist after 1423.[1] Landmale, or ground rents, as well as the profits of the borough courts, went to these officers automatically to help them finance their duties within the priory. By 1500 the priory had succeeded in becoming the leading landlord in these parts of the urban area by its acquisition of many of the freeholds of properties, and in addition, several valuable tenements elsewhere, for example in the Bailey, Clayport and St Giles, had come into priory hands. The management as well as the revenues of this large urban estate were subdivided among the priory obedientiaries: in all, eight obedientiaries had property-holding interests in Durham from which they derived what proved to be a somewhat fluctuating income. Set against this impressive priory stake in the Durham property-market, the bishop's overlordship of only one borough in the later middle ages, the Bishop's Borough, looks poor indeed, although, like the priory, the bishop held valuable properties in other boroughs as well. But it must be borne in mind that the Bishop's Borough was the most prosperous part of Durham at all periods; it contained the one marketing area for the whole town and so, in addition to court profits, it yielded a considerable income from tolls for its overlord. Furthermore, it was the most congested borough with the highest density of property and people, and the potential rent income for the bishop was considerable. All of these factors help to offset the apparent tenurial dominance of the priory in the town.

[1] Sac. account, 1423/24, Receipts.

How did the priory come to have such a leading tenurial role over much of the urban community at Durham? The origins of the priory's Durham estate are to be found in one of the forged charters attributed to Bishop William de St Calais in which land in and around Durham was divided between the bishop and the convent. In this charter, which has already been discussed,[2] the bishop granted Elvet, most probably Old Elvet, to the priory. The priory also held the area which was to become the Old Borough by the time of the episcopacy of Bishop Flambard at least. In a charter dating from *c.* 1128, towards the end of his life, Flambard handed back land which he had previously taken away from the priory, including 'land on the other side of the bridge of Durham'.[3] These two early charters, together with Bishop Puiset's restoration of the borough called 'Elvetehalge' to the monks, which seems to refer to the newly developed land at the east end of Elvet Bridge,[4] mark the extent of the priory's overlordship in Durham in the early middle ages.

This urban estate was then divided among the priory's obedientiaries as it was, for example, in Canterbury before 1170 and in most other important Benedictine communities. Similarly, the obedientiaries of Peterborough Abbey were endowed separately and the revenues of the convent's lands at Westminster were divided between at least six important obediences.[5] The earliest division of the priory's estate in Durham between its officers is unclear, to say the least. By the high middle ages, the Durham bursar seems to have been holding the largest share, for his first surviving rental of 1270 shows him receiving the farms of the Old Borough and Elvet Borough.[6] But the office of bursar at Durham does not seem to have come into existence until the middle of the thirteenth century, paralleling similar developments in other Benedictine houses in a move towards more centralised accounting. Durham chapter ordinances of 1235 and 1252 mention a sacrist, hostillar, almoner, terrar and chamberlain, but the first

---

[2] See chapter 1, p. 28; *Durham Episcopal Charters*, pp. 6–15.
[3] See chapter 1, p. 30; 2.1.Pont.1; *Durham Episcopal Charters*, p. 107.
[4] See chapter 1, pp. 28–9.
[5] Urry, *Canterbury*, p. 31; E. King, *Peterborough Abbey, 1086–1310: a study in the land market* (Cambridge, 1973), p. 88; B. Harvey, *Westminster Abbey and its estates in the middle ages* (Oxford, 1977), p. 57.
[6] Loc.iv, no.226.

documentary reference to a bursar occurs in 1265.[7] The allocation of a landed estate, including the Durham boroughs, perhaps accompanied the creation of this new obedience. The bursar's primacy of overlordship in Durham over the other obedientiaries seems to have been short-lived, however, for he had lost Elvet to the hostillar before 1302. It is the hostillar who is the most likely candidate for an earlier lordship over the Elvet boroughs, for his first surviving account roll, dating from 1302–3, shows him receiving the farms of both the Borough and the Barony of Elvet, which he did up to the Reformation. The hostillar may have surrendered, albeit temporarily, Elvet Borough to the bursar in the late thirteenth century. There is a possibility that the Old Borough was under the control of the almoner in the early medieval period. He seems to have run a court in South Street for his tenants in the thirteenth century, and to have drawn a certain number of landmale rents from tenements in the street, but later rentals and account rolls do not show him in receipt of a regular farm from this area and he did not have any jurisdiction over tenants here in the later middle ages.[8]

However, there were competing tenurial interests even in those boroughs which were under priory lordship, for overlordship of a borough did not mean ownership of all the properties within it. Private landowners, the bishop and, in the later middle ages, various chantry chaplains and religious fraternities, owned the freeholds of properties within the priory's boroughs. Indeed, it comes as a surprise to see how many tenements in priory boroughs were in private hands throughout the medieval period, owing only small, fixed, freehold or landmale rents to the priory. In the hostillar's borough of New Elvet, for example, his rent income in 1523 came from 106 rents, but of these, sixty rents were freehold ones deriving from property which remained stubbornly outside the priory's urban estate.[9] Even odder was the frequent occurrence of properties within one priory officer's borough being held by another obedientiary. Each obedientiary was responsible for the upkeep of his own estate and for producing a sizeable income which would be devoted to the maintenance of

---

[7] Dobson, *Durham Priory*, pp. 257–8; R. H. Snape, *English monastic finances in the later middle ages* (Cambridge, 1926), pp. 37–8. For variations in organisation, see R. A. L. Smith, 'The *Regimen Scaccarii* in the English monasteries', *TRHS*, 4th ser., 24 (1942), 92–4.

[8] Alm. rental, 1424.   [9] Host. rental, 1523.

his office. As there was, apparently, little oversight of the expansion of these independent estates, Durham's obedientiaries tended to compete for properties in each other's boroughs. In such cases, all that the overlord of the borough could do was to extract the small, fixed freehold or landmale rent from his brother obedientiary, who took the greater profit from, perhaps, a leasehold rent.

Durham Priory and its obedientiaries made determined efforts to increase both the physical size of their urban estates and their legal interests within them by acquiring properties in non-priory boroughs and by purchasing freeholds wherever possible so that they could be converted into leaseholds. The simple acquisition of property did not mean that the priory extended its lordship to any other Durham borough; once the lines of authority had been drawn before the end of the twelfth century, with the division of the Durham boroughs between the various overlords, the pattern of lordship was fixed. However, this strategy did give the priory an enhanced legal and economic interest in every part of the town, because it had tenants in all the boroughs by the fourteenth century, if not earlier. Although it was unable to buy out all the competing legal interests in its own boroughs, its attempts to convert freeholds into leaseholds did help to yield a higher and more flexible rent income. Unfortunately, this policy was not always of immediate financial benefit to the priory. The acquisition of new freeholds often led to additional responsibilities and outgoings in the form of small rent charges and increased maintenance costs. Nor can the physical expansion of the priory estate in Durham be equated automatically with monastic prosperity or a buoyant economy. Somewhat paradoxically, it could also be a measure of desperation, as the priory attempted to boost stagnant rent revenues and a largely fixed income with a 'spending spree' on the land market, as it did in its purchases of the later medieval period.[10] But the acquisition of properties, or of an improved legal interest in them, could, if handled judiciously, result in greatly increased receipts for the priory.

The landlord–tenant equation viewed from the Durham townsman's point of interest was no less complex. It has been said that 'all men, except a few exceptionally favoured owners, paid

---

[10] This compares with the apparent wealth of Durham Priory in terms of its annual gross income and the sense of 'financial desperation' expressed by the monks in the early fifteenth century: Dobson, *Durham Priory*, pp. 250–1.

rent to somebody for their property' in the medieval period, and Durham's townsmen were no exception.[11] The only discernible difference was one of degree; fortunate and rare was the townsman who paid only one rent for one property. Most tenants owed a multiplicity of small rents to a variety of landlords, a result, primarily, of the frequent separation of overlordship from landlordship – the lord of the borough was not necessarily the same man as the landlord of a particular property within it. Priory officers as well as private landlords also contributed their own complications to tenurial arrangements by building up small estates within priory boroughs and then sub-letting property, thus creating additional rent charges. The whole town was a veritable minefield of competing interests, with each landlord, no matter how small his holding, determined to extract the full financial obligations from his urban tenants.

The first part of this chapter analyses the different types of rents which could be extracted from the Durham townsmen, and charts broad changes in rent values which are related to the evidence from other medieval towns and the policies of other ecclesiastical overlords. In particular, the fluctuations in the rent income of the bursar, the hostillar and the almoner between *c.* 1300 and 1540 will be reviewed. These variations in income took place against a background of, it has been assumed, a fall in prices and a sharp rise in wages in the mid and late fourteenth century following outbreaks of *pestilencia* and the consequent long-term decline in population. These trends continued into the fifteenth century, with wages remaining high, prices low and a static, or perhaps slowly declining, population until *c.* 1500. Although the value of money did not remain constant through this long period as a result of recoinages at regular intervals, and its quantity fluctuated as money went abroad to pay for foreign wars, for example, it has been argued convincingly that such changes were not the main determinants of price and wage movements in the late middle ages: 'economic change in the Middle Ages must still be seen in terms of a rising or declining population'.[12] The changes in rent income of the Durham obedientiaries must be

[11] See F. Barlow in Biddle, *Winchester*, p. 8.
[12] J. L. Bolton, *The medieval English economy, 1150–1500* (London, 1980), pp. 62, 66, 72–3, 77–8, 80; J. Hatcher, *Plague, population and the English economy, 1348–1530* (London, 1977), pp. 48, 50, 52–3; Keene, *Winchester*, vol. 1, part 1, pp. 183–4, 208.

viewed against these generalised comments on the economic basis of late-medieval society.

In general, it appears from this survey that the priory was able to increase its rent income from Durham properties in the late fourteenth century and again, though on a much smaller scale, towards the end of the fifteenth century. However, the early fifteenth century was a time of mounting arrears and many waste tenements which marked a financial loss in the urban estate. The second part of this chapter deals with the cost of maintaining an urban estate. Property had to be kept in good repair or it would fail to attract a tenant; thus each obedientiary spent a considerable annual sum on building work in Durham. The acquisition of new tenements brought with it welcome additional rent income, but it also led to more long-term expenses for the priory in the form of what are known as 'resolved' rents, rents which arose out of the past tenurial history of the properties such as rent charges and pensions to former owners as well as legal costs associated with the conveyancing. Consequently, while it may at first appear that these obedientiaries reaped a good and reliable reward from their urban estates, their annual outgoings on property and rent losses shows them to be facing growing difficulties. The short-term solution, which may have been the regular practice by the late fifteenth century, was to write off debts and arrears. No long-term solution to the problems of running a diverse urban estate was found.

The main documentary sources for this chapter are the priory rentals and account rolls, both of which have their own problems of interpretation. The rentals and the section of 'assized' rents in the account rolls were often somewhat remote from reality because they were essentially retrospective in nature, and recorded rents at their original level with no account of losses through arrears, wastes, reductions or allowances. Occasionally, notes were added in the rentals giving the actual amount paid by a tenant during the year, the arrears that had accumulated and the method of payment, whether in money or in kind, and such notes show up the discrepancies between theory and practice.[13] Most of the information about the types of rent levied in medieval Durham and the methods and times of payment is derived from this source. The receipts section of the account rolls, excluding the

13 As, for example, in Host. rentals, 1523–34.

section on 'assized rents', can be used to chart the growth of an obedientiary's income from particular acquisitions of land. The expenditure section details the outgoings which were made for every property purchased, such as legal costs, the initial purchase price, which rarely bore much relation to the final sum paid for any property, the small rent charges incumbent on properties, and any pensions which were paid to previous owners. The full and detailed *Structura Domorum* part of the account, where building work was itemised, lists the money spent on maintaining property in the estate. Finally, the account rolls often reveal the scale of the problem of urban decay where other documents are silent, in their lists of tenants whose rents were in arrears, and of tenements which lay ruinous or empty.

Each of the three obedientiaries considered in this chapter kept their own account rolls and rentals as a check on the financial state of their offices. Many of these documents survive, but inevitably breaks in the series do give rise to some difficulties in charting any accurate tables of fluctuating income. The hostillar's account rolls, for example, survive only patchily before 1400 and there is no extant hostillar's rental before 1500 to fill in these gaps. The conclusions of this chapter are, in consequence, put forward somewhat tentatively. The general impression left after an examination of the evidence is that the priory obedientiaries had to run to stand still in their attempts to maintain the income from their estates. As they expanded their urban holdings, so the rent losses and outgoings increased and more properties had to be bought to cover the deficit. It was only those obedientiaries who managed to balance their losses during times of depression with the acquisition of new properties, particularly in the central areas of the town where property was more valuable, who ran their urban estates as viable concerns. The first half of the fifteenth century seems to have been a period of particular difficulty, but by the early sixteenth century, the worst of the 'crisis' noted in so many English towns seems to have been over.[14]

[14] D. M. Palliser, 'A crisis in English towns? The case of York, 1460–1640', *Northern History*, 14 (1978), 108–25; P. Clark and P. Slack, *English towns in transition, 1500–1700* (London, 1976), pp. 12–13.

THE FLUCTUATIONS OF URBAN RENTS

There were three main categories of rent charged upon the Durham holdings of priory obedientiaries. The first and largest category, in numerical if not in monetary terms, was the rent known as 'landmale' rent in Durham, a rent found in other medieval English towns such as Canterbury, Winchester, Lincoln and Bury St Edmunds, where it went under names like 'landgable', 'hawgable' or 'hadgovel'.[15] The origins and early history of this ancient rent deserve greater investigation, but at Durham it seems to have been a ground rent rather than a rent attached to buildings, and perhaps it has more claim to be called a tax rather than a rent in origin. Its size does not seem to have borne any relationship to the size of the tenement. If a tenement was sub-divided, the landmale rent was sub-divided; it was not doubled. If tenements were amalgamated, the landmale rents attached to each of the original properties continued to be distinguished in the rentals, each at its full original value. The eight burgages of the Claxton family at the west end of Alvertongate had been amalgamated into one large close by 1500, but each part owed a separate landmale rent.[16] At Durham the landmale rent does not seem to have been associated with a form of tenure as, for example, in Canterbury; there, the rent *gabulum* applied to land held in gavelkind in the early middle ages while other rents in the town were given the more general name of *redditus*.[17] The Durham landmale rent was a small sum of money, varying between 1d. and 1s. 2d. per annum, and it was fixed permanently for each tenement.[18] It was owed to the overlord of the borough in which a particular tenement was situated, so tenants living in Old and New Elvet, for example, owed landmale to the hostillar. It seems that, no matter how small or insignificant the income from landmale was, the overlord extracted it from all his tenants, even if it meant taking landmale from a fellow obedientiary. This is a sign that, as at Winchester, landmale was collected and recorded carefully in the Durham documents not necessarily for its monetary significance but rather as an 'indication or acknowledgement of dependency' on the overlord of the borough.[19]

---

[15] Similar rents in Winchester and Lincoln were called landgable rents: see Biddle, *Winchester*, pp. 7–8; Hill, *Medieval Lincoln*, pp. 56–9; Lobel, *Bury St Edmunds*, p. 7.

[16] Sac. rental, 1500.   [17] Urry, *Canterbury*, p. 36.

[18] In Winchester, it amounted to 5d. or 6d. per annum and in Lincoln and Bury St Edmunds it was only 1d. per messuage.   [19] Biddle, *Winchester*, p. 8.

A variation on the landmale rent is found in one part of the urban area. In Framwelgate, a street which was part of the Bishop's Borough although it lay on the west bank of the River Wear, those tenants holding land on its north-east side paid not only landmale to the bishop, but also a rent called 'meadowmale'. The name of this rent probably gives a reliable idea of its origin and its purpose. The bishop had a meadow lying behind the tenements on the east side of the street, near the riverside, which was called 'le Malemedow' or 'le Milnmedowe'.[20] Some of his tenants in Framwelgate may have had additional pasturage or grazing rights within this meadow, for which they paid a small rent. Clearly, meadowmale was associated with only certain tenements in the street, and like landmale, it was – according to the surviving documents, at least – a small, fixed sum of 1*d*., 7*d*. or 1*s*. 2*d*. per annum.[21]

Freehold rents form the second main category of rents owed by tenants in Durham. Unlike the landmale rents, these rents had a firm connection with a certain type of tenure, properties which were held in freehold, that is without any limit on the duration of the tenant's legal interest in the property. These rents could be slightly larger than landmale rents, although there were great variations in the amounts paid; the freehold rents owed to the almoner in South Street ranged from 4*d*. to 5*s*. per annum.[22] As with landmale, the freehold rents were fixed, and while they were usually owed to the overlord of the borough, this was not always the case. The right to levy the freehold rent could have been preserved by a previous owner of the land. The origin of freeholds in the Durham boroughs is obscure, largely because of the absence of documentary evidence, but there were many in existence before 1290, as the almoner's first surviving rent roll demonstrates. A certain number may have been created deliberately by the overlords of the boroughs to reward faithful servants and some may have arisen as a result of exchanges of land; many were held by the lesser 'gentry' or minor county families, and they remained in private ownership throughout the medieval period. Great efforts were made by the obedientiaries to buy out freehold interests, primarily to increase rent income and to restrict a tenant's interest to a life term, or even a period of years, by

[20] See, for example, 1.18.Spec.12; 1.18.Spec.20.
[21] Sac. rental, 1500, Framwelgate; 1.18.Spec.25; 1.10.Pont.6.
[22] Alm. rental, 1424.

converting the freeholds to leaseholds. But they may have had another motive. The rental evidence shows that freeholders were by far the most independent class of tenants, as they amply demonstrated by their reluctance to pay any rent at all to their priory overlords. Many freehold rents were not paid for fifty or sixty years and these arrears were never recouped, although attempts were made to bring freeholders to court to recover the money.[23] Occasionally, tenements were repossessed by landlords by writ of *cessavit per biennium* if the freehold rents and services were far in arrears and if it looked as though the case was hopeless. 'Lithfothall' (otherwise known as 'Lithfothouses' or 'le Shyrefhous') in the Bailey, once held by William de la Pole, was recovered by the priory in this way in 1371.[24] It was in the interests of the overlords of each borough to prevent the creation of any new freeholds and to try to acquire the freeholders' interest in the land whenever the opportunity arose.

Leasehold rents form the third main category of rents owed by tenants in Durham. In the priory rentals, such rents can be distinguished easily from other types by their size, for their value greatly outstripped the total income from freeholders or from landmale rents. The survival rate of leases concerning priory properties in Durham is very poor in the later fifteenth and early sixteenth centuries, and even before this there are too few leases to allow for any very detailed comments on the priory's leasing policy. In general terms, however, it seems that as soon as the priory managed to acquire the freehold of a tenement within a Durham borough, it leased out the land to tenants at a high rent. The bursar acquired four freehold tenements in Sadlergate from Richard More in *c.* 1480, and they were being leased for an annual rent of £1. 6s. 8d. by 1481. A tenement in Fleshewergate which once belonged to William Fenwyk was leased for £1. 6s. 8d. per annum by 1519.[25] The earliest surviving evidence of such priory leases comes from the middle of the fourteenth century, at a time when Dr Lomas has shown that tenure by service in other parts of the priory estates throughout the county was being converted to tenure by money rent for the customary tenants.[26] However, this policy must certainly have preceded, and in some measure have anticipated, what has been viewed as a major late-medieval

---

[23] Burs. inventories, 1446, 1464.
[24] 2.2.Elem.15.
[25] Burs. accounts, 1481/82, 1519/20, Receipts.
[26] Lomas, 'Durham Cathedral Priory as landowner', p. 32.

administrative development in Durham as elsewhere – the leasing of nearly all Durham Priory's manorial demesnes. The earliest leases of demesne lands were for relatively short terms; the earliest surviving leases of urban property on Durham Priory's estates in the late fourteenth century had terms usually extending no longer than three or five years, which compares with the position on the urban estates of Canterbury and Westminster Priories. During the fifteenth century, terms were gradually lengthened, perhaps because it was then more difficult to find tenants and to keep land in tenure consistently.[27]

In much of England it has been found that the value of leasehold rents on demesne lands tended to fall during the fifteenth century, as conditions favoured tenants. Landlords considered it more profitable to reduce rents and thereby help to prevent land becoming waste.[28] Lack of documentary evidence prevents any new contribution to this debate from the Durham urban estate, although the sacrist's rental of 1500 clearly demonstrates that many rents had been lowered. In Crossgate, the burgage leased by Alice Hyne had its rent reduced from £1 per annum to 13s. 4d. The tenement at the end of Framwelgate which had once rendered £1. 4s. produced only £1. 2s. in 1500. But the problem with using such evidence as proof of falling rent values in this late-medieval town is that it is not clear when these reductions actually occurred. The long gap in the sacrist's rentals from 1384–5 to 1500 means that the decline in leasehold income could have occurred at any time between these dates. In any case, perhaps this decline should not be seen exclusively in terms of the general economic climate prevailing in the country, but rather as the product of a combination of factors, including some purely local to Durham. Lower rents and longer, often life, terms were awarded to those who had sold their freehold interest in a tenement to the priory. Thus, for example, in 1500, Alice, widow of John Blenkarne, leased a tenement for life in Milneburngate from the priory at a rent of only 2s. per annum probably because her husband had granted it to the priory. After her death, the sacrist, released from any obligation of charity, was able to lease

[27] R. A. L. Smith, *Canterbury Cathedral Priory: a study in monastic administration* (Cambridge, 1943), pp. 192–200; Dobson, *Durham Priory*, p. 272; Harvey, *Westminster Abbey*, p. 151.

[28] See, for example, Postan's discussion of the problem in *Cambridge Economic History*, ed. M. M. Postan, 2nd revised edn (Cambridge, 1966), vol. 1, p. 589.

the tenement for a rent of 16s. per annum.[29] Leasehold rents were also lowered for a number of years when a tenant undertook his own repairs, but that, in turn, might be a sign of shrinking profits in the priory's urban estate. This was certainly the case in fifteenth-century Winchester, when returns for real property were less favourable and tenements were being let on condition that tenants did their own repair work.[30]

Furthermore, it is possible that the level of leasehold rents was also influenced by the location of a particular tenement in Durham. Where the property was in a popular street such as Fleshewergate, parts of Crossgate or in the market area, leasehold terms seem to have been short throughout the whole period and rents high because there was no difficulty in finding tenants. A comparable case is that of late-fourteenth-century Cambridge, where rent income fell, particularly in parishes which were more remote from the town centre. In contrast, 'well-placed housing was appreciated and maintained its value'.[31] Possibly leasehold rents were reduced most often in those parts of Durham where there were many waste tenements and where the urban area was receding. The sacrist's rental of 1500 does demonstrate, however, that many leasehold properties in all the Durham boroughs, in populous streets as well as streets with waste tenements, were by the later middle ages returning lower rents and this may have been part of the general trend towards reduced profits from leaseholds at the end of the fifteenth century. Nonetheless, despite these reductions, leasehold rents still provided the Durham obedientiaries with their largest and most flexible rent income from urban property.

However, it is misleading to consider their rent income in terms of its monetary value alone, precisely because few rents were being paid wholly in money by the later middle ages. Probably most of the small landmale and freehold rents were rendered in cash to the relevant obedientiary, if they were paid at all, but the larger freeholds and many leaseholds were paid, at least partly, in kind by the supply of specific goods or in services rendered to the priory. It is not clear when this system of payment in kind began, but it was fully operational by the fifteenth century and it probably had a long earlier history. Evidence for these non-

---

[29] Sac. rental, 1500; Rec.Book II, 1542.
[30] Keene, *Winchester*, vol. I, part I, p. 192; see below, pp. 117, 129.
[31] M. Rubin, *Charity and community in medieval Cambridge* (Cambridge, 1987), pp. 48–9.

monetary payments survives in some late rentals, such as the bursar's rentals of 1495, 1508 and 1538, and the hostillar's rental of 1525, where the entry for each tenant is followed by a scribbled note of how and when and where the payments were made. The payments in kind seem to bear more relation to the needs of an individual obedientiary and to the capabilities or resources of the tenant than to the location of a tenement, its value or the size of rent owed. Many tenants in the Bailey, for example, paid off their rents mostly by supplying cloth for the priory and tenants around the market place paid in spices.

Within any one Durham street, the documents reveal that there was a great variety of ways of paying rent. One of the most important non-monetary contributions was agricultural service, which is not to be confused with the agricultural services owed by customary tenants of the priory elsewhere in its estates. For a customary tenant, it was a necessary condition of his tenure which could not be avoided.[32] For the urban tenants of the priory, however, part of their money rent could be commuted into agricultural work such as mowing or railing, haymaking, weeding, ploughing and enclosing land. This form of non-monetary rent payment was common in both Old and New Elvet, where the urban tenants of the priory assisted the customary tenants with autumn work on Elvethall manor and in its extensive fields. The hostillar's rental of 1525 shows that a total of £4. 17s. 11d. (or forty-four rents) owed by tenants in Old Elvet was offset for autumn work and £1. 12s. 8d. (or twenty-three rents) for haymaking, which was a substantial proportion of the total potential income of £19. 5s. 2d. from the borough (ninety-nine rents). In New Elvet, the allowances of rent for agricultural work amounted to less (£2. 0s. 5d. from a total of £15. 4s. 2½d. in rent payments); the explanation for this discrepancy may have been that the tenants living in the streets of Old Elvet, close to the manor of Elvethall, were more likely to be called upon for work in the fields. In contrast with this flexible system of commutation, the tenants of Kepier Hospital who held burgages in St Giles' Borough seem to have had no choice but to perform agricultural services. This applied even where the bursar, for example, had purchased a small estate within this borough and had leased out tenements to his own tenants. They too were bound by the

---

[32] Customary tenants on the Durham estates owed no money rent but held *ad servicium* by labour service only: Lomas, 'Durham Cathedral Priory as landowner', p. 13.

custom of Kepier and the most common condition of tenure in St Giles' Borough, which was the performance of autumn work (*precarie*) on Kepier's demesne lands.[33]

Performing agricultural services by way of commuting rent was, naturally enough, more commonly found in those boroughs which extended out into the surrounding countryside and retained some vestiges of a manorial economy. Elsewhere in Durham, other methods of commuting rent were more popular, such as undertaking building work or providing building materials for the priory. Some of the bursar's tenants in St Giles and the Old Borough did carpentry work or tiling for their overlord, while allowances of rent were made to tenants who repaired their own houses. John Wodmose was allowed 6*d.* of his 4*s.* rent for work on a house in St Giles while John Eland was allowed 5*s.* 6*d.* of his 11*s.* rent for tiling in St Giles.[34] Some of these tenants seem to have formed part of the regular building work-force of the priory, employed on an annual basis, and they may have offered their services for part of the year freely as a way of paying rent. Other tenants serviced the priory in different ways; some provided cloth and spices or tanned hides for the priory as part of their rent. The regular band of priory servants, *famuli*, many of whom lived in the Bailey, offset the rents they owed for their properties against their annual stipends. For example, Thomas Bowman was employed by the priory as custodian of the prior's orchard in 1508, at a salary of 5*s.* per annum. Since he owed a rent of 5*s.* per annum for his house in the Bailey, he lived rent free.[35]

It is clear from the evidence of the late-medieval rentals that the proportion of urban rents paid to the priory in non-monetary ways was high. In St Giles' Borough, the total potential income the bursar could hope for in 1508 was £5. 9*s.*; out of this total, at least £1. 6*s.* 4*d.* was paid in kind and in work while 12*s.* was allowed in stipends. Only a little over half of the expected income from this borough was paid to the bursar in money. In the Bailey, the bursar's total potential income was £3. 12*s.* 8*d.* in 1508, but his rental shows that 9*s.* 11*d.* was paid in kind, 3*s.* was offset in soulsilver payments to tenants and £1. 15*s.* 8*d.* was allowed in

---

[33] 4.14.Spec.28; 1.10.Pont.6. Contrast the position in Canterbury, where tenants owing agricultural services at harvest-time paid a money commutation called evework: Urry, *Canterbury*, pp. 131–43.

[34] Burs. rentals, 1495, 1508.   [35] Burs. rental, 1508.

stipends.[36] Money payments to the bursar amounted to no more than £1. 5s. for the year. This evidence is supported by Dr Lomas' calculation that two-fifths of the bursar's total rents in Durham and elsewhere were received in kind, not in cash.[37] Many individual tenants managed to pay off almost all their rents in services; a tenant in Sadlergate who owed the bursar a rent of 8s. in 1508 paid during a half-year 2s. 8d. in cloth and only 1s. 4d. in money. John Wardon owed the hostillar 13s. per annum for his burgage in Old Elvet. In 1523 he paid 6s. 2½d. of it in autumn work, 10d. in hoeing or weeding the corn, 7½d. in railing work and 2d. in haymaking.[38] As a result of these methods of payment, the priory probably had a low cash income in any one year from its urban estates. It seems that the obedientiaries had little ready cash from this source with which to purchase new properties or to pay the obligations they owed to others, let alone finance the duties of their own offices.

On the other hand, the priory may have relied heavily on these non-monetary payments. Their Durham city tenants formed a great pool of potential local labour which could be used, for example, on priory manors at harvest-time, and these tenants also kept the priory supplied with necessary items such as cloth, food and coal without any financial expenditure. From the tenants' point of view, it was probably easier to 'work off' their rents in this way than to raise the necessary money, and the flexibility of the arrangements meant that there could be a response to the annual needs of the priory or the capabilities of the tenants. However, it was an essentially primitive form of estate management with its origins in a subsistence economy which relied on the exchange of goods rather than money. There is no sign that it had been superseded by monetary payments in the early sixteenth century; in the bursar's rental of 1538, almost half of the total rent income in the Bailey was commuted to non-monetary payments (£2. 0s. 8d. from a total of £4. 14s.). This financial conservatism compares with, for example, that of Canterbury Priory in the early middle ages and in the late fourteenth century, when the monks seem to have relied on the performance of labour services by their tenants, probably as a

---

[36] Soulsilver seems to have been a money payment made to servants or dependents of the priory: see *Extracts from the account rolls*, vol. 3, p. 967.
[37] Lomas, 'Durham Cathedral Priory as landowner', pp. 100–10.
[38] Host. rental, 1523.

result of demographic decline on their estates.[39] The importance of the non-monetary payment cannot therefore be ignored in any calculation of the rent income or indeed of the economic basis of the estate management policy of the priory throughout the medieval period.

The rentals also reveal that the priory's tenants paid their rents, whether in money or in kind, at almost any time during the accounting year, regardless of the term-days specified in their leases. The most popular term-days stated in these documents were, not surprisingly, the principal feast days of the church's year, for example the Nativity of St John the Baptist or Trinity Sunday, but equally the two feasts of St Cuthbert, which fell very conveniently at six-monthly intervals (20 March and 4 September) were ideal collecting days for rents and most appropriate for the custodians of his shrine. However, the rentals demonstrate that in practice the priory's tenants in Durham, as elsewhere in the priory's estates, paid their rents in small portions on many days during the year, probably when they had accumulated enough money or when they had suitable renders in kind. Moreover, arrears of rent were gathered in between the official days of payment, and in an attempt to keep some sort of check on this chaotic system, the rentals were brought up to date in an *ad hoc* fashion as payments were made.[40]

There were several places in Durham where tenants came to hand over either money payments or goods in commutation of rent to their landlords, depending on who the landlord was. Unlike Canterbury, for example, there was no one central receiving office for Durham Priory. Each obedientiary had his own exchequer or at least a place of receipt. The hostillar's tenants in Old and New Elvet usually came to the manor buildings of Elvethall, and rendered their dues in the new hall built for the hostillar's court, or in the hostillar's exchequer. The sacrist's tenants in the Old Borough probably paid their rents in the tolbooth in Crossgate or in the sacrist's exchequer within the priory. Most of the priory tenants in the Bishop's Borough or in St Giles' Borough seem to have climbed up to the cathedral to pay

---

[39] Urry, *Canterbury*, pp. 142–3; Smith, *Canterbury Cathedral Priory*, pp. 126–7. But Lomas found that the tenants on Tyneside had a cash economy long before Durham: Lomas, 'Durham Cathedral Priory as landowner', pp. 100–10.

[40] Lomas, 'Durham Cathedral Priory as landowner', pp. 100–10. Urry counted that in Canterbury, *gablum* was due on seventeen different days within the year: Urry, *Canterbury*, p. 38.

their rents to the obedientiary whose tenement they held; certainly the bursar's tenants in both the Bailey and Clayport paid their rents in the prior's exchequer.[41] There was no local point of collection. Freeholders, when they paid rent to their priory overlords, seem to have done so in the prior's court, although William Waynman, a freeholder living in New Elvet, paid his freehold rent in the hostillar's court in Elvethall manor in 1523.[42] The reason for this multiplicity of receiving offices lay once again in the division of lordship in Durham and the separation of overlordship from landlordship. The responsibility for the collection of landmale rents lay with the obedientiary who was the overlord of the borough in which a property lay; freehold and leasehold rents were gathered by individual obedientiaries who were the direct landlords of a particular tenant. Under this complex tenurial arrangement, the idea that any one central treasurer could account for all the priory's rent income or that all tenants should report to one central treasury to pay their rents was unworkable.

The whole business of rent payments was thus made very complicated for the tenant because any two neighbouring tenants in a street in Durham would probably owe rent to different landlords who collected it in different parts of the town. Also, many tenants would be in the unenviable position of paying a variety of rents to several landlords for one property if, for example, landmale had to be paid to one obedientiary, a freehold rent to another obedientiary and perhaps a third rent to a private landholder. William Martindale, who held a tenement in the Bailey, suffered from this problem of split lordship, and he had to pay 10s. to the master of Kepier Hospital which lay to the north of the town and £1 at the prior's exchequer on the peninsula.[43] But the priory rentals not only monitored these separate payments; they also recorded a close supervision by the obedientiaries over the business of rent collection in these small scattered estates. Arrangements were sometimes made, for example, for the bailiff of a borough or another representative of the obedientiary to go around collecting rent arrears within the boroughs. Rents would be collected at the home of a sick tenant, and if a tenant knew he was going to be away from home for a long period, he was expected to appoint a representative to hand

---

[41] Host. rental, 1523; Burs. rental, 1382.
[42] Host. rental, 1523.   [43] Burs. rental, 1382.

over his rent. John Cott paid through such a representative (*per decani mei*) when he was absent in London, for example.[44] Occasionally court action was taken against those tenants who refused to pay rents; the landlord could distrain any moveable goods in a house up to the value of the arrears or ultimately he could recover the tenement, but often the expense of bringing such a case may have outweighed the value of the property.[45] However, the long lists of accumulating arrears during the later medieval period show that even such close supervision of rent collection was not the solution to falling income from urban property.

The income which three Durham Priory obedientiaries, the bursar, the hostillar and the almoner, derived from urban rents is charted on the accompanying tables (see appendix 2, tables 1–4). The farms of the boroughs and such public buildings as bakeries and mills are included where appropriate. It would have been equally possible to analyse the sacrist's income from his Durham holdings, but the information about the urban estates of the other Durham obediences is too patchy to provide any coherent pattern of income or expenditure throughout the medieval period. Likewise, the shortcomings of the surviving evidence for the other Durham landlords and overlords, the bishop, the master of Kepier Hospital and private landholders, make it impossible to assess the size or the value of their Durham estates. In general terms, these tables show clearly that there were periods of rapid growth in each estate, for example, during the second half of the fourteenth century in the bursar's estate and the late fourteenth and early fifteenth centuries in the hostillar's estate; periods of slow growth, as in the bursar's and probably the hostillar's estates during the late fifteenth and early sixteenth centuries; and periods of stagnation or depression, as in the bursar's estate between 1400 and 1460 and in the almoner's estate in the middle of the fourteenth century and again in the early fifteenth century. The fact that these periods of depression or growth did not coincide in all three estates suggests that quite apart from any general economic trends affecting rent income there were some purely internal or local reasons for these fluctuations.

---

[44] Burs. rental, 1539.
[45] The case of William Richardson v. Joan Lilburn makes this point: Crossgate Court Book, 5 April 1503; see chapter 6, pp. 215, 225–6. Unpaid assized rents in Winchester were usually not recovered: Keene, *Winchester*, vol. 1, part 1, p. 187.

It is not difficult to account for the periods of growth in rent income at Durham, for they were clearly a direct result of physical expansion which occurred at different times in the estates of the various Durham obedientiaries. When an obedientiary was able to buy tenements outright, or to acquire at least the freehold of a tenement, his income grew rapidly. The bursar expanded his estate within St Giles' Borough between 1350 and 1382 by acquiring twenty-one properties from the master of Kepier Hospital and his income, theoretically at least, increased by over £15 as a result. His purchase of Robert Clergenett's tenement in the market place in 1515 increased his potential rent income by 16s. annually.[46] The hostillar's acquisitions of the late fourteenth century, including the estate of William Alman which was purchased in 1392, added considerably to his income. This estate alone consisted of at least seven tenements in both New and Old Elvet which rendered £4. 7s. 11d. in 1394–5. In 1394, new properties yielded a potential income of £9. 5s. 11d. which increased to £11. 3s. 11d. in 1424.[47] The almoner acquired land in the Bailey from the Bassett family in *c*. 1393 and he drew rents totalling 18s. 6d. from this land in 1424.[48] Thus a direct connection can be made between the physical growth of an urban estate and the growth of an obedientiary's rent income.

Another purely local reason for periods of growing rent income, although one which was far less important than the purchasing of properties, was the rebuilding or repairing of tenements. Thomas de Normanton built on the *placea* (a piece of land) of Richard de Hilton in the Bailey and as a result, the rent the bursar drew from it grew dramatically from 8d. to 14s. per annum between 1340 and 1342.[49] Refurbished properties were attractive to tenants and the bursar could lease them out at a higher rent. Between 1404 and 1424 the almoner rebuilt a tenement at the end of Elvet Bridge and divided it into four parts, each leased out separately. Before this work, the tenement contributed 14s. to the endowment of the almoner's chantry in St Nicholas' Church, a sum which increased to 36s. after rebuilding.[50] Similar subdivisions of tenements elsewhere in Durham provided all the obedientiaries with additional rent

---

[46] Burs. rental, 1382; Burs. account, 1515/16, Receipts.
[47] Host. account, 1394/95, *Redditus Assise*.
[48] Alm. rental, 1424.
[49] Burs. rentals, 1340, 1342.
[50] Alm. rental, 1424.

income, thereby increasing the number of leasehold rents without the expense of acquiring new property.

However, the rosy picture of the income derived from urban rents which the rentals and account rolls present conceals the harsh truth that urban property-holding was rarely of clear financial benefit to the priory. The documents merely record *potential* income, the maximum which an obedientiary could hope to raise from his estate provided all his tenants paid their full rents and all his tenements were in tenure. This ideal state was never achieved, because tenants fell into arrears, tenements became waste and land was kept in hand. Consequently, the gulf between the potential and the real income was often great, especially in the early fifteenth century: the almoner's income from 'assized rents' in Durham was stated to be £72 in the 1423 account roll, but the 1424 rental recorded the more realistic total rent income for the year to be £32. 5s. 10d. An attempt must now be made to explain this discrepancy, because it has a direct bearing on the periods of rent losses suffered by the three obedientiaries surveyed in this chapter.

One of the most intractable problems faced by the priory was the extraction of the full rent owed by each of their tenants. Many tenants fell into arrears of rent, sometimes over very long periods, and the worst offenders were the freeholders. The obedientiaries themselves identified this group of tenants as being the worst culprits; the bursar's inventory of 1446 stated several times under the entries for different streets that the shortfall in rent income was caused by the freeholders who had not paid their rents for 'forty years and more', and the almoner's arrears' lists contained the same freeholders' names year after year. As these were tenants who could well afford to pay what amounted to insignificant annual sums without any difficulty (members of the Claxton or Billyngham families, for example, who held several tenements in Durham as well as estates in the country), these arrears presumably grew because there was no effective sanction or machinery for recovering such debts. An obedientiary might take a freeholder to court for the non-payment of a debt, but usually the freeholder failed to attend; in any case, the costs of bringing such an action far outweighed the size of the rents. Eventually, most obedientiaries seem to have accepted the inevitable and they wrote off these old debts, sometimes for a nominal sum or perhaps in return for a promise to pay at a later date. In 1406, for example, the sacrist wrote off the rent arrears which a freeholder called John Cokyn had accumulated over twenty-one years for his tenement in Fleshewergate. Cokyn promised 'faithfully to pay ever after'.[51]

The general pattern of rent arrears in the estates of these three obedientiaries can be seen in the accompanying table, where certain trends quickly become apparent.[52] Long lists of arrears occur very early in the documented history of the three estates. In 1339, the almoner's account roll draws attention to the low income from Durham because 'many tenements lie waste and a great part of the farm is in arrears'; the hostillar's first list of arrears dates from 1325 and although the bursar's first list occurs later, in 1348, it records arrears of rent stretching back over the previous three years at least. These lists lengthen as the estates grow in size, a characteristic clearly shown in the bursar's accounts of the late fourteenth century after he had acquired his small estate in St Giles' Borough. Purchases of land did not necessarily mean increased rent income initially; very often new land brought a history of rent arrears, and if arrears were not inherited by the new landlord, then they soon developed. The bursar bought William Lumley's estate in St Giles' Borough in *c.* 1425, but many of these rents were in arrears by 1430.[53] The lists of arrears were at their longest in the estates of two obedientiaries in the early fifteenth century, at a time when the bursar and the almoner were unable to buy new land. In the bursar's estate, for example, the potential rent income for 1404 was £15. 15s., of which £5. 15s. 7d. was lost in unpaid rents. In 1408, arrears of rents due to the almoner totalled £13. 13s. 6d. This is a pattern which has been noticed in Newcastle-upon-Tyne at the same period.[54] It was a problem which none of the obedientiaries managed to solve. Although the lists were never again as long as in the early fifteenth century, many tenants were still in arrears at the end of the medieval period, including nearly all the almoner's freeholders. Moreover, the shortening of the arrears' lists may be attributable to new accounting procedures, such as the writing off of long-

[51] Sac. account, 1406/07, *Allocationes*.
[52] Appendix 2, table 5.
[53] Burs. account, 1425/26; Burs. rental, 1432, fol.40r.
[54] Butcher, 'Rent, population and economic change', pp. 70–2.

term arrears on the change of obedientiary, rather than any recovery of debts.[55]

It is also clear from a more detailed analysis of the arrears' lists that certain parts of each obedientiary's urban estates were more prone to the problem of arrears than others. The worst-affected area in the bursar's estate was St Giles' Borough, where many tenants seem never to have caught up with rent payments, while South Street was a particular problem for the almoner. In 1353, some thirteen rents in this street were in arrears; many of these debts seem to have been written off by the almoner and they were recorded perhaps as a matter of historical record rather than as a practical proposition for recovery. Parts of Alvertongate and Crossgate were also affected badly by this problem. Why should this be? Areas where arrears were high shared two common characteristics. There were sizeable numbers of freeholders holding tenements in these streets; and the streets concerned lay at some distance from the market place. In South Street, for example, seven freehold rents were owed to the almoner, and of these, six were in arrears in 1353 and continued to be in arrears for most of the medieval period.[56] Wherever there was a concentration of freeholds, there was a concentration of rent arrears, but this was exacerbated when a street was located near the edge of the urban area and far from the market. Although the priory held many freeholds in the Bishop's Borough, arrears do not seem to have accumulated to the same extent, and tenements in the centre of the town seem to have yielded high rents throughout the medieval period.[57]

By the late fourteenth century another category of rent arrears, called 'decayed' rents, appears in the obedientiaries' account rolls, perhaps marking a development in estate management rather than a new problem. A comparison of the names of tenants appearing in arrears' lists with those in the lists of decayed rents suggests that those who were persistent offenders, such as freeholders, were added or transferred to the decayed rents' list after many years in the arrears lists. This situation parallels, though at a later date, the

---

[55] Alm. account, 1533/34, Arrears. Arrears also accumulated gradually in Newcastle until the backlog was written off in 1470 and 1484/85, in an acknowledgement that they could never be recovered: Butcher, 'Rent, population and economic change', p. 70.

[56] Alm. account, 1353/54, Arrears; Alm. rental, 1424.

[57] This compares with Oxford: *VCH Oxfordshire*, vol. 4 (London, 1979), p. 39.

practice of Oseney Abbey in Oxford. There, rents which had
been in arrears from the late thirteenth century were allowed to
'decay' in the early fourteenth century.[58] In other words, decayed
rents were those which were recognised by an obedientiary as
being impossible to recover (something which the almoner
acknowledged in his description of them as *non-levabilia*) and
which, in effect, he wrote off, although he retained a record of the
debts.[59] In the bursar's estate, separate rolls listing decayed rents
accompanied the account rolls from 1395; in the hostillar's
accounts they first appeared in 1396. Year after year they
contained the names of the same tenants and often the sums
involved changed little; the sum of the bursar's decayed rents in
Elvet and Clayport was the same in 1404 and 1406, and the total
in the hostillar's accounts was the same in 1396 as it was in 1397.
However, the fact that such lists were kept at all is a mark of
defeat for the obedientiaries in their attempts to extract the full
rent income from all their Durham tenants.

'Waste' rents or tenements were a second important source of
lost rent revenue for a priory obedientiary which had to be offset
against the idealistic assessments of rent income in the account
rolls. The bursar considered that a tenement became waste if no
repair work had been done or there had been a failure to find a
suitable tenant to take on the property. The hostillar's rental of
1523 widened the definition of a waste tenement to include three
categories: those tenements which returned no rent, had no
tenant, or were held in hand.[60] Such tenements could, presumably,
cease to be classed as 'waste' if a suitable tenant was found or if
sufficient repair work was done to the tenement so that it could
be leased again. Hence this form of rent loss may have been less
entrenched than rent arrears because it held out to an obedientiary
the hope of future recovery. The accompanying table shows the
general pattern of waste rents in the estates of three obedientiaries.[61]

Some of the characteristic features of rent arrears recur in the
case of waste tenements and waste rents. The 'wastes' presented
problems from the beginning of the documented period, as the
almoner's account roll of 1339–40 reveals: in that year 'many

---

[58] *VCH Oxford*, vol. 4, p. 39. In York, some 20 % of the rents assigned to the upkeep of
Ouse Bridge were 'decayed' by 1445: *VCH Yorks., City of York*, p. 85.
[59] Alm. account, 1392, dorse.
[60] Burs. inventory, 1446; Host. rental, 1523.   [61] Appendix 2, table 6.

tenements lie waste' (*multa tenementa iacent vasta*). However, they do not seem to have had much monetary significance until the late fourteenth century, when separate waste and decay rolls were being kept by both the bursar and the hostillar (the earliest surviving list of wastes from the bursar's estate dates from 1395 and in the hostillar's estate from 1396). The keeping of such lists may, of course, simply mark a change in estate management policy to compare with the development of the category of 'decayed' rents; mounting rent losses may have been subdivided under new headings according to the likelihood of recovery. Equally, they may mark a recognition of a rapidly growing problem. These lists of waste rents, like rent arrears, were at their longest between 1400 and 1460. By 1404, waste rents amounted to a third of the bursar's total rent income from Elvet; and the hostillar's waste rents were at their highest in 1400, 1422 and between 1440 and 1448. The long lists of waste rents at this period contributed greatly to the decline in rent income in the early fifteenth century.

The obedientiaries were never able to solve fully the problem of rent losses from waste tenements even though, on the face of it, it seemed a less intractable problem than that of rent arrears. The sacrist tried to extract some revenue from waste tenements at little if any cost to himself by amalgamating two or three into closes or orchards and leasing them at a reduced rent.[62] The bursar was able to rebuild some of his waste tenements, especially in the Bishop's Borough, in the late fifteenth century, and these he leased at higher rents. A simple comparison between the bursar's inventories of 1446 and 1464 shows how much repair work had been done to reduce the number of waste tenements at a time when rent revenues were depressed. Both the bursar and the almoner reduced rents on waste tenements at the edges of the boroughs as a way of attracting tenants, but all of these methods were comparatively unsuccessful. Although there was a general improvement in the overall condition of the estate, with shorter lists of waste rents in the late fifteenth century, the bursar's rental of 1538 shows that waste tenements were still a serious problem in some parts of his urban estate. Ten of the almoner's fifteen tenements in South Street were waste in 1501. Only the hostillar's estate shows any real progress, with decreasing lists of wastes in

---

[62] The evidence for this policy is clear in Sac. rental, 1500.

1509, 1510 and 1528; but even this apparent improvement may have been on paper only, with the waste rents being transferred to another category.

Waste tenements and waste rents were, like rent arrears, concentrated in certain specific parts of the priory estates, and not spread generally through all the boroughs. These concentrations were to be found, not surprisingly, in streets such as South Street and St Giles Street, where there was little attempt at rebuilding. Tenements here remained waste or were amalgamated into larger units of open land by the bursar. Yet waste tenements in other parts of Durham, in the Bailey, Silver Street, Clayport or Souterpeth, for example, were frequently repaired and rebuilt by the almoner and the bursar, often at great cost. It seems that some parts of the priory's estates in Durham had a greater priority for expenditure than others; any money that was available for repair work was spent on the central area where property was more valuable and higher rents could be charged. Consequently, this pattern of waste rents during the medieval period can be seen to have wider implications for the history of the city as a whole. Tenements situated in streets on the edge of the urban area were more likely to become waste, and once this happened, they were rarely rebuilt or reoccupied. Instead, these tenements were amalgamated into larger units and turned over to agricultural use, thus indicating both a shrinking of the urban area and a possible reduction of Durham's population. Again, a parallel can be found in late-medieval Oxford, where a similar gradual contraction of the built-up area has been observed as the number of waste tenements increased.[63] The growth of these lists of waste rents in early-fifteenth-century Durham perhaps marks the gradual erosion of the urban fringe of the boroughs.

The priory also suffered a loss of rent income in a variety of ways which were less widespread than arrears and wastes and which were probably the result of purely local factors. Several tenements were kept in hand, sometimes for many years if it was impossible to find a tenant, or for a few months while essential repair work was carried out, with a consequent loss of revenue. The bursar had some tenements in hand in Elvet in 1396, as did the hostillar in the early fifteenth century, but rent losses from this source were very small in comparison with wastes and arrears, and the effect on the whole urban estate was negligible. Rent

[63] *VCH Oxford*, vol. 4, p. 26.

losses also occurred when one obedientiary transferred tenements or some other source of income from the town to another obedientiary's estate. In the fifteenth century, such transfers resulted in a consistent loss of income for the bursar. Between 1421 and 1426, the bursar exchanged his income from landmale, fines and amercements collected from the Old Borough and the rents of two tenements in Crossgate for a regular pension of £2. 13s. 4d. from the sacrist, which was an unprofitable if secure deal. In 1446, he transferred four tenements in Old Elvet to the cellarer with no financial compensation, and other transfers were made which gave the bursar no benefit.[64] There may have been a connection between this shedding of properties and the financial crisis in the bursar's estate which culminated in the division of his duties between three obedientiaries from 1438 to 1445.[65] Finally, there was a certain loss of revenue each year because rent reductions and allowances of rents were made to tenants who were busy with their own repair work, or were unable to pay the full rent for a specified reason, or had given tenements to the priory. The hostillar reduced rents in Old Elvet by £1. 8s. in 1351 because repair work had been done by the tenants, and the almoner reduced the rents owed by Roger Diker (an allowance of 5s.), William Plausworth (an allowance of 2s. 6d.) and Ralph Sissor (allowed 10d.) because of repair work on their houses in 1378.[66] These allowances were relatively rare occurrences and lasted for only a short time, perhaps for one rent-paying term, and the effect on total rent income was small. There does not seem to have been any policy of making systematic large rent allowances in the early fifteenth century, as there was, for example, in some monastic estates in York and Oxford. In York, it was the bursar of Fountains Abbey who allowed his tenants a substantial proportion of their rents in the 1450s, and in Oxford, Oseney Abbey reduced its rents between c. 1435 and 1449.[67] Small rent losses of similar origins occurred in the estates of the Durham obedientiaries from time to time, but they had a limited impact on income and cannot be associated with any general economic decline in the priory's urban estate.

[64] Burs. rental, 1427: Loc. xxxvii, no.87; Burs. accounts, 1423/24, 1426/27; Sac. account, 1423/24; Burs. account, 1446/47, Receipts.
[65] Dobson, *Durham Priory*, pp. 285–8.
[66] Host. account, 1351/52, Repairs; Alm. accounts, 1378/79, Repairs; 1398/99, *Allocationes*.
[67] *VCH Yorks., City of York*, p. 85; *VCH Oxford*, vol. 4, p. 42.

The general impression which remains after both the potential income and rent losses from the three priory estates in Durham have been surveyed is that although the physical size, the legal interest and even the income from rents increased at certain periods, even during good years urban property was not greatly profitable because of mounting losses, especially in the form of rent arrears and waste tenements. In particular, the evidence of falling income and increasing numbers of waste properties between 1400 and 1460 suggests a time of economic difficulty. The bursar's income from properties in Durham fell from £54. 19s. in 1396 to £29. 0s. 2d. in 1427 and to £30. 6s. by 1446.[68] The worst losses occurred in Crossgate, St Giles Street and the Bailey. At the same time, arrears of rents rose from £1. 7s. in 1395 to £6. 7s. 8d. in 1429 and the number of waste tenements in his estate was substantial. The difficulties of using account roll and rental evidence to supply accurate totals of losses are obvious. The occasional writing-off of arrears distorts the picture, as does any variation in the method of accounting (for example, the inventing of new categories of losses such as non-leviable rents). However, it does appear that the priory's urban estate was going through a period of falling income and increasing difficulties during this time.

How does this depression of the early fifteenth century compare with other medieval towns and the urban estates of other ecclesiastical corporations? In the north, there are many examples of falling rent income and property values particularly during the early fifteenth century: in Newcastle-upon-Tyne, the accumulating totals of arrears and allowances indicated falling property values in at least one urban estate in this period.[69] In York, the income the Vicars' Choral derived from 250 properties declined from £160 per annum in 1426 to c. £100 in 1456. Their total income from rents fell by 55 per cent between 1399 and 1472, and by 66 per cent by the end of the fifteenth century.[70] Nor was the depression confined to urban areas. Rents and farms on the Percy family's Northumberland estates fell by between a third and a half in the early fifteenth century, although this was partly the result of repeated confiscations of their lands by the crown, which led

---

[68] See appendix 2, table 1.
[69] Butcher, 'Rent, population and economic change', pp. 67–77.
[70] J. N. Bartlett, 'The expansion and decline of York in the later middle ages', *EcHR*, 12 (1959/60), 28; *VCH Yorks., City of York*, p. 85.

to a lack of consistency in estate management policy. The bishop of Durham was not immune from the general economic trend, however, for there was a comparative decline in his estates at this period.[71] Moreover, this economic depression in urban and country estates was not limited to the north. In Canterbury, there seems to have been a decline in rent income during the early fifteenth century, but by 1473 there was some recovery.[72] Both Oseney Abbey and St John's Hospital reduced their rents on many properties in Oxford in the early fifteenth century, and the reorganisation of the manorial economy of Ramsey Abbey at the same time was accompanied by 'the deepest and most prolonged depression in manorial revenues in any period of its history'.[73] The rental value of Westminster Abbey's estates fell in the fifteenth century, many properties were empty and income sagged in its urban as well as its rural estates. By the late fifteenth and early sixteenth centuries, however, the signs of a slow recovery and some growth in rent income which were noticed in Durham are there to see in many of the estates which have been mentioned.[74] Set against this background, the fluctuations of rent income in Durham Priory's urban estates are not untypical of general trends in revenue in the rest of the country, and lend some support to the theory of a general contraction in the economies of many English towns in the early fifteenth century.

THE COSTS OF MAINTAINING AN URBAN ESTATE

The ever-widening gulf between real and potential income from an urban estate in the early fifteenth century was only part of the problem faced by Durham Priory's obedientiaries. The hidden expenses of being an urban landlord were considerable, for the management of any estate involved financial outlay, and these outgoings also affected the opportunities for expansion. It is the costs of increasing and even maintaining an urban estate which will be considered in the last part of this chapter, and these can be divided into three categories. First, before any new properties

---

[71] J. M. W. Bean, *The estates of the Percy family, 1416–1537* (Oxford, 1958), p. 35; Bolton, *Medieval English economy*, p. 222; Lomas, 'Durham Cathedral Priory as landowner', Conclusion.   [72] Smith, *Canterbury Cathedral Priory*, p. 13.

[73] *VCH Oxford*, vol. 4, p. 42; J. A. Raftis, *The estates of Ramsey Abbey* (Toronto, 1957), p. 292.

[74] Harvey, *Westminster Abbey*, p. 64; Rosser, 'The essence of medieval urban communities', p. 95.

could be acquired, an initial purchase price had to be raised, a sum which might be high in relation to any anticipated rent income. Second, after purchase, some land brought with it rent charges or other financial obligations to third parties, the *redditi resoluti*; these might amount to very little each year, but they had to be paid, whether or not the tenement was leased out or lying waste, unless the priory succeeded in buying out these interests. Third, all newly acquired land increased the financial burden of building and repair work on an obedientiary's estate, work which was essential to keep land in tenure. Only when the monetary significance of each area of hidden expenditure has been assessed will it be possible to make any judgement about the economic viability of the priory's urban holdings and the success of individual obedientiaries in managing their Durham properties.

The priory purchased tenements throughout its history, but little is known about the costs involved or the methods of payment until the purchase prices began to be recorded under the section of the account rolls called 'necessary expenses'. Once again, this evidence has to be treated with a certain degree of caution; the fact that the account roll states a property has been bought might disguise what was, in effect, a device for borrowing money, a mortgage, not a straightforward purchase.[75] Furthermore, the price mentioned in the account was not always the full purchase price paid out for the land. It did not include items such as the payment to 'brokers' or feoffees who acted for the priory in the conveyance. It excluded hidden expenses such as pensions to former owners. Moreover, the initial acquisition could be followed by litigation over many years, and legal costs could add considerably to the cost of buying a property. Consequently, these purchase prices cannot always be considered a reflection of the true value of newly acquired land. However, with these reservations and in the absence of other sources for the priory's purchasing policy, the following comments on the Durham evidence can be offered.

Durham Priory's obedientiaries purchased properties, or at least an increased legal interest in them, either by means of one lump-sum payment or in a series of smaller payments spread over a number of years. In one very expensive accounting year for the bursar, 1376, he bought an Elvet tenement from John Killinghall

[75] Harvey, *Westminster Abbey*, p. 169.

for £5. 6s. 8d. and he paid £16 to John de Castrobernardi for his properties in Elvet and all legal rights connected with them (*pro iure quod habuit in domibus in Elvet*).[76] It was a measure of the bursar's sound finances in that year that he could afford to spend such large sums on property in Durham. Where the purchase price was high, an obedientiary usually had difficulty in raising or allocating such a large sum from one year's revenues, and his solution was to spread his payments over several years. Hugh de Chilton's Durham holdings were considerable and they were located in several Durham streets. The almoner acquired this private estate in 1376. The full agreed purchase price, according to the account roll, was £20, but the almoner could not pay the whole amount in one year. So we find him paying £13. 6s. 8d. in 1376, 10s. 7d. the following year and subsequently the remainder of the purchase price.[77] The purchase of de Chilton's land was one of the most expensive recorded in the accounts, as might be expected because of the size of this estate, but the purchase of single tenements could also be costly, as the example of Killinghall's tenement shows. The purchase price of Richard Lumley's tenement in Old Elvet is recorded as being £6. 13s. 4d. in the hostillar's account for 1474.[78] With such high purchase prices, it took many years for an obedientiary to recoup his initial outlay in rent income from his new properties. Killinghall's tenement brought in an income of £1 per annum; provided that it was in good repair and tenants were found to pay this high rent, then the bursar could hope to recover his expenditure on it in five years.

A number of subsidiary charges arising from the purchase of property had to be paid by a priory obedientiary. First among these were the payments for legal work associated with conveyancing, such as the purchase and drawing up of title deeds and the acquisition of a licence from the bishop (if necessary) granting permission for an alienation of land to be made to the priory. When the hostillar bought William Alman's land in Old and New Elvet in 1392–3, he paid an additional sum of 16s. 8d. to the bishop for the alienation of the land and for the 'farm'.[79] Furthermore, payments sometimes had to be made to relatives or kinsmen of the grantor to purchase any right or future claim they might have in a tenement. William Alman's widow was paid

---

[76] Burs. account, 1376/77, *Expense Necessarie.*   [77] Alm. account, 1376/77, Expenses.
[78] Host. account, 1474/75, Expenses.   [79] Host. account, 1392/93, Expenses.

£13. 6s. 8d. for renouncing her claim to his Elvet estate, but after the hostillar had bought the estate, she was still allowed to occupy the 'principal tenement', probably rent free, as long as she lived. When she died in c. 1396, the entry under the assized rents section of the hostillar's account concerning this estate specifically mentioned the principal tenement for the first time, showing that it had become a disposable part of the hostillar's property. The difference in rent income which this widow's legal interest made for the hostillar is starkly apparent in a comparison of the account rolls for 1392 and 1396. In 1392, the hostillar only received £2. 5s. 9½d. from this land, which was so much lower than might have been expected from such a large estate, that he had to explain it by saying that the principal tenement was still in the tenure of Matilda Alman. By 1396, rent income from this estate, now with the principal tenement included, was £2. 16s. 8d. for one term alone, and this rose to £4. 2s. 10d. by 1417.[80] The acknowledged right of a relative to remain in a tenement without paying rent was a hidden loss of income for the priory which might continue for many years.

Unfortunately, purchases of land often involved an obedientiary in a secondary form of expenditure on the estate, the subsidiary rents with which the land was charged, variously called 'resolved rents', 'pensions', 'necessary expenses' or 'stipends' in the account rolls. Several 'resolved rents' were quite large and they amounted to a regular, fixed loss of income from the Durham estates. Whatever type of subsidiary rent was owed, it rarely lapsed from its creation to the end of the medieval period, because it was valued by its holder, not necessarily for its monetary significance but rather for its acknowledgement of legal and tenurial rights. The landmale rent, mentioned earlier, fell into this category of subsidiary rent. Whenever an obedientiary extended his estate into a non-priory borough or even into a borough held by another obedientiary, he found himself saddled with a number of these small landmale payments on a permanent basis. This was one area of expenditure which the hostillar managed to avoid altogether, because unlike the other obedientiaries, he did not purchase property in boroughs other than those over which he held the lordship. According to the rentals and account rolls, the bursar paid only one regular landmale rent

<hr>

[80] Host. account, 1392/93, Expenses; 1396/97, *Redditus Assise*; 1417/18, *Redditus Assise*.

before 1400, a payment of 7*d.* per annum to the bishop for the tenement next to Clayportgate, which is first mentioned in 1390, although other landmale payments may have been owed for property acquired in St Giles' Borough which were subsumed in the pension the bursar paid to the master of Kepier Hospital.[81] By 1538, the bursar was paying five regular landmale rents, four to the bishop for land in his borough and one to the sacrist for land in Bellasis.[82] They amounted to a mere 4*s.* 7*d.* per annum, a tiny fraction of the bursar's total expenditure on his Durham estates. By 1450, the almoner paid eighteen regular landmale rents to other obedientiaries for tenements in the Old Borough and in Elvet, which amounted to 10*s.* 11*d.* in 1533.[83] It may seem strange that these small landmale payments owed by one obedientiary to another were not waived; but the landmale rent, however insignificant, was a sign of the tenurial dominance of one obedientiary over another, territorially at least, and was therefore worthy of preservation.

The rent charge was the second 'resolved rent' inherited or created when an obedientiary purchased a tenement. When the almoner bought a valuable holding in the Bailey from the Bassett family in 1393, a rent charge alternating between 3*s.* and 3*s.* 4*d.* per annum was created.[84] This payment may have been negotiated as part of the purchase price of the property, thus reducing the size of the lump sum the almoner had to pay in one accounting year, but more likely it represented the wish of the Bassett family to retain some legal interest in the property. A rent charge could be inherited by an obedientiary, as, for example, when the bursar bought the tenement next to Clayportgate in the 1380s. This property was charged with an annual rent of 13*s.* 4*d.* payable to the Billyngham family, who were probably the original owners of the land.[85] Some rent charges could be very small, such as the 1*s.* per annum which the almoner paid the chaplain of St Mary's Chantry in 1428; others, such as the 15*s.* per annum which the hostillar paid the abbot of Blanchland in 1455, were more onerous, and probably more than offset any profits to be made

---

[81] The payment to Kepier Hospital amounted to £1. 9*s.* 11½*d.* in 1388: Burs. account, 1388/89, *Expense Necessarie*. For landmale owed for the tenement next to Clayportgate, see Burs. account, 1390/91, *Expense Necessarie*.

[82] Burs. rental, 1538.

[83] Alm. rental, 1424, resolved rents; Alm. account, 1448/49, resolved rents; Alm. rental, 1533.   [84] Alm. account, 1393/94, Payment of Farms.

[85] Burs. account, 1386/87, *Expense Necessarie*.

from leasing the land to tenants.[86] Of the three obedientiaries discussed here, the hostillar had the greatest number of rent charges on his tenements. By 1512, he was paying eight such rents regularly, mainly to religious organisations like chantry chaplains or fraternities, and none to private families. By 1542, these payments amounted to £1. 10s. 11d. per annum. Although in some ways these rent charges resembled landmale payments, there was a crucial difference. Rent charges, like other legal interests in property, could be, and were, bought out by obedientiaries. The bursar's tenement by Clayportgate is an example of this policy: the bursar paid the Billyngham family £10. 13s. 4d. in 1416 as a once-and-for-all payment to end their legal interest in the land.[87]

'Pensions' were the third and largest category, in monetary terms, of subsidiary payments which an obedientiary had to make after expanding his estate. They usually arose as a result of an agreement between two obedientiaries where land was exchanged in return for a fixed annual payment. The payment of pensions was rather like spreading the purchase price of property over several years, but of course the instalments never came to an end. However, it seems that these pensions did include all the other hidden payments which land acquisitions entailed, in addition to the purchase price of the property. The bursar's expansion of his estate into St Giles' Borough was arranged in this way. He agreed to pay the master of Kepier an annual pension, a sum intended to cover any freehold rents or rent charges and services such as suit of court and autumn work which Kepier was entitled to levy from this land. This annual pension increased slightly as other tenements in the borough were added to the bursar's estate; in 1388 it was £1. 9s. 11½d.: in 1395 it was £1. 10s., rising to £1. 17s. 6d. in 1400 and £1. 18s. 3d. in 1407. By 1420, it stood at £1. 18s. 8½d., a sum which seems to have become fixed subsequently.[88] Other examples can be cited from the account rolls. In the 1420s, the sacrist paid the bursar an annual pension of £2. 13s. 4d. in exchange for two tenements in Crossgate and landmale, fines and amercements from the Old Borough.[89] The almoner made annual payments of £2 to the priory's feretrar for a tenement in the South Bailey after 1516.[90] Such pensions arose as a direct result of

---

86 Alm. account, 1428/29, Payment of Farms; Host. account, 1455/56, Pensions and Stipends.   87 Burs. account, 1416/17, *Expense Necessarie*.
88 See Burs. accounts for these years, *Expense Necessarie*.
89 Burs. rental, 1427.   90 Alm. account, 1516/17, *Redditus Resoluti*.

the wish of an obedientiary to extend his estate, but recognising that he lacked the capital to purchase properties outright in a given accounting year, he was forced to come to these expensive arrangements with his fellow monks. For these pensions were the most onerous of the subsidiary payments. They continued indefinitely whether or not the land was leased and regardless of any fluctuations in the rent. Furthermore, this arrangement meant that another obedientiary retained some legal interest in the land.

Finally, an obedientiary might find himself making other more miscellaneous subsidiary payments for a particular property, where, for example, special services or privileges incumbent on a tenement were commuted for small sums of money. The bursar owed suit to the court of the Bishop's Borough in the tolbooth for properties he held in that borough, and he commuted this obligation by paying 1s. 6d. in 1425.[91] Similarly, in 1399 he made a monetary rather than an agricultural contribution to autumn works on Kepier's land, a service he owed by virtue of holding property in St Giles' Borough.[92] Lastly, the bursar made a small contribution to the bishop's coroner for a right of way from the back of his orchard in Sadlergate on to the motte of the bishop's castle.[93] All of these miscellaneous payments seem to have been fixed in amount by earlier convention; they were small and they made no significant impact on the total budget of any one obedientiary.

Although most of the financial outgoings on property considered in this section of the chapter, apart from the initial purchase price, have been within the category of 'hidden' payments, a final area of expenditure for the priory could hardly be concealed. As an obedientiary accumulated an urban estate, so the costs of maintaining it in building or repair work mounted. Any neglect of this important area of expenditure had obvious effects. The gradual run-down of the physical fabric of an urban estate was marked by ruinous properties; these in turn would discourage new tenants from taking up leaseholds and, above all, they would imply shortcomings in estate management. Expenditure on building and repair work was a necessary concomitant of property ownership, especially when that property was situated in a prestigious ecclesiastical centre, and the

[91] Burs. account, 1425/26, *Redditus Resoluti*.
[92] Burs. account, 1399/1400, *Expense Necessarie*.
[93] Burs. rental, 1538, *Redditus Resoluti*.

high priority such work received is reflected in the expanding section called 'repairs to houses', *structura* or some similar title in the various account rolls during the medieval period. An examination of this section of the accounts reveals not only the amounts of money which obedientiaries spent annually on building work in Durham, but also the priorities within their estates – repair work was more frequently undertaken in streets where properties were in demand at all periods. It ought to be said, however, that to use the priory account rolls and rentals alone to trace fluctuating expenditure on repair work gives a rather one-sided impression of the priory's estate management policy. For it was not only the landlord who spent time and money on repairing properties; the tenant had an interest in, and a responsibility for, maintaining his tenement. The few remaining priory leases from this period show the extent of the tenant's obligations. Robert de Merington's lease, already discussed,[94] is a case in point. While the sacrist undertook to provide the largest timbers and stone for the foundations, Merington had to build the house and carry the building materials to the site at his own expense. Furthermore, he had to pay for all future repairs and maintenance work on this tenement. The poor survival rate of leases tends to lead to an underplaying of what was clearly the important role of the tenant in repair and building work on the priory estates.

In the early fourteenth century, the brevity of entries concerning domestic building work and the relatively small expenditure on it in the Durham Priory account rolls is suggestive of a fairly low level of activity in the priory's urban estates. But by the middle of the fourteenth century, the repairs section of the accounts had grown with the expansion of the estates. Repairs continued at a high level throughout the fifteenth century (except in the hostillar's estate where, apparently, little money was spent on repairs until the late fifteenth century), but there was a lessening of recorded building activity in the early sixteenth century. The pattern of building work is much the same in the estates of all three obedientiaries considered in this chapter, which implies a similarity of policy. A comparison between the periods of intense building work and the periods of expansion in the estates suggests that the level of building work can be directly

---

[94] 2.2.Sac.3a; see chapter 3, pp. 82–3.

138

correlated to the acquisition of new tenements. During periods when considerable amounts of money were spent on acquiring land, few tenements were rebuilt extensively. When the bursar's estate expanded rapidly in the late fourteenth century, repair work was limited; and during the 1390s, when the hostillar purchased several small estates, his repair bill was small. After new land was acquired, however, there was a surge in building activity (as in the bursar's estate in the fifteenth century), perhaps to bring the new tenements up to the standard of the rest of the estate.[95]

However, the pattern of building work in these three estates was not connected solely with the acquisition of land. Other factors had a bearing on the work, and one of the most important was the number of 'public' buildings within an obedientiary's estate, buildings such as the mills and bakehouses, for whose upkeep he was financially responsible. Major repair work had to be undertaken on these buildings almost every year because it was vital to the priory's income and to the obligations of lordship to keep them in working order.[96] There were churches to repair, such as St Oswald's, the responsibility of the hostillar, and St Mary Magdalen, which was maintained by the almoner. Other public buildings like the hostillar's Elvethall manor buildings and the almoner's infirmary in the Bailey had to be maintained. In years when expenditure was high on the public buildings in an obedientiary's estate, there was not enough money available to undertake significant rebuilding of domestic property. In 1347, for example, the bursar had to find £7. 15s. 2d. to reconstruct the *Meysondieu* in the Bailey and at least £4. 12s. for rebuilding the monks' infirmary. He also spent small sums on Scaltok Mill and the bakehouse in Elvet in that accounting year, and, not surprisingly, there was no surplus money to spend on domestic property repairs.[97]

Each obedientiary seems to have had a clear estimation of the priorities in repairs to domestic property in different parts of his own estate, and to have followed a policy of selective building work which can, perhaps, be demonstrated most clearly among the widely scattered holdings of the almoner. In the middle of the

---

[95] For the hostillar, see Host. accounts, 1393–7, Repairs. For the bursar, see Burs. accounts, 1423/24, when £4. 0s. 2d. was spent on rebuilding two tenements in New Elvet; and 1425/26, when a tenement in the Borough of Durham was rebuilt at a cost of £4. 18s. 2d.

[96] See chapter 3, pp. 100–2.   [97] Burs. account, 1347/48, *Structura*.

fourteenth century he financed the repair of tenements in Elvet; in the late fourteenth century, tenements in the Bailey and Souterpeth (where his estate had grown recently); and by the early fifteenth century he spent more money on the street near his chapel and hospital of St Mary Magdalen. It is significant that there is no record of repair work in streets like South Street and Crossgate, where the rentals show that many tenements were lying waste. Clearly, the almoner had abandoned all hope of again letting land in this part of his estate, as the categorising of rent arrears here as 'non-leviable' shows. He put any money that was available into restoring buildings in those parts of the town where he considered tenements could be let easily for higher rents.[98] After the bursar bought twenty-one properties in St Giles' Borough in the early 1380s, expenditure on repairing and rebuilding in this street was high, perhaps marking an attempt to bring these properties up to a suitable standard for letting. But this part of his estate proved to be unprofitable; arrears were always high, tenements lay waste and there was a shortage of tenants. Consequently, the bursar relegated St Giles to the lowest priority in building repairs for the rest of the period.[99]

It is noticeable that there were two levels of building work in the priory's urban estate. First, there was the complete reconstruction of a tenement, involving presumably the demolition of the existing structure and the rebuilding of a new house or houses on the site. When Richard More's four tenements in Sadlergate were acquired by the bursar in *c.* 1480, they were rebuilt, as was the almoner's tenement at the end of Elvet Bridge in Souterpeth in the early fifteenth century at a cost of at least £3. 14s. 7d. in 1404.[100] Second, there was repair and maintenance work such as the pointing or roofing of a house and the renewal of guttering or doors, the kind of small-scale building work which can be found in every surviving account roll.[101] Of the two types of building work, the first had more significance in terms of the management of the urban estate. Comprehensive reconstruction work was very expensive, and would have been undertaken only when there was a healthy surplus in the account, when an obedientiary had no other major demands on his

[98] See above, pp. 125, 128.   [99] Burs. accounts, 1388–1390, Repairs.
[100] Burs. accounts, 1476–1480, Repairs; Alm. account, 1404/05, Repairs.
[101] See, for example, the repairs to tenements acquired by the hostillar in exchanges with the feretrar and the master of the infirmary: Host. accounts, 1389/90, 1392/93.

resources, or when parts of his estate were in dire need of improvements.

Three reasons for the relatively high priority given to domestic building work in any obedientiary's estate can be deduced from the account rolls. First and most obviously, obedientiaries wished to improve tenements to attract tenants on to their estates. It was easier to find tenants to take up a lease if the buildings on the land were in good repair, and it was easier to increase rents if the tenements were well maintained. In 1446, for example, two tenements in Framwelgate were lying waste because no repair work had been carried out (*propter defectum reperationis*), and there was a loss of 18s. rent income. By 1464, one had been repaired and it alone rendered 16s. per annum.[102] Second, tenements which were rebuilt could be subdivided into separate dwellings by the obedientiary; where previously he had levied only one rent from the tenement, the reconstructed tenement might produce three or four and thus increase his revenue. An example of this strategy was the almoner's rebuilding of his tenement in Souterpeth, with its new division into four separate holdings.[103] Third, a tenement might have to be rebuilt after some disaster, like a fire. In 1355, the hostillar spent over £5. 9s. rebuilding four houses in Old Elvet which had been burnt down at the time of a fire in St Oswald's Church.[104]

The total expenditure on repair work in the Durham estates of the priory varied widely from year to year; there were years when the allocation to domestic building work was low, although expenditure on public buildings might be high, and years when much money was spent on rebuilding houses. It might be assumed that these fluctuations would correspond with the fluctuations of rent income from the estate and that years of high expenditure on domestic building work would coincide with years of high rent revenues, as in the late fourteenth century or the later fifteenth century. But this was not the case. The bursar's repair bill rose dramatically between 1400 and 1450 at a time when, as we have already seen, there was little growth in the estate, mounting lists of wasted and decayed rents and a diminishing rent income.[105] In the early fifteenth century, when the bursar could not afford to

---

[102] Burs. inventories, 1446, 1464.
[103] Alm. account, 1404/05, Repairs; Alm. rental, 1424.
[104] Host. account, 1355/56, Repairs.
[105] See, for example, Burs. accounts, 1416/17, 1419/20, 1423/24, 1443/44, Repairs.

buy new tenements and he was actually transferring properties to other obedientiaries, he seems to have put money into the repair of his remaining Durham properties, perhaps to ensure that they would remain in tenure. It seems that the bursar spent more money on repairs at times when his rent income was low – no doubt in an attempt to improve what he already possessed and to lessen the number of rents lost from waste tenements in his estate. During periods of high rent revenues, as in the late fourteenth century, when the market value of land was high and there was no shortage of tenants wanting to lease properties in the town, the priory could pass on much of the burden and cost of repairs to its tenants. The priory could exploit this keen land market by insisting that their tenants repaired properties at their own expense. In times of greater difficulty in the estates, when rents were falling into arrears, tenements were waste or in hand, and there was a shortage of tenants, then the priory had to take over the repair work to make a holding more attractive to would-be tenants. It was only when urban property-holding became a 'buyer's' market in periods of economic depression that the priory was forced to step up its financing of building work. Perhaps it could be argued that the lengthening sections of property repairs in all three obedientiaries' account rolls during the fifteenth century are not only the natural corollary of the physical growth of an estate, but also the indicators of increasing difficulty in finding sufficient tenants to lease priory land and to maintain it at their own expense.

This analysis of the economic relationship between the priory and its urban tenants bears some resemblance to the methodology of the medieval account rolls themselves, in both form and structure. Throughout the chapter, the fluctuating income from urban rents has been set against the landlord's expenditure on his properties, and it only remains now for the balance to be drawn. Was the account in arrears or did urban property-holding give the priory a profit to carry into the following year? Could, indeed, any consistent balance be struck? It is clear that the ownership of an urban estate brought certain financial gains to the priory from time to time, particularly in the late fourteenth century and again in the late fifteenth century. During these periods, revenue from urban rents seems to have been relatively high; there was sufficient money in the account for the priory to acquire new properties and to extend its legal interest in tenements. Properties in the central Bishop's Borough in particular seem to have been coveted, because there was no problem in finding tenants to occupy them and higher rents could be extracted from these desirable commercial premises. However, the possession of an urban estate created certain problems and financial liabilities which, even at times of high rent income, could not be avoided. Some tenants were always reluctant or unable to pay their way; certain properties were situated in less popular or prosperous streets and were more difficult to lease. Buildings needed a minimum amount of repair work at all times and many properties were burdened with rent charges to others. These financial obligations and difficulties could be more than counterbalanced by the profits from the estate in good years, but when, for various reasons, there was economic depression in the estate as a whole, as there was in the early fifteenth century, the priory probably had to subsidize its urban estate fairly heavily, resigning itself to making a loss.[106]

It is difficult to see how these problems could have been overcome by the priory, given the complications of overlordship in the different Durham boroughs, the allocation of properties between several obediences and contemporary accounting procedures. The priory did try various remedies, some purely cosmetic, such as writing off arrears or 'decayed' rents after a number of years, some more drastic, such as directing much of the money for repair work into certain streets near the centre of the town rather than the outskirts. However, despite the expense of maintenance and the undoubted difficulty in extracting rent payments from tenants, the priory obviously never considered ridding itself of this urban estate, even in its blackest hours. Why did it persist with its often unprofitable Durham estate? It needed to retain a financial and legal stake in the town surrounding it, for it wanted properties with which it could, perhaps, reward its lay servants and relatives of its inmates. It had a financial interest in maintaining a tenurial relationship with the Durham inhabitants, a relationship in which it exercised legal and financial dominance through its borough courts. Individual obedientiaries may have relied more heavily than it at first appears on their rent incomes to maintain their offices. Furthermore, they may have depended

---

[106] See R. B. Dobson, 'Cathedral chapters and cathedral cities: York, Durham and Carlisle in the 15th century', *Northern History*, 19 (1983), 35-6.

on the commutation of money rents for renders in kind,
agricultural services or food, for example, to keep the priory's
own internal economy working. For a variety of reasons, it seems
that the priory had a vested interest in retaining and maintaining
its Durham estate. Perhaps even more significant than any
economic or practical explanation was the desire common to any
religious corporation to preserve its holdings, urban or otherwise,
intact for the future. As M. D. Lobel has commented, using the
Benedictine monastery of Bury St Edmunds as an example, the
administration of urban property was regarded as a trust, and the
monks always considered the interests of their successors in
office.[107] It was this philosophy which goes furthest to explain
why, against all the odds, and with the insoluble problems of
mounting wastes and arrears in the early fifteenth century, the
large outgoings on property and the difficulty in finding tenants,
Durham Priory and its obedientiaries went on investing time and
money in what was so frequently an unprofitable venture, the
administration of an urban estate.

[107] Lobel, *Bury St Edmunds*, p. 31.

Chapter 5

Trades and occupations

The economic success of a medieval town naturally depended, to a great extent, on the variety of industries and trades it offered to the surrounding countryside and on the market it provided for the exchange of goods. A prosperous town acted as a magnet upon its immediate area, drawing a supply of labour and produce from the country and giving in return goods which were un-obtainable in village communities and services which were dependent on the town's craftsmen. To anticipate the conclusions of the following survey, late medieval Durham emerges as a comparatively small market town with a limited range of trades. These trades or occupations were geared to the servicing of the urban community as a whole, and the two great ecclesiastical households of the bishop and the prior on the peninsula in particular, as well as to the needs of the agricultural communities nearby. Durham was still small enough to retain several characteristics of an agricultural community well into the sixteenth century: many open spaces, orchards and closes were to be found in the outer boroughs; and probably a significant proportion of the town's inhabitants were employed as seasonal agricultural labourers, working, for example, on the priory hostillar's manor of Elvethall.[1] Durham was closely bound to its immediate hinterland and to a purely local market; it thus bears close comparison with a town such as fourteenth-century Colchester, where local trade predominated and agrarian-based occupations were important in the town's economy.[2]

However, attempts to quantify accurately the volume of trade which passed through, or was generated by, Durham's market, or even to estimate the number and size of the different occupational groups operating in the town, are fraught with difficulties because of the lack of any one significant medieval source which is

[1] Lomas, 'A northern farm', pp. 26–53.
[2] Britnell, *Colchester*, pp. 12, 16.

continuous throughout the whole period under study, with the possible exception of the priory bursar's account rolls. It is possible to form a general, and probably reasonably accurate, impression of trends in Durham's economy in the later middle ages by scanning a very wide variety of documents including these accounts, title deeds, chancery enrolments and court rolls, and using relevant archaeological reports. Nevertheless, it has to be admitted that none of these sources provides, for example, a comprehensive picture of industries or craftsmen in Durham. The witness lists of deeds are perhaps the most fruitful and accessible source of documentary information about the latter, although the few surviving craft ordinances, such as the weavers' ordinances of 1450, contain lists of craftsmen working at that time.[3] There are, however, no extant surveys of occupations in the town to rival those derived from the 1379 poll tax returns for three of Stamford's parishes, for example.[4] The priory rentals, the only surviving documents which come close to a survey of landholding in the town, do not give the trades of many tenants. Consequently, it is impossible to make a fully accurate assessment of either the number of trades in medieval Durham or the numbers of people involved in one particular craft at any one time. The poor survival rate of any documents relating to the Bishop's Borough is a particular cause for regret, since this area clearly was the commercial centre of Durham throughout the medieval period.

Surname evidence can be used to amplify and extend the documentary evidence for the existence of many Durham occupations, particularly in the late thirteenth and early fourteenth centuries. However, it has to be treated with a degree of caution: occupational surnames no doubt first emerged as an accurate description of a man's trade, but by about the middle of the fourteenth century many such designations had become family names which were inherited by later generations who had no connection with the trade.[5] It can be assumed, for example, that

---

[3] PRO Durham Chancery Enrolments, 3/44, m.10, 11.

[4] Rogers, 'Medieval Stamford', p. 47; Durham has no extant local lay poll tax returns.

[5] In Winchester, for example, many occupational surnames seem to have become hereditary by the end of the fourteenth century: see A. R. Rumble, 'The personal name material', in Keene, *Winchester*, vol. 2, appendix 1, p. 1409. In contrast, it has been suggested that many people with occupational surnames in late-fourteenth-century Oxford actually practised the trade of their surnames: R. A. McKinley, *The surnames of Oxfordshire* (London, 1977), pp. 29–30. See also R. A. McKinley, *Norfolk and Suffolk surnames in the middle ages* (London, 1974), pp. 52–4; Kelly and others, *Men of property*, p. 13.

John le Barber who held land in Fleshewergate and Crossgate in 1318 was by trade a barber, but John Barbour who witnessed a charter in 1422 was a tailor.[6] By the middle of the fourteenth century, contemporaries with the same occupational surname might be involved in completely different trades. John Bacon, who held land in Elvet Borough in 1374, was, predictably enough, a butcher, but John Bacon who held land in Framwelgate in 1354 was a potter.[7] It is only when other documentary evidence can be assembled in support of these occupational surnames that they can be used reliably to provide information about the variety of trades in a medieval city in the later middle ages.

The following chapter attempts to survey the variety of Durham's trades and industries as a means of assessing the scale of the town's role as a market for its region and its position on a notional league table of wealth relative to other medieval towns.[8] It is possible to identify specialised trade quarters within the city and to suggest some reasons for the development of given trades in these areas. Some estimate, albeit rather primitive, of the number of craftsmen or traders involved in each industry, their wealth and status and family connections, will be made. Finally, there will be a discussion of the organisation of trade in Durham, its craft guilds and the part they played in the ceremonial as well as the economic life of the town. One important omission in this survey of occupations is that of the clergy and their retainers (*veredarii*) and servants. The large and influential group of clerks who worked for the priors and bishops of Durham held considerable numbers of tenements in the town and played an important part in all aspects of town life. For the purposes of this chapter, however, it is not proposed to deal with their professional role in the town's society, but rather to view this group, like the majority of Durham's inhabitants, primarily as consumers of goods produced by the craftsmen and traders.

THE RANGE OF TRADES AND INDUSTRIES IN MEDIEVAL
DURHAM

A rapid and somewhat cursory survey of the available documentary evidence, however imprecise, reveals the existence of at

[6] 1.2.Sac.35; Misc.Ch.2209; 3.15.Spec.42.   [7] 4.2.Sac.3c; 2.2.Sac.3b.
[8] See the table which appears in W. G. Hoskins, *Local history in England*, 2nd edn (London, 1972), appendix 1.

least fifty-four different named trades or occupations in Durham by *c.* 1300.[9] Taking this figure as merely an indication of the scale of the town's economic activities, it suggests a very restricted manufacturing base when compared with the 305 occupations collected from twelfth- and thirteenth-century Coventry deeds and the over 125 crafts found in Norwich in the 1390s.[10] Most of the occupations found in Durham at this period fall into the three broad categories common to the majority of English medieval towns: leather workers, textile workers and members of the victualling trades, who between them provided most of the necessities of life for the town dweller. Within these categories, there were several more numerous or distinctive groups of craftsmen, such as the saddlers, tanners and skinners within the leather workers' group, and the butchers, millers and cooks among the victuallers. However, some rare examples of the more specialised branches of these same crafts are to be found in surname evidence contained in undated but probably late-thirteenth-century deeds. Among them are Richard Felter of the Bishop's Borough; Roger Parmentarius of Framwelgate; Ralph Vinetarius of Elvet Borough; and James Apotecarius of Clayport.[11] The luxury trades were well represented in Durham at this period by several goldsmiths and spicers, but references to other specialists bearing more unusual occupational surnames like William Vaginator, Richard, son of David Wolpuller, Roger Harousmyth and Alexander Parchementator, die out by the later fourteenth century.[12]

Limited as the list of occupations in early-fourteenth-century Durham is, it is much more extensive than any compiled for the later middle ages. Using three main sources originating from Durham Priory, deeds, rentals and account rolls, by *c.* 1400 a very approximate total of thirty-eight different occupations can be collected, revealing fewer specialists and traders in luxury items; and this total was to be reduced even further, to nineteen, by 1500.[13] The list could, no doubt, be amplified from other sources, but even so, the trend of the evidence points to a narrowing range of occupations in the late-medieval town which compares

---

[9] See appendix 2, table 7.
[10] *VCH Warwicks.*, vol. 8, pp. 152–3; Campbell, 'Norwich', p. 14.
[11] Loc.xxxvii, no. 20; 1.18.Spec.13; Misc.Ch.2230; Misc.Ch.1853.
[12] Misc.Ch.2006 (1309); Misc.Ch.2372 (1294); 3.18.Spec.6 (1320); 2.3.Elem.17 (undated).
[13] See appendix 2, tables 8 and 9.

unfavourably not only with provincial centres such as York and Norwich but also with smaller towns like Colchester.[14]

This reduction in numbers does, of course, conceal the fact that many closely related crafts were probably operating under an umbrella organisation; the scabbard maker and the woolpuller of early-fourteenth-century Durham may have been subsumed into the larger general categories of smith and textile worker. It is quite possible that the term *faber* in the late fifteenth century included many specialists such as wheelwrights, locksmiths and arrowsmiths, craft designations which seem to have disappeared from the Durham documents. The dispute between two groups of Durham weavers in 1468 demonstrates this same point. It emerged there that the weavers produced a variety of textured cloths of varying quality, presumably employing different techniques and skills. The 'wolnewebsters' wove woollen cloth, linen 'called Playn lyn', 'Caresay' or kersey, sackcloth and cilicia, or rough, hair-cloth. The 'chalonwebsters' made higher quality fabrics such as coverlet, tapestry work and say as well as worsted, motleys, 'tweled work' – probably a form of tweed – and diaper.[15] In the early medieval period, probably all these individual products were made by men with different, specialist occupational names, but by 1463 they had come under the aegis of two main craft organisations. This situation compares with Winchester in the fourteenth century, where the tailors made and mended a variety of garments, including gowns, tunics, doublets, hose, hoods and gloves. In late-medieval York, the tailors' craft organisation seems to have included specialist producers (the hosiers or the cappers, for example) while other members acted as wholesalers, such as the drapers. In other towns, it can be shown that some craftsmen were involved in the production of goods entirely unrelated to their original occupational designations.[16] The result is that the true variety of different occupations in late-medieval towns is hidden and reliance on, for example, evidence

---

[14] There were more than forty-three crafts in Colchester in 1428–c. 1434: Britnell, *Colchester*, p. 244.

[15] Say is a coarse cloth like serge. PRO Durham Chancery Enrolments, 3/50, m.10.

[16] Keene, *Winchester*, vol. 1, part 1, p. 318; H. Swanson, 'Crafts and craftsmen in late medieval York' (unpublished DPhil thesis, University of York, 1980), p. 72. In London in the fourteenth century, the linen armourers may have made bedding and tents and the glovers also made purses: E. M. Veale, 'Craftsmen and the economy of London in the 14th century', in A. E. G. Hollaender and W. Kellaway (eds.), *Studies in London history* (London, 1969), p. 144.

such as a list of craft organisations – as a guide to the numbers of
different trades or to the range of goods produced by a town – is
both misleading and limiting.

However, it is also true to say that in some cases men who
produced the same work might be given different occupational
names, thus redressing the imbalance of the evidence to an extent.
Two well-known examples of this naming confusion are the
tanners with the barkers and the souters with the cordwainers. In
Winchester, shoes were made not only by men described as
cordwainers, but also by corvesers and cobblers (*sutores*) by the
late fourteenth century. The London quilters and stuffers did
exactly the same job at a similar period.[17] Although the Coventry
deeds of the fourteenth and fifteenth centuries record some 739
different trades, on closer examination it can be seen that between
a quarter and a third were simply subdivisions of the cloth and
wool crafts.[18] Perhaps such duplication of activities, if not of
organisation, also applied to Durham, if on a much smaller scale,
although the surviving evidence does not allow for detailed
quantification of the activities of its craftsmen.

In a town which was so dominated by its ecclesiastical
overlords, overlords who were, in the case of Durham Priory and
Kepier Hospital, resident and whose bishop maintained a
permanent household in Durham castle, it is hardly surprising that
service industries, especially the victualling trades, were a
dominant force in its economy, as they were in medieval
Westminster or in Norwich, where they formed more than 14 per
cent of the known trade population.[19] The butchers are
particularly well represented in the Durham documents, as they
were in King's Lynn and Winchester, where they provided more
than 20 per cent of the recorded occupations before 1530.[20] The
Durham butchers are called variously *carnifici*, *macrerarii* and
'flesshewers', the last title giving a vivid impression of their main
activity. Whereas much of the concern of the overlord in
Westminster was to control the butchers' activities in matters such
as the disposal of offal, the Durham butchers seem to have been
left to pursue their trade without interference from the local

[17] Keene, *Winchester*, vol. 1, part 1, p. 289; Veale, 'Craftsmen and the economy of
London', p. 139.

[18] *VCH Warwicks.*, vol. 8, pp. 152–3.

[19] Rosser, 'The essence of medieval urban communities', p. 96; Kelly and others, *Men of
property*, p. 25.

[20] Parker, *King's Lynn*, p. 16; Keene, *Winchester*, vol. 1, part 1, p. 251.

courts.[21] This could, of course, be a reflection of the paucity of evidence for the Bishop's Borough, where most of the butchers lived, but it is their status as urban property-holders and borough office-holders which comes across most strongly from the documents, and perhaps this status protected them from close regulation by the overlords. From the many references to butchers in conveyances dating from 1280 to 1527, it seems clear that butchers were to be found holding land at any period in each Durham borough – for example, Ellis Carnificus in Milne-burngate (probably in the late thirteenth century) and the Tudhow family in Clayport (in the fourteenth century).[22] Their activities in the Durham land market suggest that the butchers were men of means. By contrast, Canterbury butchers' names rarely occur in twelfth-century charters or rentals, which may indicate that they lacked the landed wealth or status of their Durham counterparts.[23] The number of butchers working in Durham at any one time is difficult to assess from the documents, but surname evidence suggests there were at least seventeen in the early fourteenth century. This figure compares favourably with an average of eleven butchers in Winchester between 1300 and 1500, although in York some forty-nine butchers were presented in 1304 alone for offences against the assize.[24]

The Durham cooks (*coci* or 'coks') and bakers (*pistores*) do not seem to have had either the landed wealth or the social status of the butchers, although some members of the trade were property-holders. Bertram, son of Gilbert Cocus, held land in Fleshewer-gate (probably in the late thirteenth century) and Nigel Pistor had land in St Giles (1316); but some of these men, such as Waldenus de Pistrino of the abbey who held land in Old Elvet in the late thirteenth century, were not ordinary bakers, providing bread for the townsmen. They were employed by the priors' or the bishops' households.[25] Private baking was strictly controlled by the priory, which had its own communal bakehouses in New Elvet and Crossgate; and most of the bakers appearing in the documents were probably those who operated the priory bakehouses.[26] Consequently, their opportunities for making substantial profits which could be converted into land-holding would be limited.

[21] Rosser, 'The essence of medieval urban communities', pp. 96, 99.
[22] 1.5.Elem.5; Misc.Ch.1857.   [23] Urry, *Canterbury*, pp. 111–12.
[24] Keene, *Winchester*, vol. 1, part 1, p. 256; Swanson, 'Crafts and craftsmen', pp. 144–5.
[25] 2.3.Elem.19; 2.11.Spec.50; 4.14.Spec.20.   [26] See chapter 3, pp. 100–2.

Brewing was an occupation common to many Durham households, although it is unlikely that many livelihoods depended exclusively on the sale of home-brewed ale. It was usually a part-time activity which supplemented the family's income, and it was one of the few trades in which women were involved. The Marshalsea court roll for New Elvet contains what may be a complete list of brewers in the borough in 1395. Some thirty-four brewers appeared before the prior's representative to display their measures and this list of *communes brasiatores* included the names of five women: Christine de Pittingdon, Agnes Vessy, Mabel Porter, Alice de Boynton and Margaret de Barneby. The list of brewers in the Old Borough that year included six women among the sixteen names.[27] This small but significant proportion of female brewers compares with York, where twenty women out of a total of seventy brewers were presented in 1304 for breaking the assize of ale, and with late-medieval Winchester, where 23 per cent of those presented for breaking the assize of ale in 1351 were females, and between 1380 and 1433, 10 to 20 per cent of tapsters and brewers presented for such infringements were women.[28] However, it is clear that most of the Durham brewers had another trade as well and, as in Winchester and York, brewing may have been simply a secondary occupation. Roger White, for example, who appeared before the Elvet Marshalsea court, was a fuller of cloth; and among those summoned to appear in court in 1395 were seven bakers, two weavers, a butcher and a spicer. For those who brewed ale surplus to the requirements of their own family or neighbours, the main outlets would be the ecclesiastical establishments on the peninsula, to judge by the Canterbury evidence.[29]

In contrast to the relatively well-documented brewers, only one vintner appears in the Durham deeds (Ralph Vinetarius, who held land in New Elvet probably at the end of the thirteenth century),[30] although the demand for wine within the monastic precinct, at least, was great, as the account rolls show. It is clear from the latter source that the monks either bought wine from local merchants who had, presumably, organised its shipment and transport to Durham, or that they by-passed local suppliers altogether and instead bought direct from the wine importers at

[27] Loc.IV, no.140.
[28] Keene, *Winchester*, vol. I, part I, pp. 265–6; Swanson, 'Crafts and craftsmen', p. 160.
[29] Urry, *Canterbury*, p. III.   [30] Misc.Ch.2230.

ports such as Newcastle and Hartlepool or even Hull.[31] A survey of the Durham bursar's accounts has shown that it was the same merchants who exported wool from the region and dealt in corn sales who supplied him with, among other luxury products, wine and malt. To give just two examples, John del Cotes, a Durham wool merchant from whom the priory also borrowed quite heavily, supplied wine to the bursar in 1331. Robert de Castro, a Newcastle-upon-Tyne merchant, exported wool from Newcastle in the 1330s, and he supplied Durham Priory with wine in 1334–5 and with barley malt in 1335–6. It seems that the bulk of wine sales was in the hands of the merchants, not Durham vintners, by the later medieval period, as it was in both York and Winchester.[32]

Many different types of leather workers are mentioned in the Durham documents, and although it does appear that they formed a significant proportion of the Durham craftsmen, it is not possible to estimate accurately the size of this group, or even to compare it with the number of Durham victuallers, for example. During the late thirteenth and early fourteenth centuries, a sizeable community of saddlers (*sellarii* or 'sadelers') was living in Sadlergate and perhaps gave its name to the street. The names of at least eight saddlers survive from this period.[33] There were considerable numbers of men described as barkers or tanners in Durham, holding property in, for example, Crossgate and Framwelgate throughout the medieval period. This part of the urban area was also popular with skinners (*pelliparii*); Roger de Ask and Richard de Bolum held property in Crossgate in 1316.[34] Footwear was a significant product of the Durham leather workers from the earliest days of the town, as the Saddler Street excavations demonstrated. Scraps of shoe-making leather and worn soles and uppers from boots were found among the artifacts in a house dating from the late tenth or early eleventh century.[35] The names of souters or cordwainers occur regularly in title deeds to properties in most of the Durham boroughs, although not, as

---

[31] See below, pp. 172–4.

[32] Burs. accounts, 1331/32, *Emptio vini*; 1334/35, 1335/36; C. M. Fraser, 'The pattern of trade in the north-east of England, 1265–1350', *Northern History*, 4 (1969), 45, 53, 65; Swanson, 'Crafts and craftsmen', p. 163; Keene, *Winchester*, vol. 1, part 1, p. 272.

[33] These were: Absalon Sellarius (also known as Absalon de Dunelm.); Nicholas Sellarius, burgess; Nicholas de Newerk, saddler; Adam de Newerk, saddler; Ralph Sellarius (also known as Ralph de Flasceby); Robert Sellarius, burgess (also known as Robert de Lychefeld); John de Hilton, saddler; and Wydon Sellarius.

[34] 1.16.Spec.15.   [35] Carver, 'Three Saxo-Norman tenements', pp. 1–80.

the street name might suggest, in Souterpeth. Their numbers can be assessed more accurately in the middle of the fifteenth century, for when the souters' craft regulations were drawn up in 1463, some eighteen souters, presumably the total membership of the craft at that time, witnessed their ordinances.[36] This number compares favourably with Winchester, another ecclesiastical centre, where there may have been fifteen shoe makers at work *c.* 1367–71 and probably the same number in the sixteenth century, and where leather workers were the third most numerous group of tradesmen. However, it was a small-scale manufacturing activity in comparison with York, where fifty-nine members were listed in the cordwainers' ordinances of 1387.[37]

If leather working cannot be claimed as the dominant industry of late-medieval Durham, the next most likely candidate is the textile industry. Here again, the evidence is sparse, but it is sufficient to show that at no period did this industry approach the scale it did, for example, in Norwich, Stamford or York during the later middle ages.[38] There are occasional references to Durham townsmen who were involved in all stages of cloth manufacture, the first process being represented by two wool 'pullers', Thomas Wullepuller, who witnessed a charter in 1260, and Richard, son of David Wolpuller, who lived in Crossgate in 1294.[39] A small weaving industry seems to have developed in Durham by the fifteenth century, when twenty-three weavers could be marshalled to witness their craft regulations in 1450. They included William Nesse of Framwelgate and John Frank of Clayport, who were chosen as wardens for the year. Probably the other twenty-one, whose places of work were not specified, were drawn from all the Durham boroughs, and this list may constitute the total number of weavers working in Durham at this time.[40] There seem to have been fewer fullers than weavers in late-medieval Durham, although there is no surviving complete list of fullers for any one year. Many of those mentioned in the

36 PRO Durham Chancery Enrolments, 3/50, m.6.
37 Keene, *Winchester*, vol. 1, part 1, pp. 285, 290; *York Memorandum Book*, vol. 1, ed. M. Sellers, Surtees Society, vol. 120 (1912), p. 73.
38 In Norwich, the worsted industry provided 25–30 per cent of those admitted to the freedom of the city in the early sixteenth century: Campbell, 'Norwich', p. 16. The largest group of traders in Stamford in 1379 was clothworkers: Rogers, 'Medieval Stamford', p. 48. There were seven craft guilds in York concerned with textiles and five of these contained 325 masters: *York Memorandum Book*, vol. 1, p. xxvi.
39 4.18.Spec.17; Misc.Ch.2372.
40 PRO Durham Chancery Enrolments, 3/44, m.10–11.

documents may have worked for the priory at its fulling mill below the cathedral or, for its brief life, at the South Street fulling mill. The finishing trades were represented by several tailors and glovers (*talliatores* or *cissores*) like John Karlele, glover, who lived in Sidegate in the Bishop's Borough in 1386, but they were an insignificant presence in the town when compared with, for example, the fourteenth-century York guild of tailors with its 128 members.[41] As with the production of wine in Durham, so too the production of cloth locally was affected by the purchasing policy of its largest consumers, such as the priory. The account rolls show that the Durham bursar tended to by-pass local producers of cloth in favour of buying wholesale further afield, at regional fairs, for example at Boston in Lincolnshire, or from merchants and drapers based in Yorkshire.[42]

A small market town like Durham might be expected to generate a community of metal workers to manufacture and repair agricultural as well as domestic implements. However, the documentary evidence does not support this theory, although it is clear that there were some smiths (*fabri*) in the town throughout the medieval period. For example, in a deed dated 1313 John Scot of Horslawe granted Robert de Belford, *faber*, a tenement in Old Elvet which he had bought from Ralph Faber of Brancepeth.[43] However, there may have been specialists in the trade in Durham in the late thirteenth and early fourteenth centuries, catering for the needs of the military garrison in the castle. The occupational surname held by Roger Rasursmith (or Rasurschmyth) demonstrates a degree of specialisation, and his alternative surname, Harousmyth, suggests that he would be in demand in wartime as well as peace (1320).[44] Also connected with Durham's small-scale metal trade were cutlers such as Robert le Cuteler (1353), a scabbard maker, William Vaginator (1309) and farriers such as Ellis Mariscallus (1242).[45] Such specialisation compares unfavourably with York, where the ordinances of thirteen separate mysteries of metal workers survive from the fourteenth century. But none of these York organisations contained many members; the total membership amounted to only seventy-nine, an average of eleven members per guild.[46] The lack of any significant

[41] 2.2.Sac.4d; *York Memorandum Book*, vol. 1, pp. 95–6.   [42] See below, pp. 171–4.

[43] 4.17.Spec.51.   [44] 3.18.Spec.6; 3.18.Spec.4.

[45] 4.16.Spec.167; Misc.Ch.2006; 4.3.Elem.8.

[46] *York Memorandum Book*, vol. 1, pp. xxxiv–v, xlii, 93; Swanson, 'Crafts and craftsmen', p. 179.

numbers of metal workers in the Durham documents suggests the same was true there. Furthermore, in the later middle ages, the references to specialist branches of the craft decrease and the generic term 'smith' covers most metal workers.

The organisation of the building trade has been subjected to detailed scrutiny in a previous chapter, but a rapid survey of the variety of types of building craftsmen in the town gives a clearer impression of the size of the trade in comparison with others and its importance in Durham's economy.[47] The elite of this group were the masons (*cementarii*), employed, as they were in York, on large-scale building works such as churches, the cathedral priory and the castle buildings. Some may have been itinerant experts, skilled men brought in by the bishop or the prior to supervise specific projects, craftsmen who may have stayed in the town only for the duration of the work, as was the case in late-medieval Winchester. However, as in Norwich, several masons seem to have been permanent members of the community and some of them, like John de Ulkyliston (1314), held land and their own quarries in the Old Borough.[48] On the evidence of occupational surnames alone, there were twelve masons in Durham during the fourteenth century. But there are more references in the account rolls to the more lowly workers of stone, the layers, setters and wallers, who were considerably beneath the masons in the hierarchy of building craftsmen; these were men such as Richard Farne or John and William Kay who repaired houses and built their foundations.[49] Carpenters seem to have been more numerous in late-medieval Durham, to judge by the account roll evidence; indeed, as in medieval Winchester, they may have been the largest category of building craftsmen because of the number of timber houses which were in constant need of repair.[50] Certainly, they are found living in all parts of Durham: to give two examples, John de Alverton had property in Clayport (1353) and Thomas de Meryngton leased a tenement in South Street (1403).[51] Undoubtedly, the building trade provided a secure livelihood to many townsmen; as we have already seen, the priory employed a group regularly to maintain its city properties, and if the

[47] See chapter 2, pp. 90–2.
[48] 4.15.Spec.24; H. Swanson, *Building craftsmen in late medieval York*, Borthwick Paper no. 63 (York, 1983), pp. 7–8; Keene, *Winchester*, vol. 1, part 1, p. 283; Kelly and others, *Men of property*, p. 29.
[49] Alm. account, 1472/73, Repairs; Burs. account, 1368/69, Repairs.
[50] Keene, *Winchester*, vol. 1, part 1, p. 283.   [51] Misc.Ch.1880; 1.3.Sac.5(7).

evidence allowed, similar groups would no doubt be seen working for the other Durham overlords.[52]

The social composition of Durham, with its large communities of clergy, administrators and legal advisers, as well as, from time to time, visiting church dignitaries and county families, demanded other more specialist service industries and goods than were common in many other small medieval towns. Luxury items, such as furnishings and fine cloth, were brought into Durham by the men described as *mercatores* or mercers, terms which seem to cover every category of general trader from the wealthy land-holding merchants such as Reginald Mercator, in the late thirteenth century, to men like Thomas Burton, mercer, who rented the Cornerbooth from the priory to sell his wares in 1438.[53] This resident 'merchant class' was relatively small in comparison with many towns, partly because the priory at least tended to buy from merchants from Newcastle, Hartlepool and even Darlington for such transactions, particularly in the fifteenth and early sixteenth centuries,[54] but in terms of the size of Durham, the small scale of its manufacturing trades and the restrictions of its hinterland, there was a significant merchant presence at least in the early fourteenth century.

Furthermore, a few Durham merchants had extensive, even international, trading connections and dealt in a wide range of commodities. In the middle of the fourteenth century, for example, John del Cotes, the Durham wool merchant mentioned earlier, was issued with Dordrecht bonds amounting to £708, a sum which was larger than that owed to most merchants elsewhere in England. It was surpassed in the north only by those owed to William de la Pole of Hull and Henry Belton and Henry Goldbeter of York.[55] These merchants, and others like them, helped to keep the priory afloat financially by entering into credit transactions and loans with the bursar. The bursar borrowed £79. 10s. 1½d. from Robert de Coxside, another Durham

[52] Burs. accounts, 1464/65, 1471/72, Repairs. See chapter 2, pp. 91–2.

[53] 5.2.Elem.2; Misc.Ch.1700. In sixteenth-century York, the terms 'mercer', 'merchant', 'grocer' and 'chapman' overlapped considerably, and the same may have been true in late-medieval Durham: D. M. Palliser, *Tudor York* (Oxford, 1979), p. 161.

[54] See below, pp. 172–4.

[55] See, for example, *CClR 1337–9*, pp. 429, 433; *CPR 1338–40*, p. 425; *CPR 1340–43*, p. 14; Fraser, 'The pattern of trade', p. 53; information supplied by Edward Miller. On the York wool merchants and their financial arrangements, see E. B. Fryde, *Some business transactions of York merchants*, Borthwick paper no. 29 (York, 1966).

wool merchant, in 1341, for example. He in turn sold the priory malt in 1338 and spices in 1344, and he secured the contract for supplying cloth for the liveries of all the prior's household in 1340, 1343 and 1344 (a contract amounting to £83. 13s. 4d. in 1340). He was one of the farmers of the wool customs in 1343, and he held Dordrecht allowances for £180. 16s. 7d. at Hull, £200 at Hartlepool and £160 12s. 4d. at Newcastle.[56] Coxside's partner, Robert de Gretewych of Durham, and John de Morpath of Durham sold cloth extensively to Durham Priory in the middle of the fourteenth century; they supplied cloth for livery for the priory's household in 1336, for example, at a cost of £27. 12s. 6d. They also dealt in luxury foodstuffs such as almonds, saffron, rice, sugar and wine.[57] The credit arrangements entered into by the priory and these merchants revolved around the tithes of grain and wool, which seem to have been bought in advance from the priory in return for these loans. In 1328/29, for example, John del Cotes and Ralph de Whitwell, another Durham merchant who traded from outside the North Gate of Durham castle, bought nine sacks and fourteen stones of wool from the priory bursar, and subsequently, Cotes was to be found in the account rolls supplying the bursar with almonds, a barrel of sugar, wax, wine and cloth.[58] These men may not have been resident in Durham for more than a few weeks each year owing to their widespread trading commitments, but they described themselves as Durham merchants, perhaps because of their family connections, or their property-holding in the town, or because they counted the prior and the bishop as two of their best customers.

The influence of a wealthy clientele can also be seen in the growth of a small but significant community of goldsmiths situated close to the castle gate in the early fourteenth century.[59] Another luxury item, spices, was not only imported to the town by the international merchants; there were resident suppliers and sellers of spices in Durham in the earlier medieval period, and it was clearly a profitable and prestigious trade. James le Espic, also known as James Apotecarius (1295), presumably dealt in spices as

---

[56] Burs. accounts, 1338/39, *Empcio Bras. et Cervise*; 1340/41, *Garderoba*; 1341/42, *Mutuaciones*; 1343/44, *Garderoba*; 1344/45, *Garderoba*; *CClR 1337–9*, pp. 424, 429; Fraser, 'The pattern of trade', p. 54.

[57] Burs. account, 1336/37, *Garderoba*.

[58] *RegPalDun* 3, pp. 415–16; Burs. accounts, 1328/29, 1329/30, 1330/31, 1337/38; Fraser, 'The pattern of trade', p. 53.

[59] See, for example, Alan Aurifaber's tenement in Sadlergate: Misc.Ch. 2001, 2003, 2004.

well as in medical potions. He held property in Fleshewergate, and he was referred to as a 'burgess' of Durham; he also held the office of bailiff of the Bishop's Borough several times.[60] Other Durham occupations which were clearly linked with the needs of this distinctive urban community were a parchment maker, a hatter, a furrier and several barbers. In 1468, the bishop gave a charter to 'all them that occupy the Barber's Craft, Waxmakers and Surgeons in the said city', setting out the regulations governing their trade. Twenty-eight men of these amalgamated trades witnessed the charter, including Robert 'barber of the Abbey', which suggests that there was plenty of work available for this specialised and somewhat peripheral service industry in the town.[61]

The evidence is sparse, but it is reasonable to assume that the size of most Durham professions was small relative to many other medieval towns, although perhaps not to those towns which were ecclesiastical or administrative rather than manufacturing centres. Furthermore, it was in keeping with the size of the resident population of the town, which, as we have already observed, was never very great.[62] The composition of the jury which examined the quarrel between the 'wolnewebsters' and the 'chalonwebsters' in 1468 may give an indication of the comparative importance, if not the sizes, of different trades in Durham. The jury was, apparently, drawn from representatives of all the main Durham crafts, excluding any cloth workers, presumably because they were not considered to be impartial, and any victuallers. The jury contained two glovers, two carpenters (one from St Giles), one smith, four tanners (including one from the Old Borough and one from Élvet), one mercer, one baxter, and a man whose trade was not given.[63] On this admittedly slender evidence for the relative sizes of Durham crafts, leather workers appear to have been predominant, with building workers a poor second and metal workers very few and far between. However, this document does not take into account the presence of many victuallers in the town which the deeds, for example, reveal. It is likely that the victuallers occupied a prominent place in the hierarchy of trades in the town, as they did

[60] Misc.Ch. 1879.
[61] This charter is transcribed by C. E. Whiting, 'Durham trade guilds', *TAASDN*, 9, part 3 (1943), 408–10.   [62] See chapter 1, pp. 35–6.
[63] PRO Durham Chancery Enrolments, 3/50, m.10.

in Winchester and Westminster, because of the peculiar
circumstances of Durham, with its large ecclesiastical presence and
its pilgrim trade.[64]

Despite the small size of the Durham crafts, there was a
considerable variety of occupations in the town, especially in the
thirteenth and fourteenth centuries, a variety which compares
with other smaller provincial towns such as Winchester in the
twelfth century, with more than forty different trades, or Bury St
Edmunds, which had seventy-five bakers, ale-brewers, tailors,
washerwomen, shoe makers, robe makers, cooks, porters and
abbey retainers in 1086.[65] It is unlikely that any one of these
individual trades could be classed as a dominant industry in
Durham; as it has been commented about Canterbury in the early
middle ages, 'the evidence available does not suggest that there
was any one outstanding characteristic trade or industry'.[66]
Durham's trades seem to have been primarily service industries,
designed to satisfy a local rather than a wider market, and there
was little investment in them. However, this limited industrial
base made Durham less prone to fluctuations of demand for any
one product, in the way that the downturn in the fortunes of the
wool or cloth trades seems to have produced a recession in towns
such as Leicester, Coventry or Northampton in the late fifteenth
and early sixteenth centuries. A slump in any one trade had
presumably no disastrous effect on Durham's diversified service
industries as a whole.[67]

[64] About half the tradesmen in Winchester may have been involved in feeding and
clothing the population: Keene, *Winchester*, vol. 1, part 1, p. 251. But the market for
food and luxury items in Durham may not have been regular, being dependent on
visitors to the peninsula. Compare with Westminster, where the flow of visitors was
probably more consistent: Rosser, 'The essence of medieval urban communities',
p. 96.

[65] Darby, *Domesday geography of eastern England*, p. 198; Biddle, *Winchester*, p. 430.

[66] Urry, *Canterbury*, p. 109.

[67] *VCH Northants.*, vol. 3, pp. 26–31; P. Clark and P. Slack (eds.), *Crisis and order in
English towns, 1500–1700* (London, 1972), pp. 8, 11–12; C. V. Phythian-Adams,
Desolation of a city: Coventry and the urban crisis of the late middle ages (Cambridge, 1979),
pp. 40–50.

THE OCCUPATIONAL TOPOGRAPHY OF
LATE-MEDIEVAL DURHAM

The location of this wide variety of small service industries and trades reflects two apparently contradictory topographical tendencies which were not unique to medieval Durham. The first is the growth of specialist quarters with the concentration of one trade in a particular street or area, as in fourteenth-century Salisbury, for example. The second is the dispersal of some trades, with one or two representatives scattered through the town, as was the case in late-medieval Stamford.[68] Somewhere between these two extremes lay towns such as Norwich and Winchester which lacked any marked zoning of occupations in quarters but where different parts of the town were noted for their characteristic trades. As Dr Keene comments, referring to late-medieval Winchester, 'individual trades rarely predominate to the exclusion of all the others in any one area' but most trades had a characteristic pattern of distribution.[69]

The location of tradesmen and craftsmen in medieval Durham, what we might call the 'occupational topography', provides examples of both concentration and dispersal. The most obvious evidence for the existence of trading quarters in Durham at an early stage comes from the five occupational street names found in the city: these were Sadlergate, Fleshewergate, Silver Street, Souterpeth and Walkergate. It is striking that all five streets were situated within the Bishop's Borough; there are no occupational street names recorded in the other Durham boroughs, a fact which serves to reinforce the comments already made on the economic predominance of the central urban area. Although the earliest written record of these names dates from deeds of the late thirteenth century, they were probably in use long before this date, suggesting that distinct trading quarters for the butchers, goldsmiths and others had been established in the Bishop's Borough, more precisely in the streets leading into the market place, in the early middle ages.[70] Naturally, street-name evidence has to be treated with caution; it may indicate merely that a trade was located there at one particular time in the town's history

---

[68] M. D. Lobel, 'Salisbury', in M. D. Lobel (ed.), *The atlas of historic towns*, vol. 1 (London, 1969), no. 8, p. 5; Rogers, 'Medieval Stamford', p. 48.

[69] Keene, *Winchester*, vol. 1, part 1, p. 335; Kelly and others, *Men of property*, p. 32.

[70] See chapter 2, pp. 60–1, 63–4.

when the street acquired its name. Unless it is supported by other corroborative evidence from a variety of different sources, an occupational street name in itself is not a reliable guide to the trades in a given street.

However, in the case of the location of the Durham butchers, the evidence of the street name Fleshewergate is supported by a number of title deeds which show land in the street passing from one member of the trade to another. One butcher in particular, William, son of Walter de Essh, accumulated a large collection of tenements in this street in the early fourteenth century which eventually became part of the priory's urban estate. William held land in other Durham boroughs, as, for example, in the Old Borough near Crossgate, but this was much more a tribute to his own personal wealth than evidence for the distribution of his trade.[71] Such small private estates were property investments made by wealthy tradesmen and should be differentiated from properties which were used for specific trading purposes. It is clear that Essh's principal dwelling was actually within Fleshewergate, whence he managed his business, and other butchers leased stalls and shops in that street not only for their trade but also for their private dwellings. Durham's butchers, like those at York, seem to have congregated in this one place from an early date, for they appear in the deeds and rental entries relating to this street from the late thirteenth century to the end of the medieval period. This continuity of documentary evidence presumably implies that the trade remained located in the same area throughout the medieval period.[72]

Sadlergate adjoined Fleshewergate, and here again we seem to have an occupational street name which accurately reflected its predominant trade, at least in the early medieval period. In an appropriate topographical juxtaposition, saddlers and other leather workers lived alongside the suppliers of their hides, the butchers of Fleshewergate. The deeds of the late thirteenth and early fourteenth centuries show, as with the butchers, that neighbouring tenements in Sadlergate were conveyed from one saddler to another through several generations. Absalon of Durham, saddler, had acquired his land in Sadlergate from a

---

[71] See, for example, his land in Fleshewergate: Misc.Ch.2002; Misc.Ch.2022; Misc.Ch.2024; Misc.Ch.2032. He held land called Farthyngcroft and Slateracre in the Old Borough: Misc.Ch.1967; Misc.Ch.1986.

[72] Swanson, 'Crafts and craftsmen', p. 144.

furrier called Nicholas de Roxysborough. Absalon's daughter, Matilda, sold the burgage to Nicholas de Newerk, saddler, who in turn granted it to his nephew, William de Blythe, saddler; William de Blythe sold the land to Ralph de Flasceby, saddler, in 1302. There was thus a proven continuity of trade in this tenement.[73] Archaeological excavations on the west side of Sadlergate (modern Saddler Street) added further support to the theory of a distinct historical zoning of the leather-working trade in the early middle ages. Shoe making, at least, if not saddlery as well, continued without a break on this site from possibly the late tenth century to the thirteenth.[74] After the middle of the fourteenth century, however, such meagre evidence for the location of Durham leather workers as survives suggests that the trade had become dispersed through all the boroughs. In 1424, William Harpour, a saddler, was living in Souterpeth, a street adjoining Sadlergate, and Hugh de Stafforth, saddler, leased 'le Cornerbooth' in the market place in 1403.[75] In the later medieval period, it is no longer possible to discern any significant pattern of landholding by leather workers, but this may in part be a reflection of the changed status of several members of the trade from freeholders to leaseholders after the fourteenth century.

Sadlergate would thus seem to be a good example of a fossilised occupational street name which bore little relationship to the trades its inhabitants followed in the later medieval period. Silver Street is, however, a positively misleading occupational street name. There is no surviving evidence, documentary or otherwise, to suggest that silver or goldsmiths lived or traded in this street at any time. It is possible that gold or silver articles were sold in Silver Street in the early middle ages, as Ekwall surmised about London's similarly puzzling street name, Silver Street.[76] But according to the deeds, the small community of Durham goldsmiths seems to have lived as close as possible to their chief clients, near the main gateway to the castle and the monastic precinct in Sadlergate, in the late thirteenth and early fourteenth centuries at least, a location comparable to that of the goldsmiths

---

[73] Misc.Ch.1706; 4.2.Sac.14; 1.16.Spec.28.
[74] Carver, 'Three Saxo-Norman tenements', pp. 1–80.
[75] Alm. rental, 1424; Misc.Ch.2012.
[76] E. Ekwall, *Streetnames of the city of London* (Oxford, 1965), pp. 76–7; K. Cameron, *English place-names* (London, 1961), p. 199.

of Bury St Edmunds.[77] Alan Aurifaber had his principal house on the east side of Sadlergate in 1340 although, like the wealthier butchers, he also held property elsewhere in the town, particularly in the Old Borough, property which he seems to have leased out to tenants unconnected with his craft.[78] William de Hedley, goldsmith, bought a burgage from William de Beautrove in Sadlergate in 1370.[79] There are few references to goldsmiths in Sadlergate after this date; by 1505, the goldsmith Robert Lytholl held a tenement in the market place, and in 1526 Thomas Blakden, goldsmith, lived in Walkergate.[80] Perhaps the four-teenth-century group of goldsmiths in Sadlergate had been disbanded, moving down the hill towards the market place, where their luxury goods would be more accessible to a wider audience on market days. Such a migration may mark a shift in their activities from supplying mainly an ecclesiastical market on the peninsula (hence the location in Sadlergate) to a secular market. It may also indicate the increasing security of life in the town and a growing feeling of confidence among craftsmen who could leave the safety of the castle gate for the market place, which had its own walls by the early fourteenth century.

Probably few of the other Durham crafts had a sizeable enough membership to make any trade concentration particularly noticeable in the documentary sources, but there are signs of a zoning of tanners and skinners. Although there is no surviving appropriate occupational street name, deeds and leases of the late fourteenth and fifteenth centuries show that most tanners lived on the east side of Framwelgate and the north side of Crossgate, with only one or two representatives of the trade in Old and New Elvet and in St Giles. Like the saddlers and the goldsmiths, certain tenements were held successively by members of the same trade, although not necessarily by members of the same family. Alice, widow of Richard Brake, tanner, granted Robert Hogeson of Durham, tanner, a burgage on the east side of Framwelgate in 1486, presumably because she had no male heir to take over the business.[81] John Halywell, barker, conveyed his two burgages in Framwelgate to William Nicolson, barker, in 1443; Nicolson in

[77] R. S. Gottfried, *Bury St Edmunds and the urban crisis, 1290–1539* (Princeton, 1982), p. 84.
[78] For his land in Sadlergate, see Misc.Ch.2001. For his property in Crossgate, see Misc.Ch.1981; 1.2.Sac.4. He also held land near Chiltonpool in the Old Borough: Alm. accounts, 1345, 1352/53.   [79] 1.2.Spec.34.
[80] Loc.xxxvii, nos. 32,34,35,36; PRO Durham Chancery Enrolments, 3/74, m.4d.
[81] 2.2.Sac.17.

turn granted them to Richard Baxter and John Yowdale, barkers, in 1444.[82] Such continuity of trade in certain tenements was desirable because equipment associated with tanning, like lead cisterns and other vessels, seems to have passed with the land. Sixteen lead cisterns contained in the barker John Yowdale's tenement in Framwelgate were conveyed with the land, for example.[83] Consequently, such tenements would be more attractive propositions to members of the same craft.

The reasons for this apparent concentration of tanning activity in Framwelgate and Crossgate are not difficult to surmise: tanners needed a constant supply of running water, and the tenements they occupied in Durham extended from the street of Framwelgate down to the River Wear or from the north side of Crossgate to the Milneburn stream. The occupational topography of Norwich is directly comparable with Durham in this respect: more than half the conveyances involving tanners in the late thirteenth and early fourteenth centuries concerned property with river frontages, and the deeds stipulate the 'right to water course'. Tanners were also to be found living near water in Winchester, York and Coventry.[84] Furthermore, it was highly desirable that tanners or barkers should not live too close to the centre of the urban area, for their trade was noxious and at the very least anti-social. Some towns, such as Coventry, passed regulations banishing these trades to certain areas; in 1457, for example, the leet ordered that leather was not to be curried within the walls.[85] In Durham the lack of any one overall authority or of any measure of self-government by townspeople probably prevented any formal arrangements for the zoning of such unpleasant activities, but it is likely that the overlords exerted an informal development control through their borough courts and their leasing policy which led to the location of the trade on the edge of the urban area. Indeed, it is possible that the tanning industry had been forced to relocate by the middle of the fourteenth century. In 1336, there was at least one tannery in Sadlergate, from which John Tunnak was alleged to have stolen three hides.[86] It was appropriate for the tanners to work alongside the saddlers and the butchers in this part of town, but the growth in population

---

[82] 1.18.Spec.3; 1.18.Spec.4.   [83] 1.18.Spec.12; 1.18.Spec.25 (1467).
[84] Kelly and others, *Men of property*, p. 23; Keene, *Winchester*, vol. 1, part 1, p. 287; *VCH Yorks., City of York*, p. 89; *VCH Warwicks.*, vol. 8, pp. 152–3.
[85] *VCH Warwicks.*, vol. 8, pp. 152–3.   [86] Loc.IV, no.52.

and perhaps a desire to improve the approaches to the peninsular forced the tanning industry to seek a new home. In any case, Sadlergate had a limited water supply, and this difficulty probably influenced the tanners' removal to Framwelgate.

The other trades and occupations of medieval Durham provide plenty of examples of the dispersed type of occupational topography. This is particularly noticeable in the case of the cloth workers, who, as in Angevin Canterbury, had no one identifiable locality. Weavers are found in Clayport and Alvertongate, with tailors in Sadlergate, the market area, St Giles, and Old and New Elvet; and there were tenting frames in St Giles' Borough.[87] The absence of a clear quarter or focus for the textile industry, in contrast with other medieval towns such as Norwich which were known for their cloth production, again makes the point that it was not a manufacturing industry of great significance in Durham.[88] The few metal workers in medieval Durham were also scattered around the boroughs, although most lived in Clayport and Old Elvet; this contrasts with York, where 48 per cent of those recorded lived in one of the four parishes where metal workers occurred, as the evidence of wills demonstrates.[89] Most building workers were widely dispersed, although the masons were more localised and, not surprisingly, seem to have lived near the quarries which they worked. John de Ulkyliston, for example, held a croft and a quarry in South Street in 1314, and other masons held land in Elvet.[90] Most Durham merchants or mercers seem to have lived near the market place or in Fleshewer-gate, some occupying their own homes and others, such as William Clerk in 1433, leasing shops from the priory. However, in the late thirteenth and early fourteenth centuries, some merchants, such as Hugh de Querington, burgess and merchant, lived on the north side of Clayport, and a few held property in the outer Durham boroughs. John Sotheron had property in Sidegate in 1382, and Adam de Stanhop, mercer, granted his burgage in New Elvet to Robert othe Howe, mercer, in 1339.[91] This scatter of merchant properties is not entirely random, however. Tenements

---

[87] Urry, *Canterbury*, p. 122; Burs. rentals, 1427, 1495, 1507–17.

[88] The majority of Norwich cloth workers lived in the central area and the dyers, in particular, were concentrated in one sub-leet: Kelly and others, *Men of property*, p. 24.

[89] Swanson, 'Crafts and craftsmen', p. 459.   [90] 4.15.Spec.24.

[91] William Clerk leased a stall from the priory commoner: Misc.Ch.2426. For Querington's property, see 5.2.Elem.2 (undated charter). For property in Sidegate and New Elvet, see 2.2.Sac.2; 3.3.Elem.6.

near to and around the market place were obviously most desirable from the commercial point of view – hence the preponderance of merchants living in the Bishop's Borough. But merchants, just as any other urban landlords, also invested in property elsewhere in the town which they could lease out for profit.

The fact that any one occupation had a specific trading quarter in the town did not mean its members were debarred from living and working in other parts of Durham, and even the butchers, one of the clearest examples of a zoned trade, had representatives dispersed throughout the boroughs. The Tudhow family of butchers, for example, lived in Clayport in the fourteenth century,[92] and in the late thirteenth and early fourteenth centuries butchers held land in Framwelgate, South Street, Alvertongate, Crossgate and New Elvet. This dispersal can be explained in the light of the peculiar administrative divisions within the town. Despite any centralising influence exerted by the Bishop's Borough on traders and craftsmen, the division of Durham into separate borough communities meant that there would always be members of the different crafts or trades in each part of Durham, a generalisation which is only belied by the producers of luxury goods who lived and traded as close as possible to their main consumers. It is likely that each borough had at least one butcher, for example, who catered for the immediate needs of the local community. The victualling trades in particular were subject to fairly heavy and regular consumer demand, a demand which was, perhaps, reflected in the widespread scatter of butchers. Dr Swanson made this connection between demand and dispersal in her work on the York bakers, tailors, smiths and building workers in the later middle ages.[93] Yet the random presence of butchers in any Durham street should not hide or detract from the very clear concentration of this trade in Fleshewergate throughout the medieval period.

This very general survey of the location of some of Durham's craftsmen and traders has revealed a number of influences on occupational topography. Most obviously, the physical characteristics of an area determined, to a large extent, which trades would develop. A good water supply drew the tanners to Framwelgate and Crossgate rather than, for example, to Old Elvet, although concern for public health and for the cleanliness of the water

[92] Misc.Ch.1857.   [93] Swanson, 'Crafts and craftsmen', p. 454.

supply probably weighed in the balance. The open spaces on the edge of St Giles' Borough were ideal for long tenting frames. Man-made features presumably accounted for the siting of the goldsmiths, attracted by the security of a castle gate and the later town wall. The site of the one Durham market place drew a wide variety of trades and most of the merchants to the Bishop's Borough. The majority of potential customers would be found in this area; and most Durham traders seem to have attempted to purchase or to lease shops and stalls if not in the market place itself, then in the streets leading into it.[94] The bridgeheads were also good sites for shopkeepers and traders, because traffic built up at these crossing points. Furthermore, it was no coincidence that many of the victuallers lived alongside the main route to the castle and the priory, near the principal castle gate, a road frequented by monastic servants, administrators and pilgrims alike.

However, it may have been something altogether more contrived which led to the concentration of many trades and traders in the Bishop's Borough. It was, after all, within the power of the overlord, the bishop of Durham, to create the most favourable conditions for trade, conditions which would encourage economic growth in his borough perhaps at the expense of the priory's or Kepier Hospital's boroughs. Bishop Puiset's charter appears to have done this, by granting certain liberties and freedom from toll to his burgesses living there.[95] The inhabitants of the priory's Old Borough seem to have lacked a charter altogether, and accordingly to have been deprived of any economic advantages such a document might have provided. The limited freedom bestowed by Prior Bertram on his Elvet burgesses does not seem to have been enough to counteract the attractions of the Bishop's Borough and its market.[96] Consequently, it was the latter which was the hub of economic activity in Durham throughout the middle ages, just as in Coventry the earl's part of the town was more prosperous than the monks' part because the latter lacked the active promotion of trade by its overlord.[97]

---

[94] Compare this policy with Norwich, where there were 48 stalls for butchers, 28 for poulterers and 44 for fishmongers in the market place: Campbell, 'Norwich', p. 14.

[95] Reg.i, part 2, fol.3; see chapter 2, pp. 46–8.

[96] Cart.ii, fol.251; see chapter 2, pp. 46–8.

[97] J. Lancaster, 'Coventry', in M. D. Lobel (ed.), *The atlas of historic towns*, vol. 2 (London, 1975), no.3, p. 5; A. and E. Gooder, 'Coventry before 1355: unity or division?', *Midland History*, 6 (1981), 1–38; A. and E. Gooder, *Medieval Coventry: a city divided?*, Coventry and Warwickshire Pamphlets, no.11 (Coventry, 1981); *The*

THE DURHAM MARKET

An attempt can be made to evaluate the role of Durham in supplying goods, even if not locally manufactured, to consumers through its market place. The principal outlets for products in the town were the great households of the bishop and the prior, followed by the lesser establishments of Kepier Hospital and the county families. Unfortunately, the patchy survival of documentary sources concerning the bishop's household, and the lack of any evidence at all about the running of other larger establishments in the town, which has been lamented more than once in this study, prevents any reliable estimate of the range and origin of goods with which they were being supplied in the medieval period. But the remarkably detailed account rolls of various Durham Priory obedientiaries can be used to demonstrate the place of Durham's market in provisioning a large corporate consumer within the urban community. Of the three obediences mentioned in the preceding chapter, all of whom, it might be assumed, would need to make substantial purchases locally for the upkeep of their offices, only the bursar seems to have kept consistent records of the amounts and types of goods purchased, the expenditure on individual items and the names of places or people from whom provisions were bought. Under the expenditure section of the bursar's accounts, which, as the accounts become longer and more complex, is subdivided into sections such as 'wardrobe', 'purchases of wine', 'purchases of iron' and 'necessary expenses', occur lists of goods purchased annually by the bursar on behalf of the prior, with, in most cases, the name of a merchant or dealer, and the place where the goods were purchased. Consequently, it is these account rolls which have been used as the basis of the following survey.

Of course, there are problems of interpretation when relying so heavily on a single documentary source, and it cannot be claimed that the account rolls themselves contain all the answers to the questions raised by an analysis of trade and marketing in medieval Durham. One obvious difficulty is that the place of origin of merchants or dealers who sold goods to the priory is not always supplied, and so it is difficult to ascertain whether we are dealing with Durham merchants or men without local connections. If the

early records of medieval Coventry, ed. P. R. Coss, Records of social and economic history, new ser., vol. 11 (1986), pp. xxxi, xxxiv.

evidence of surnames derived from place names is used to identify origins, it can be positively misleading; Robert de Coxside was clearly identified as a merchant of Durham in the account of 1341, as were John de Morpath and Robert de Gretewych in 1336. Thomas del Holme was called a Beverley merchant in 1330, but in the ultimate misleading surname William de Durem belonged to Darlington, not to Durham.[98] A second problem of this source is that many of the victuals purchased by the bursar were not linked to a particular place of origin or manufacture; the lists of provisions and the sums of money enable us to know how much the priory spent in a given year on these items, but not always where the money was spent – in Durham market place or elsewhere. However, with these reservations in mind, it is possible to use the bursar's accounts to make a somewhat rough-and-ready analysis of the town's role in the supply of goods to the priory.

In the late thirteenth and the early fourteenth centuries, it is clear that the Durham bursar relied quite heavily on Durham's market and on local producers to provision the priory with a wide variety of goods. The three broad categories of purchases he made in Durham were wine, cloth and spices. In 1298, for example, he bought saffron, fennel, dill and peony seeds in the town; in 1302 he bought a selection of cloth, including blue cloth (*bluetto*), blanket cloth, russet, cloth for the poor and canvas in which to pack wool. He purchased wine in Durham in 1318 and 1331, and ale in 1333, 1338 and 1344. In 1335, he was buying fourteen pounds of sugar, and in 1336, ginger and sugar, rice, sweetmeats and olive oil.[99] At this period, all the signs are that goods of a high quality were available in the local market place, as were luxury items which were brought in for sale, although few of these items, with the possible exception of the cloth, were manufactured by Durham craftsmen. However, this evidence tends to reinforce the conclusions made earlier in this chapter about the greater variety of tradesmen working in Durham in the high middle ages and the significant numbers of members of the luxury trades, such as the goldsmiths and spicers who lived in the town at this period. After the middle of the fourteenth century, the purchasing policy of the

---

[98] Burs. accounts, 1330/31, *Mutuaciones*; 1336/37, *Garderoba*; 1341/42, *Mutuaciones*; Fraser, 'The pattern of trade', pp. 50–4.

[99] All these references, and subsequent ones, come from the Burs. accounts of the given years, under the sections of the accounts variously entitled *Expense Necessarie*, *Garderoba*, *Emptio Vini* etc.

bursar had changed, and other sources of supply were tapped, as we will see. Furthermore, by the later middle ages it is clear that the bursar was using Durham market only for smaller-scale purchases of goods of inferior quality. The finer cloths he had bought in the early fourteenth century were replaced by purchases of sackcloth and worsted, as in 1373, and more canvas, as in 1422. The wine purchased in the fifteenth century was not of any particular distinction or quality, and more common were purchases of malt and ale locally brewed, as in 1399. The basic commodities necessary to sustain monastic life were bought in Durham, such as bread, wax and candles, but for goods of a higher quality and a more professional finish, the bursar was looking elsewhere.

It is not hard to elicit from the bursar's account where most of the priory's purchases were being made. Even in the early fourteenth century, when the bursar was buying a substantial amount of produce in Durham's market, he had other sources of supply, in particular the great local fairs where he made bulk wholesale purchases. The bursar patronised three fairs in the region: these were Durham, Darlington and Boston fairs. In 1338, for example, the bursar bought fifteen ells of cloth of various colours at Durham's fair for making hose, at a cost of £1. 6s.; in 1342, he was buying black fur for the prior's tunic, hood and cloak at a cost of £13. 4s. 4d., as well as altar cloths and towels. The sums spent at Darlington's fair were comparable, and again the goods bought there were chiefly cloth of various types: the bursar spent £7. 19s. 11¾d. on cloth there in 1293, for example. He was still using this fair to supply livery for members of his household in 1371, when he purchased green and striped cloth. At regular intervals in the early fourteenth century, the bursar, travelling with one servant at least, went all the way to Boston fair in Lincolnshire to buy provisions for the prior: in 1336, for example, he spent £4. 16s. 6¾d. on provisions and the wardrobe, and he bought twine or cord, cloth and stockfish. The latter were shipped to Newcastle, and then transported overland to Durham. It has been calculated that in 1298 the bursar spent £2. 14s. 6½d. on cloth, furs and haberdashery at Darlington fair, and he bought £148. 1s. 0¼d.'s worth of wine and spices at Boston, which is a measure of the reliance of the priory on sources of supply external to Durham itself.[100] So at the time when the priory was making

[100] Fraser, 'The pattern of trade', p. 50.

a substantial number of purchases in Durham's own market place, it was still relying heavily on the large regional fairs to buy wholesale. Large-scale purchases of cloth, in particular, were made through such means, something which should be borne in mind when considering the comments already made about the lack of a significant cloth industry in the town itself.

By the late fourteenth century, the regional fairs had had their day, but the bursar had kept a third option open for purchasing goods. He had made extensive use of merchants as middlemen, and from the earliest surviving account rolls he can be seen purchasing goods from them, often on credit. The priory maintained connections both with merchants who were described as Durham merchants, who, presumably, had a home in the town itself, and merchants from wider afield, principally from Newcastle-upon-Tyne, Hartlepool, Darlington, York and Hull. The Durham merchants have already been mentioned earlier in this chapter;[101] gradually these locally based merchants were replaced by those from further afield. In the middle of the fourteenth century, for example, the priory was dealing with William de la Pole of Hull, who supplied three casks of wine in 1355, and John Spycer of Newcastle, who provided sweetmeats and five quires of paper in 1360 and 1363.[102] Fish had always been purchased in bulk from non-Durham sources, mainly from Hartlepool merchants such as the Bromptoft family in the early fourteenth century, or direct from the fish quays at Shields at the mouth of the River Tyne as in 1416, when the bursar bought white fish, lobsters, crabs and lamprey there. Salmon came from Berwick and Holy Island, brought by sea to Newcastle by, for example, John Doxforth, mariner, in 1510, and then transported overland to Durham. But one of the most popular fish with the Durham monks, to judge from the account roll evidence, dogdraves, was being bought in vast quantities from Hartlepool men in the sixteenth century. In 1523, Percival Conyars alone supplied 690 dogdraves at a cost to the bursar of £17. 13s. 4d.[103] London merchants or suppliers were rarely used by the priory in the fourteenth century, but the supply of spices, for example,

---

[101] See above, pp. 157–8, 170.

[102] The wine from Hull and its transport cost the bursar £17. 6s. 8d.: Burs. account, 1355/56, *Emptio Vini*.

[103] Fraser, 'The pattern of trade', pp. 51–2; Burs. accounts, 1416/17, *Emptio piscium*; 1510/11, *Expense Necessarie*; 1523/24, *Emptio piscium*.

seems to have passed to them from local merchants in the fifteenth century. Robert Marchell, a London grocer, supplied the bursar with ginger and cinnamon in 1437 at a cost of £2. 4s.[104]

By the fifteenth century, the supply of certain items to the priory, chiefly good quality wine and cloth as well as spices and furs, had been cornered by merchants without a Durham base. Wine purchases were made mainly at Newcastle: Roger Thornton of Newcastle supplied red Rhenish and Gascon wine to the bursar between 1403 and 1422, and he also had a side line in the supply of Spanish iron to the priory. In 1440, the bursar spent £6. 13s. 4d. on wine bought from Thomas Bee, John Hunter, Thomas Hedlam, Thomas Wardley, Thomas Hudson and Thomas Smyth, all Newcastle merchants.[105] Salt was another commodity not handled in the Durham market: Robert Oliver of Newcastle supplied the bursar with salt from Poitou in 1381 and 1383, as did the Newcastle merchant William Hedlam in 1419.[106] Meanwhile, an interesting shift in the sources of supply of cloth for liveries for members of the prior's household was taking place. Fourteenth-century supplies had come from Durham merchants or from the regional fairs. In the fifteenth century, the bursar transferred his patronage to Yorkshire sources of supply; at first these were York merchants or drapers such as Thomas Kerr, who supplied broad cloth, blue and green cloth at a cost of £10 in 1419, or John Marchall who supplied cloth in 1449 and 1457. But with the rise of the new cloth towns of Yorkshire, the bursar began to purchase cloth from Halifax and Leeds. Richard Clyff of Halifax, draper, supplied the cloth for liveries in 1484; Thomas Richardson of Leeds in 1492 and 1499; and Nicholas Best in 1514. By the sixteenth century, however, some Durham merchants or 'clothmen' had retrieved this contract: in 1513 and 1515, William Myghlay supplied cloth to the priory, and in 1536 George Heddon was paid £4. 10s. for broadcloth for liveries.[107]

In view of all these purchases of goods from other trading centres in the north and beyond, and from many merchants who had no local Durham links, what then was the role of the town in supplying produce to its largest consumers in the later middle ages? It seems clear enough that the late thirteenth and early

[104] Burs. account, 1437/38, *Expense domini Prioris.*
[105] Burs. accounts, 1403/04–1422/23; 1440/41, *Emptio Vini.*
[106] Burs. accounts, 1381/82; 1383/84; 1419/20, *Expense Necessarie.*
[107] All these references to the supply of cloth come from Burs. accounts, *Garderoba.*

fourteenth centuries were periods of wider economic opportunities for local merchants and local producers of goods; the market place in Durham was being used by at least one large household for a wide range of products of high quality, both for expensive luxury items as well as for the more mundane necessities of life, and this would have encouraged the development of a wide variety of trades with greater specialisation in Durham. At the same time, the priory bought wholesale from the large regional fairs and it forged some connections with merchants based principally in the local ports. But after about 1350, increasingly the priory turned away from Durham for provisioning. Durham's market ceased to supply it with the majority of purchases of cloth, wine and spices in particular, and consequently less money, or, at least, fewer credit transactions, were generated within the town. In the earlier period, the priory bought not only goods which had been manufactured in the town by local craftsmen but also goods which had been transported to Durham for sale by Durham merchants. By the late-medieval period, it purchased in the market place simply a small selection of basic items produced by the local inhabitants, such as ale, candles, wax and bread. If the priory account rolls are a fair reflection of the situation in the other Durham households, it cannot be claimed that a great deal of money was flowing into the town's industries, or that the presence of two large ecclesiastical communities and several smaller private establishments in the town did much to stimulate such trade or industry as there was. Consequently, the narrowing of the range of occupations in the late-medieval city already observed can be, to some extent, explained by the lessening of trading opportunities for Durham men. Further, it leads to the inescapable conclusion that Durham's own local industries had not proved themselves capable of withstanding the competition from producers elsewhere; the Durham bursar still found it more economical to travel throughout the north of England to purchase goods and to arrange for their shipment or transport overland over substantial distances.

MERCHANTS AND CRAFTSMEN: ORIGINS, WEALTH AND SOCIAL STATUS

Despite the comparatively small scale of commercial and industrial activity at medieval Durham, the profits of trade were obviously considerable for at least some of the merchants and the skilled craftsmen, particularly in the late thirteenth and early fourteenth centuries. The clearest sign of this urban wealth was the ability of such men to purchase tenements and to amass small estates within Durham itself, probably for investment. The level of wealth required for such purchases was attained only by the most prosperous craftsmen or traders, foremost among whom were the Durham butchers. Thomas, son of Lewyn, for example, held considerable amounts of land in Fleshewergate, Sadlergate and Framwelgate in the late thirteenth century; and William, son of Walter de Essh, had numerous tenements on either side of Fleshewergate, some of which he bought from other butchers such as Gilbert Pyle in the 1320s.[108] Traders dealing in luxury items were also able to invest in urban property. James Apotecarius and Geoffrey de Catden, spicer, both held small estates in the streets surrounding the market place in the late thirteenth and early fourteenth centuries. John, son of Alan Aurifaber, had land in the Old Borough and in Sadlergate in the middle of the fourteenth century.[109] Merchants, or mercers, as could be anticipated, invested heavily in land, particularly in the Bishop's Borough. Reginald Mercator owned several tenements in Clayport and in other parts of the Bishop's Borough, and he drew rent from other properties in the late thirteenth century. The most obvious indication of his wealth was his stone hall or house in the market place near St Nicholas' Church; stone-built domestic properties were a rarity at any time during the medieval period in Durham and the possession of this house alone identifies Reginald as one of its most successful entrepreneurs.[110]

Most categories of craftsmen within the building trades were less notable for amassing land, but Richard More, a carpenter who worked for the priory in the late fifteenth century, held several

---

[108] 2.11.Spec.27; 2.11.Spec.49; Misc.Ch.2002, 2019, 2022, 2032.

[109] See, for example, Catden's property: 3.18.Spec.1; 3.18.Spec.3; 3.18.Spec.4; 3.18.Spec.6; 3.18.Spec.27. For Aurifaber's land in Sadlergate: Misc.Ch.2001, 2004. For his land in Crossgate: Misc.Ch.1917, 1981, 1988.

[110] 6.1.Elem.6★★ (the undated foundation charter of his chantry); Alm. rental, 1424; see chapter 3, pp. 80–1.

tenements in Clayport and Sadlergate which eventually passed to the priory.[111] Masons seem to have been well rewarded for their highly skilled work, and those who worked for the bishop, such as John Lewyn, the principal mason for Durham Cathedral in the late fourteenth century and for several northern castles, were given land as well as office. Peter Dryng, a mason employed by the priory contemporaneously with Lewyn, was granted twenty acres of exchequer land near Bearpark for his work in 1386–7; Lewyn was given four acres in Framwelgate in 1367–70 and the custody of the lands of Thomas Coxside in 1371 pending the majority of his son.[112] In addition to these grants, both men held other land in Durham which they may have purchased independently: Peter Dryng, for example, held four tenements including some shops at the west end of Framwelgate Bridge in 1375. These passed, by way of his daughter, Agnes Markby, to William Whelpdale, a large private landowner, and so to the sacrist's endowment by 1500.[113]

Some of the wealthiest Durham traders accumulated small urban estates, not to provide material benefits for their families or their business associates in any direct monetary sense, but rather for the spiritual benefits which might accrue to them in the next world. They earmarked the income from this property and often the property itself to found and endow private chantries within Durham churches. Furthermore, the chantries would stand, it was hoped, as permanent reminders and memorials to the founder's success in business. The butcher, Thomas, son of Lewyn, founded a chantry chapel at the west end of Elvet Bridge at the end of the thirteenth century and endowed it with land and rents from his property amounting to over £2. 10s. per annum.[114] Much of Reginald Mercator's property was handed over into the custody of the almoner before 1300 on the understanding that he would establish a chantry to St Mary within St Nicholas' Church in the market place.[115]

---

[111] For his land in Clayport, see 3.15.Spec.47. For his land in Sadlergate and elsewhere, see 3.15.Spec.43; 3.15.Spec.45; 3.15.Spec.46; Misc.Ch.2243.

[112] PRO Durham Chancery Enrolments, 3/32, m.8d; 3/31, m.2,3; for the careers of these masons, see J. Harvey, *English mediaeval architects: a biographical dictionary* (London, 1954), pp. 88–9, 166–9; Salzman, *Building in England*, pp. 413–14.

[113] Misc.Ch.2334; 4.18.Spec.16; 4.18.Spec.57; Loc.xxxvii, no.51; Sac.rental, 1500.

[114] Foundation charter of St James' Chapel, c. 1312, 2.11.Spec.49.

[115] Foundation charter of St Mary's Chantry, undated, but endorsed with the date 1271 in the fifteenth century: 6.1.Elem.6**.

Whether or not a Durham merchant or craftsman had made formal or informal arrangements to hand his urban estate over to his descendants, or to use it to found a chantry, most of the surviving documentary evidence demonstrates that private property acquisitions did not usually survive for more than two generations at most in a trader's family. One reason for this relatively rapid turnover of land may have been a shortage of male heirs who could continue the trade, a characteristic of the London merchant class. The failure of heirs among the burgesses has also been advanced as an explanation for the high percentage of newcomers among the York freemen.[116] Two Durham cases can be cited in support of this theory. One concerns the small Fleshewergate estate of the butcher Gilbert Pyle. Pyle had a son, Roger, who inherited some of his father's land in the late thirteenth century, and three daughters, Emma, Christine and Alice, each with a share in his estate. William de Essh, a neighbouring butcher, bought out the daughters' interests in 1295 and possibly that of the son as well (his name does not appear again), and so added Pyle's properties to his own growing estate in Durham. All William's property passed, on his death, to his heiress, his daughter Margaret Drayton, and before the end of the fourteenth century it had been conveyed to the priory.[117] By the late fourteenth century, William Whelpdale held a considerable amount of property in both the Bishop's Borough and the Old Borough, property which had been accumulated by successful business dealings (the nature of which is not revealed in the documents) and well-chosen marriage partners. In the early fifteenth century, after the untimely death of his only son, William, the inheritance passed to his three granddaughters, Sibil, Margaret and Isabella. Sibil married William Stokdall of Sherburn, near Malton, York and probably moved away from Durham. Durham Priory bought out Sibil's share of the inheritance and that of her sister Isabella for at least £36 in 1490, and William Whelpdale's estate became part of the sacrist's endowment.[118]

The Tudhow family of butchers, holding land in Clayport, may be an exception to this emerging pattern of rapid changes in

[116] S. L. Thrupp, *The merchant class of medieval London* (Chicago, 1948), pp. 41–52; *VCH Yorks., City of York*, p. 41.
[117] Misc.Ch.2002, 2019, 2020, 2022, 2023, 2024.
[118] 3.18.Spec.31; 3.18.Spec.33; 3.18.Spec.41.

private property-holding: they managed to retain their possession of a tenement in Clayport for much of the fourteenth century, perhaps because there were sons to inherit both the land and the butchery business. John de Tudhow, butcher, held a burgage in Clayport from 1311 and he granted it to his son, William, in 1336. William's son, John, a butcher, held the tenement in turn, and granted it to Thomas de Tudhow, possibly another relative, in 1359.[119] However, we should be wary about dubbing the Tudhows as an exceptional case; the limitations of the surviving evidence render any conclusions about family landholding in Durham tentative. After all, most of the conveyances which are extant today were preserved simply because they related to land which was acquired by the priory during the middle ages and gave it firm evidence of title. Histories of those tenements which remained in private hands throughout the medieval period remain obscure and largely undocumented; it is more than likely that they were held by the same family, particularly where the family belonged to the gentry of the county, over many generations. The picture of private landholding in Durham is too incomplete to give more than an impressionistic view of family structure and inheritance patterns.

Some analysis of the places of origin of Durham traders and craftsmen can be attempted from the documentary evidence. Title deeds are a useful source of such information, revealing, for example, that Thomas de Wardon, a cutler living in Clayport in 1388, came from York, and that Thomas de Aula, residing in St Giles' Borough in 1338, was not a servant of Kepier Hospital as his surname might suggest but a merchant originating from Whitby in Cleveland, where he retained family connections.[120] In other cases, the surname itself suggests the area of a trader's origin, although this is not a very reliable guide to a man's home village after about the middle of the fourteenth century, when many surnames had become hereditary: the duplication of several place-names in medieval England brings a certain element of doubt to any conclusions on this subject.[121] However, bearing these difficulties in mind, it appears that the majority of Durham traders

[119] Misc.Ch.1849, 1852, 1857.   [120] 4.2.Sac.17; 3.14.Spec.58; 1.15.Spec.29.

[121] McKinley, *Surnames of Oxfordshire*, pp. 67, 90; P. McClure, 'Patterns of migration in the late middle ages: the evidence of English place-name surnames', *EcHR*, 2nd ser., 32 (1979), 168. The misleading nature of such evidence has already been observed in the names of merchants: see above, pp. 169–70.

or craftsmen holding surnames derived from place-names came from Durham or nearby villages such as Tudhoe, Chilton and Esh. The butchers John de Tudhow and William de Essh fall into this category, as does the tanner William de Chilton and the merchant Robert de Fery (all found in deeds of the late thirteenth or early fourteenth centuries).[122] This impression reinforces Professor Dobson's evidence that about two-thirds of the locative surnames borne by Durham monks in the early fifteenth century related to villages in the centre and east of the county, and it compares with the pattern of local immigration to small market towns such as Stratford and larger communities such as Leicester and Nottingham.[123] Durham, as was the case in so many other small urban centres, was drawing on its immediate hinterland for both skilled workers and unskilled labourers to maintain its limited industries.

The pattern of immigration to Durham was not exclusively local, however. Using the same evidence, it can be shown that another group of craftsmen or traders came from more distant places, perhaps drawn by the possibilities of work and clients in an ecclesiastical and administrative centre. Interestingly, this group included several merchants and mercers, men such as William de Gysburgh (1359), Richard de Novo Castri (late thirteenth century) and John de Hexham (1366) who originated from towns outside the bishopric of Durham.[124] However, perhaps the most exotic collection of locational surnames was held by the Durham leather workers in the late thirteenth century. Among the saddlers was a group from the Lincolnshire area, including Adam and Nicholas de Newerk and William de Blythe. There was also a skinner from this area, William de Lincoln. Robert de Lichefeld came from further afield; and a Scot, Nicholas de Rokysburg, a furrier, seems to have been acceptable as a Durham trader although later craft regulations show a strong anti-Scottish bias.[125] Such evidence suggests that while one craftsman's family

---

[122] See, for example, John de Tudhow, butcher, 1311 (5.2.Elem.23); Robert de Fery, merchant, 1339 (Misc.Ch.1889); William de Chilton, tanner (undated deed, D/Sa/D366).

[123] Dobson, *Durham Priory*, p. 57. A survey of 1251 showed that 90% of Stratford burgesses were drawn from a sixteen-mile radius of the town: E. M. Carus-Wilson, 'The first half-century of the borough of Stratford-upon-Avon', *EcHR*, 2nd ser., 18 (1965), 54; McClure, 'Patterns of migration', p. 177. The majority of incoming freemen to York were drawn from the Vale of York and the Hull area: *VCH Yorks., City of York*, pp. 40, 108. [124] 5.2.Elem.23; 1.18.Spec.13; 3.2.Sac.32.

[125] 1.16.Spec.28; 2.17.Spec.3; see below, pp. 187–8.

might die out in Durham, replacements from several areas of the country were available, at least in the thirteenth and fourteenth centuries.[126]

The accumulation of property and the endowment of private chantries were two outward signs of a craftsman's wealth and success in business. Equally, office-holding marked out the more 'substantial' traders, those who in the eyes of their fellow citizens were judged suitable or worthy of positions of authority in the town. Several Durham craftsmen held office in their boroughs, giving them rights, however limited, over their fellow townsmen and duties, however burdensome, as well as a certain social standing. Office-holding could be financially crippling and was strenuously avoided in both York and Leicester, for example, in the late fifteenth century, where heavy fines had to be imposed on those who would not serve.[127] But there is no surviving evidence of any such difficulties in recruiting office-holders in Durham, where, in any case, the lack of urban independence severely restricted the number of offices which were open to townsmen. The position of farmer of the Bishop's Borough, which was probably not strictly speaking an 'official' position, was perhaps the most financially hazardous. The farmer was responsible for raising the annual sum required by the overlord from borough landholders, from tolls or other sources, and any deficit had to be met from his own pocket. The innate problems of this position can be seen in the case of William Couper, barker, and William Snayth of Durham, mercer, who were appointed farmers of the Bishop's Borough in 1435. By 1441 they were facing legal action because the annual farm of £62. 13s. 4d. was in arrears by £41. 3s. 4d.[128]

The office of bailiff of a borough did not carry with it a similar threat of financial ruin, for it seems to have been largely an administrative and legal position. These officials were responsible, for example, for finding juries and bringing offenders to the local court. The qualification for this office seems to have been that a man should be considered 'upright and substantial' by his peers,

---

[126] As was the case with most towns in the north: G. W. S. Barrow, 'Northern English society in the early middle ages', *Northern History*, 4 (1969), 24.

[127] R. B. Dobson 'Urban decline in late medieval England', *TRHS*, 5th ser., 27 (1977), 13–16; *Records of the Borough of Leicester, 1103–1327*, vol. 1, ed. M. Bateson (London, 1899), p. 328; J. I. Kermode, 'Urban decline? The flight from office in late medieval York', *EcHR*, 2nd ser., 35 (1982), 179–98.

[128] PRO Durham Chancery Enrolments 3/36, m.15; 3/37, m.13; 3/46, m.6.

and several craftsmen passed this test. The butcher Thomas, son of Lewyn, was bailiff of the Bishop's Borough in the late thirteenth century, as were James Apotecarius and Geoffrey de Catden, the spicer, in 1295; and the goldsmith John, son of Alan Aurifaber, was bailiff of the Old Borough in 1351.[129] The victualling and the luxury trades seem to have provided most of the holders of this office, not the merchants, as was the case in late-fourteenth-century Colchester.[130] Property-holding seems to have been an important qualification for those judged eligible for the position of borough bailiff. Certainly, most of the craftsmen who were appointed bailiffs held more than one tenement in Durham and may have been the wealthier members of their own crafts. But there seem to have been few suitable candidates for office-holding in medieval Durham, for the same names occur with great frequency in the position of bailiff. James Apotecarius, for example, was bailiff of the Bishop's Borough in 1295, 1304 and 1306 while John Aurifaber was serving as the bailiff of the Old Borough in 1350, 1351 and 1353.[131] However, it is impossible to make any firm deductions about the relative status and wealth of individual craftsmen who held office in Durham because no records of a freemen admissions policy (if it ever existed) have survived.

A contemporary acknowledgement of greater status may possibly have been manifested in the use of the title 'burgess', a designation which applied to a select few of the inhabitants of each borough. 'Burgesses' were not necessarily those who held or had held office. Some traders or craftsmen were habitually referred to as burgesses, including the butchers William Gray, Gilbert Pyle and Thomas, son of Lewyn, for example, in the late thirteenth and early fourteenth centuries. Other tradesmen who were called burgesses of the boroughs were Reginald Mercator, the saddlers Robert de Lichfeld and Absalon de Dunelm., and the souter Alan de Neuton. Richard More, the carpenter who held land in Clayport and Sadlergate, was a burgess of St Giles' Borough and two tanners who witnessed the agreement between the 'wolnewebsters and the chalonwebsters' in 1468 were described as burgesses (John Mosdale and Thomas Bidylstone).[132]

[129] 5.3.Elem.3c; D/Sa/D365; 4.2.Elem.17**.
[130] Britnell, *Colchester*, p. 110.
[131] D/Sa/D365; Misc.Ch.1875, 1881; 4.15.Spec.27; 4.2.Elem.17**; 4.18.Spec.34.
[132] PRO Durham Chancery Enrolments, 3/50, m.10.

How much significance should be accorded to this title is debatable; in the priory sacrist's rental of 1500 and in the Crossgate court records, it is occasionally stated in the entries concerning property conveyances in the borough that by right of holding a certain tenement or burgage, the tenant became a burgess of the borough. Presumably, such burgesses enjoyed all the privileges attached to burgage tenure, as well as its duties, which included the annual payment of rent and probably regular attendances at the borough court. Yet tenants who were not called burgesses owed similar services to their overlords, so it does seem that, by the later middle ages at least, the term had ceased to have any great legal or tenurial significance. However, the names of those craftsmen or borough inhabitants who were called burgesses in the late thirteenth and the first half of the fourteenth century headed or came near the top of witness lists to charters, indicating that at this period they had some standing within the borough community if not much power in the running of the town.

There were, in fact, comparatively few opportunities, apart from the limited office-holding already described, for Durham craftsmen to share in the town's government. No merchant oligarchy emerged in Durham at all comparable to those of Beverley or York, partly perhaps because of the lack of great fortunes to be made in the town and partly because the scale of industrial activity was so restricted. The merchants with international connections do not seem to have taken any active part in Durham's internal politics nor to have served the bishop or the priory in any administrative or advisory capacity. The crafts, as we shall see later in this chapter, apparently enjoyed little freedom of organisation independent of the borough overlords. But it is possible that in the late thirteenth and early fourteenth centuries, at a time when, as we have already observed, local trade and industries seem to have been booming, Durham craftsmen made a more individual contribution to town life. The number of craftsmen who appeared as bailiffs, farmers of the boroughs or on special commissions gradually became more infrequent after 1350; and by the fifteenth century they seem to have been largely replaced by an expanding class of officials, clerks and notaries of the bishop and the prior and members of the local gentry who retained a town house in Durham. In the late thirteenth century, for example, it was a merchant whose land endowed a chantry in St Nicholas' Church and a butcher who endowed St James' Chapel; but in the early fifteenth century it was a family of clerks, the de Elvet brothers, who endowed a chantry in St Oswald's Church with their land. It is noticeable that no craftsmen are recorded among those who refounded the most prestigious guild in later-medieval Durham, the Corpus Christi Guild, in 1437. This contrasts with York, where craftsmen were still involved in the founding of chantries in the fifteenth century.[133] But the rise of the professional elite in the government of Durham's boroughs can be paralleled in the fifteenth-century freemen's registers in York and in late-fifteenth-century Colchester, where the merchant class was gradually replaced with minor gentry from the countryside.[134] Any influence which the craftsmen of Durham might have gained in town government had apparently been displaced by that of the clerical families by the fifteenth century.

It should come as no surprise that there are few traces of any craft organisation in Durham before the fifteenth century. It could be argued that this results from the meagre survival rate of relevant documentation rather than any more tangible contemporary factors. But it is highly doubtful that Durham craftsmen were formally organised before the later medieval period. Industrial activity in the town was very small scale; few workers were employed in these industries; moreover, independent groupings of townsmen for any purpose whatsoever were not encouraged by the town's overlords. The earliest extant set of guild ordinances is that of the weavers, which was confirmed by the bishop of Durham and enrolled on 1 August 1450.[135] The phrasing of these regulations might suggest that they were not the earliest prescribed for this craft; they begin with the assertion that they have been made to maintain the Corpus Christi procession and play 'eftir the old custume', although this old custom may refer to the plays and not to any former ordinances of the craft. The

[133] See above, p. 176. The chantry of St John the Baptist in St Oswald's Church was founded in 1404: 4.16.Spec.34. For the refounding of the Corpus Christi Guild, see PRO Durham Chancery Enrolments, 3/36, m.11. For York, see Swanson, 'Crafts and craftsmen', pp. 432–3.
[134] *VCH Yorks., City of York*, pp. 46–7; Britnell, *Colchester*, p. 210.
[135] PRO Durham Chancery Enrolments, 3/44, m.10–11.

weavers' ordinances may have been used as a model by the other Durham crafts because there are many similarities between subsequent regulations. Next in the craft chronology are the souters' ordinances, enrolled in the bishop's chancery in 1463, followed by a charter of 1468 from the bishop to the barbers, surgeons and waxmakers.[136] The remaining craft organisations seem to have had a much later formal organisation; the ordinances of the company of butchers and fleshers date from 1520 and those of the goldsmiths, plumbers and their coalition from 1532.[137] This last amalgamation implies that each constituent member craft possessed some independent organisation of its own before 1532. Other Durham trades, such as the skinners, glovers, carpenters and fullers, are known to have had rule books, but none of these are now extant. The early-nineteenth-century antiquarian Robert Surtees saw the skinners' books, which began in 1600, although some sixteenth-century material was incorporated into them. Whiting quotes a somewhat unlikely tradition that the skinners were incorporated in 1327; but there is no original evidence to substantiate this claim.[138]

This brief review of the earliest surviving documentary references to craft organisations in medieval Durham tells us little about their early history and development and it is inadequate in many other ways. It is especially regrettable that none of these ordinances or charters survives in their original form, but rather as enrolments, confirmations or later transcripts, thus adding to dating problems. It is difficult to assess the real role of these associations within the town from such sources because they are the 'official' records of the craft, the ordinances, which had to conform to the policy of the town's overlords.[139] By their very nature, they are unlikely to say anything controversial or to

---

[136] The souters' ordinances are to be found in PRO Durham Chancery Enrolments, 3/50, m.6d. The original charter of the bishop to the barbers was held by the warden of the company when it was transcribed by Whiting: Whiting, 'Durham trade gilds', p. 408.

[137] The butchers' ordinances survive in a transcript which is part of the Mickleton and Spearman MS in Durham University Library, vol. 49. They are transcribed by F. J. W. Harding in *TAASDN* 11 (1958–65), 98–100. The original was stated to have been signed on 14 June 1403, but no corroborative evidence for this dating survives. The ordinary of the goldsmiths was confirmed by Bishop Tunstall and it is transcribed in Whiting, 'Durham trade gilds', p. 397.

[138] Surtees, *Durham* 4, p. 21; Whiting, 'Durham trade gilds', p. 172.

[139] This was also the case in York in the later middle ages: Swanson, 'Crafts and craftsmen', pp. 310–15. See C. M. Barron, 'The parish fraternities of medieval London', in C. M. Barron and C. Harper Bill (eds.), *The church in pre-Reformation society* (London, 1985), p. 21.

challenge the Durham concept of lordship. They reveal little of the daily workings of a craft organisation or of its membership. But what sources can supplement them? For Durham, the only other remaining evidence would seem to be a few cases which came before the Crossgate court in the late fifteenth and early sixteenth centuries. Here, offences against the craft ordinances, such as bad trading practices or unacceptable standards of workmanship, were prosecuted by the local borough court. These cases are the only measure of how successfully the crafts' rules were being enforced.

However, the ordinances do have some value in revealing the preoccupations of both traders and overlords in the fifteenth century and their apparent priorities in regulating Durham's trade. The first common element in all the surviving ordinances is the internal structuring of the craft organisation itself. Officials were to be elected to oversee the conduct of a particular trade. The weavers were to gather together annually to choose two of 'the most conyng and discreit men' to be wardens and 'serchours' for that year and all members of the trade were to obey these wardens for the good of the craft or be fined 4*d*. The butchers were 'to fulfill mainetaine support and doe every thing…that shall be devised or advised by the sayd wardens'. Similar guidelines for the election of officials were used by the souters, the barbers and goldsmiths; the latter added that every member of the craft 'after being lawfully warned' should attend every meeting unless he had a reasonable excuse or was on a journey out of the bishopric. These elected officers, the warden and the searchers, were responsible for maintaining the honest working practices of their craft, for protecting their members against unfair competition, and for ensuring that a high quality of workmanship was preserved. Any defaults in workmanship had to be remedied by the order of the warden and the searchers.

A second preoccupation was with the rules governing entry to the trade and the system of apprenticeship. Most important of all was the regulation – for example, in the weavers' ordinances – that no man was to set up in business until he had obtained the consent of the wardens, paid a fine of 6*s*. 8*d*. to go towards the cost of maintaining the light of the craft and 6*s*. 8*d*. to the bishop and had been sworn in. A solemn oath was to be sworn before the bishop's officers: each weaver swore 'to be true, to use and occupy his craft truly to the profit of the common people, to use no deceit in his craft and to fulfill the ordinances'. The penalties for not taking this oath were severe: a fine of £1 to the bishop and £1 to the craft, or imprisonment. An element of examination is revealed in the souters' ordinances, where the wardens had to judge whether a would-be souter had the 'cunning' to 'be able to wyrk for profit of the common people'.[140] The rules for the taking of apprentices and their period of service were strict. No less than seven years' apprenticeship was considered sufficient for the goldsmiths. When a man ended his apprenticeship in the barbers' craft, he had to pay a fine of 1s. 8d. to the bishop and 3s. 4d. with one pound of wax to the craft. The fine was greater for those not apprenticed in Durham (6s. 8d. to the bishop and to the craft in the barbers' ordinances, for example, and 10s. in the goldsmiths' craft). No member of the goldsmiths' craft in Durham was to 'Tyess [entice] procure exhort nor hier the prentice nor Servant pertenynge or belonging to any other Brother' without licence from his last master. However, there seems to have been no rule limiting the number of apprentices each craftsman could take, as was the case in some guild regulations in other towns.

Also ubiquitous in the surviving ordinances was the concern with regulating the working practices of craftsmen and protecting them against unfair competition from within the town or from outsiders. No barber was to shave a man outside his shop for less than 1s. and a minimum price of 8d. was set on shaving within the shop. In a nice gesture which was as much an acknowledgement of Durham's close connections with the surrounding countryside as a recognition that many of its inhabitants were still involved in agriculture, shaving was permitted on Sundays only during harvest time. Butchers were not allowed to slaughter animals on Thursday afternoon or on Sunday before one o'clock.[141] According to the weavers' ordinances, no 'brother' was to seek another man's customers; or, as the barbers' ordinances put it, 'if any Brother of the said Barbers craft have [sic] a Customer that

---

[140] Compare this test with that contained in the York fullers' ordinances, where no one was allowed to set up as a master unless he had appeared before the mayor with the searchers of the guild to testify that he was of good character and abilities: *York Memorandum Book*, vol. 1, pp. 70–2.

[141] Compare this regulation with that of the York ironmongers which prohibited Sunday working, but the York founders were allowed 'smetyng de lour metall' by night. The glovers were not allowed to make a noise to attract customers before the first stroke of the bell for matins in the parish churches. See *York Memorandum Book*, vol. 1, pp. xxxvii, 93, 49.

passes from him and comes to another brother, that he shall lovingly enquire that Man and say "Art ye agreed with him that ye come free for the time that ye were shaven with him?" And if he find that he be not agreed with him, he shall say "Hold me excused, I will not take you to that ye be agreed and then ye shall be welcome"'. Consequently, it would be difficult for a Durham inhabitant to change his barber, no matter how badly he was shaved!

Finally, there were instructions about the procession on Corpus Christi day. The importance of this particular ordinance was emphasised by its position in each guild's regulations. For example, it was the second rule in the weavers' and souters' ordinances. Furthermore, in the preamble to these regulations, it was stated that they were made 'in the worship of God and the sustentacion of the procession and play on Corpus Christi day in Durham'. This day's events will be described in more detail later in the chapter, but each guild ordinance concerning the Corpus Christi day celebrations contained three elements: first, all members of the guild were to assemble 'in best array', although reasonable excuses for absence were allowed. Second, there was to be a procession of guild members to the cathedral; and third, there was to be the performance of a play which belonged to that particular craft.

The rules outlined so far are patently very similar to those of craft guilds in other medieval towns. But the Durham craft ordinances differ from many others in two important respects. The first is the strong anti-Scottish prejudice they express in the ban on the taking of Scottish apprentices and the heavy penalties for disobeying this injunction. The weavers' and the souters' ordinances state baldly that no Scotsmen are to be apprenticed. The fines for disobeying this regulation were large: 6s. 8d. to the bishop and 6s. 8d. to the craft for the weavers, and a massive £2 for the souters. The reasons for anti-Scottish feeling at Durham are all too clear: on several occasions in the early middle ages, Scottish armies had been responsible for destroying the homes of Durham inhabitants. But by the fifteenth century any fears of military dominance must have passed and economic protectionism may have replaced them as an explanation for such discrimination. At the end of the fifteenth century, the Crossgate Court Book shows that various wandering traders, including Scots, had taken up residence in the 'bakdwellyngs' of houses in the Old Borough and probably many of them were seeking work. The craft regulations were, perhaps, an attempt to protect Durham's own townsmen from unemployment or undercutting in the job market by 'foreigns' who might be cheaper to hire. Similar restrictions on 'foreigns' rather than Scots in particular were a feature of some York craft regulations of the fifteenth century when protectionism was a clear motive for their compilation.[142]

The second important difference between Durham's craft regulations and those of many medieval towns was the involvement of one overlord, the bishop, and his officials in the oversight of trade. In towns such as Winchester and York it was the city authorities who controlled the powers of crafts and ensured that their regulations conformed to a standard acceptable to the ruling body. In Durham it was the bishop who, indirectly, controlled craft membership and upheld the standards of manufacture in the town by delegation to the wardens and searchers of individual guilds. Most of the fines imposed on careless or disobedient members had to be split between the bishop and the craft, whereas in York, the division was between the city and the guild.[143] As we have seen, before a man could become a member of a craft he had to swear an oath in the presence of the bishop's officer; and in the weavers' ordinances, disobedient members were reported to the bishop's temporal chancellor. The goldsmiths' ordinances went further and stated: 'If one refuses to pay forfeits or duties, or will not swear obedience to the rules and ordinances before the steward of the borough court, complaint shall be made to the bishop's chancellor, who shall compel the offender by imprisonment, if necessary, to do what he ought.' This episcopal control no doubt helps to explain why the craft guilds never wielded great political power in Durham: their role was limited to the regulation of a particular trade and there was little opportunity for them to assume a position of leadership in town government. Although they had their own elected officials, ultimately each member of the trade

---

[142] In 1508, all those having *le Bakdwellys in domibus* were ordered to remove them and all Scots living there: Crossgate Court Book, fols. 100, 108v. The rules of the York tapiters (1419) include the injunction that no master was to take an apprentice unless he was English born and a free man. Foreigns had to pay £2. 13s. 4d. to the council for setting up in trade in York: *York Memorandum Book*, vol. 1, p. xxxii.

[143] Swanson, 'Crafts and craftsmen', pp. 318, 310–16; *VCH Yorks., City of York*, p. 91; Keene, *Winchester*, vol. 1, part 1, p. 333.

was responsible to the bishop for his behaviour, and his allegiance was to the bishop over and above the warden of his craft.

The surviving regulations imply that they applied equally to all craft members, no matter in which borough they lived and worked. The list of witnesses to the weavers' ordinances contained the names of craftsmen from all Durham's boroughs and included some who worked in the prior's or bishop's households.[144] The precedent for enforcing trading regulations across borough boundaries had been set by *le Convenit* (*c.* 1229), which established that prices and measures were to be the same in all boroughs. Hence, no trader could make a profit at the expense of his fellow in a different borough.[145] Nor could he escape the consequences of fraud or bad measures by fleeing to another borough, for *le Convenit* outlined a judicial procedure whereby the bailiffs of the prior's and the bishop's courts could exchange offenders who would then be brought before their local court and fined for their crimes. The prices of grain, ale and other foodstuffs were fixed regularly in the borough courts, and traders living in the priory boroughs were required to appear before special Marshalsea sessions in Elvet and the Old Borough to display their measures.[146] But the courts did not operate only for the protection of the consumer; there is evidence that craft officials took some trouble to police their members for the good reputation of the craft and for their own self-protection. In 1509, the proctors brought Thomas Pavy before Crossgate court and accused him of selling wax candles without the craft's permission and Richard Davyson was found guilty of practising his craft in Durham without coming to an agreement with the proctors of the 'Tailyourcraft'. Five glovers were accused of buying up and forestalling sheepskins in the market.[147] However, it is significant that the craft guilds relied on the machinery of the borough courts to enforce their own regulations, and not on their own administration. Despite their ferocious fines and the threats of expulsion from the craft for certain offences, any sanctions were toothless without the backing of the overlords and the legal processes available through their courts.

Given the lack of political power which the crafts possessed in

---

[144] PRO Durham Chancery Enrolments, 3/44, m.10–11.
[145] *Feodarium Dunelm*, pp. 212–17.
[146] Loc. IV, no.140; see chapter 6, pp. 200, 220–1.
[147] Crossgate Court Book, fols. 109v, 112v, 114v.

Durham, it is hardly surprising that there are no references to any discord between the overlords and craftsmen in the surviving documents. Disputes between members of a craft were a different matter, however, although only one, a quarrel between the 'wolnewebsters' and the 'chalonwebsters', subdivisions of the weavers' craft, seems to have been serious enough to come to the attention of the bishop. This was a controversy about the division of labour within the craft and the products which each group of weavers could manufacture, and it illustrates the rigid demarcation which was necessary to preserve enough work for all members of a craft. The final compromise was based, according to the enrolled record of the agreement of 1468, upon precedents: the 'wolnewebsters' had 'time out of mind' been accustomed to make certain types of cloth which were listed, followed by those which were made by the 'chalonwebsters'. The penalty for any future infringements was to be £5, which perhaps illustrates the strength of the temptation there was for the weavers to take each other's work.[148] This demarcation was paralleled in several towns. In York, textile manufacturing was divided between two main crafts: the weavers, who manufactured broadcloth, and the tapiters (who included chaloners and coverlet weavers) who manufactured worsted. In Norwich, there was a distinction made between the bed or coverlet weavers and the worsted weavers. In times of economic difficulty, there were quarrels between the York textile crafts, who were competing for what became a shrinking market with very low profit margins. Perhaps the quarrel in Durham marks a similar period of difficulty in the industry with a consequent struggle for survival by individual craftsmen.[149]

One of the most important contributions made by the craft guilds was less to the economic than to the ceremonial life of Durham, for upon them fell the responsibility for the Corpus Christi day procession and plays. The arrangements for the procession were probably made by the religious guild of Corpus Christi, a guild which was refounded in 1437 by Bishop Langley.[150] No contemporary account of Corpus Christi day in Durham survives, but the reminiscences of a quondam Durham

---

[148] PRO Durham Chancery Enrolments, 3/50, m.10.
[149] Swanson, 'Crafts and craftsmen', pp. 33–5, 52–4.
[150] Bishop Langley gave a licence to several townsmen *de novo incipere inire facere fundare et ordinare* this guild: PRO Durham Chancery Enrolments, 3/36, m.11.

monk writing late in the sixteenth century give a detailed narrative of the ceremonies as they were on the eve of the dissolution of the priory: 'Baley of town did stand in the towle bowth and call occupations that was inhabites in town every occupation to bring forth banner with all lights appertinant to Banner and to go to abbey church door every banner to stand in a row from abbey church door to Wyndshole yett on west side all Banners and on east all torches pertinant to banners.'[151] The Corpus Christi shrine from St Nicholas' Church was carried in the procession up to the cathedral with the guilds and their banners following. The monks, bearing the standard of St Cuthbert before them, met the townsmen at the north door of the cathedral and led them into the church. A service was held, then the craftsmen processed round the shrine of St Cuthbert, and later accompanied the Corpus Christi shrine back to St Nicholas' Church. Apart from its religious significance, clearly this day was most important in town ceremonial. It marked a direct and visible link between the craft organisation, town government in the person of the bailiff of the borough, who was the bishop's representative, and the cathedral priory; it was Durham's equivalent to what has been called Coventry's 'communal ceremonialisation'.[152] The hierarchical structure of town life was on display and the relationship between the craftsmen and their town overlords was most graphically illustrated on this occasion. But the procession and the following plays also gave the crafts an opportunity to add dignity and honour to their daily work, and to display themselves to their best advantage before the assembled townspeople.

Once the Corpus Christi shrine had been returned to St Nicholas' Church, it seems that each craft had to perform a play, probably on the lines of the York cycle, although on a much smaller scale. The ex-monk ends his account of the day's proceedings before this most colourful and entertaining, but undoubtedly more secular, part of the festival took place, and further evidence for the plays is slim indeed. No record of their content survives, but the craft ordinances, unspecific as they are,

---

[151] *Rites of Durham*, ed. J. T. Fowler, Surtees Society, vol. 107, no. 2 (1902), p. 107.
[152] C. V. Phythian-Adams, 'Ceremony and the citizen: the communal year at Coventry, 1450–1550', in P. Clark and P. Slack (eds.), *Crisis and order in English towns, 1500–1700* (London, 1972), pp. 58, 75; M. E. James, 'Ritual, drama and the social body in the late medieval English town', *Past and Present* 98 (1983), 3–29.

reveal some of the more prosaic backstage arrangements for their production. Each craft obviously took the same episode of the cycle every year. The barbers, for example, had to 'go together in Procession and to play the play that of the old Custom belongs to their Craft'. The weavers had to perform 'the play which of old tyme belonged to their craft' and the goldsmiths' ordinances emphasised the long history of these plays 'after the old and laudable custom'. The cost of performing the plays was borne by the individual craft guilds: the weavers were to play the play 'at their own expense' and the goldsmiths' play was to be 'at their owne Costes and Charges after the Ordynance of the Wardens and Serchers'. The costs of such plays could be considerable, as the evidence from York and Coventry shows, but there is no sign that the Durham guilds appealed for financial help either from the Corpus Christi Guild or from the bishop, or that as in Coventry the crafts were allowed to join together to reduce expenses.[153] Corpus Christi day seems to have been the one occasion in the year when the Durham craftsmen and their organisations had a direct and visible part to play in town life. After the civic procession was over and the religious services completed, then the day was assigned to the craftsmen.

THE DURHAM ECONOMY IN A NATIONAL CONTEXT

It only remains to attempt an assessment of Durham's role as a market town and to place it in the wider context of national trade and industry. The small size of Durham's trades and the limited numbers of craftsmen in the town have been one of the main themes of this chapter. Durham harboured no one industry of any national importance in the middle ages to compare with, for example, the characteristic cloths produced in Lincoln or Norwich. It has been claimed that Durham's first genuinely distinctive industry was the production of mustard in the 1720s.[154] Nor was Durham able to participate in direct overseas trade, as did the east-coast ports such as Newcastle-upon-Tyne, Boston or Norwich, because it lacked a navigable river. The absence of riverine traffic and limited overland communications hampered

---

[153] Phythian-Adam, *Desolation of a city*, pp. 44–5, 263–4; *Coventry Leet Book*, ed. M. D. Harris, EETS, vols. 134–5, 138, 146 (1907–13), pp. 172, 185, 559.

[154] Hill, *Medieval Lincoln*, p. 325; Campbell, 'Norwich', pp. 15–16; Pocock and Gazzard, *Durham*, p. 16.

the development of widespread inland trade which towns such as York enjoyed. As Robert Surtees was to remark in the early nineteenth century, 'the Trade of Durham has never been much extended beyond the establishment of many substantial shops for the supply of the City and neighbourhood with the usual articles'.[155]

Durham was, however, a local market of real significance in its surrounding area. Produce was brought from the neighbouring small agricultural communities to be sold in the weekly market in exchange for goods and food produced by the town. The list of tolls to be charged on goods entering the market shows the range of products as well as produce passing through Durham. Although grain and livestock were obviously of prime importance, wool, wine, bread, sea fish, salmon, herring, potash and spices were all mentioned in the tolls of 1379.[156] Dr Fraser has pointed to the difficulties of using murage tolls as an accurate indicator of the range of commodities in a market, but in conjunction with other sources, like the account rolls of priory obedientiaries, they can give a rudimentary guide to the trade in Durham market.[157] If any credence can be given to Bracton's dictum that a 'reasonable' day's journey to a market averaged twenty miles, then Durham was well positioned. The nearest market towns were Newcastle, Darlington, Hartlepool and Barnard Castle, each within an approximately twenty-mile radius of Durham and each with their own hinterlands filled with small agricultural communities. The appetite of Durham citizens for food supplies and labour from its region was probably considerable, and this alone would help to stimulate agriculture in the area. However, this hinterland can in no way bear comparison with, for example, the rich and wealthy grazing lands of East Anglia which surrounded Norwich; and the needs of the small Durham communities were relatively limited. Hence the range of trades which developed in Durham was fairly basic.[158]

However, Durham did not exist to serve its hinterland alone, for, just as Winchester and Westminster did, it had at its centre great ecclesiastical households and, from time to time, a considerable military garrison. The town provided for the needs of these separate communities, which in turn generated some

---

[155] Surtees, *Durham* 4, part 2, p. 25.
[156] PRO Durham Chancery Enrolments, 3/31, m.13.
[157] Fraser, 'The pattern of trade', pp. 45–6.   [158] Campbell, 'Norwich', p. 14.

wealth within the town and provided work for many. The priory
account rolls demonstrate the range of goods purchased in the
market and the heavy financial reliance of the monks on some
Durham and many northern merchants. Many of the priory's
basic foodstuffs were bought in Durham, as well as luxury items
such as wine, barley for malt, wax and some cloth in the early
middle ages. It is likely that the bishop's administrators and staff
also bought essential goods in Durham at this time, although
documentary evidence does not survive to prove it. No wonder
that so many butchers had stalls near the market and the
victualling trade was so important in Durham. Further, local
traders and inn keepers would profit from the visits of countless
pilgrims to St Cuthbert's shrine, just as indeed they do today.
Durham had a considerable internal market which had to cater for
a wide variety of consumers.

R. S. Gottfried argued not so long ago for the uniqueness of
Bury St Edmunds among late-medieval provincial towns.
Although industry and commerce on a small scale existed within
it, because of the abbey it was also able to support a range of
specialised crafts which ordinary towns could not.[159] It appears
from this survey of Durham's crafts and industries that this
cathedral and palatinate city bears close comparison with Bury, as
it does with other ecclesiastical centres such as Canterbury and
Winchester. While it may have lacked a significant manufacturing
industry, Durham was able to support, for example, a substantial
community of goldsmiths serving not only the local wealthy
inhabitants, like the county families holding tenements in the
town, but also the religious community with its demand for
ecclesiastical ornaments. Although it was never more than a small
market town at any time during the medieval period, it was
elevated in status, if not in economic wealth or size, in a way not
achieved by towns such as Bury because it was the ecclesiastical
and administrative centre for the whole region. It had a certain
'economic as well as honorific ascendancy between Tees and
Tyne' and although the problems of the evidence are considerable,
it repays study as an example of a town whose reputation
probably outran its economic importance.[160]

[159] Gottfried, *Bury St Edmunds*, p. 115. [160] Dobson, *Durham Priory*, p. 36.

Chapter 6

Lordship in action: the maintenance of law and order in late-medieval Durham

Although Durham was a town dominated by its religious communities, in the same way as its more secular counterparts it was equally in need of firm government and even-handed justice to restrain the excesses of its citizens and to arbitrate in their disputes. Late-medieval Durham never experienced civil unrest as severe as the rioting at, for example, Coventry or Beverley; nor did the legal battles between the town and its ecclesiastical overlords ever reach the proportions they did in Bury St Edmunds, Norwich or York. Nonetheless, the whole structure of town life was shaped by regulations or restraints on townsmen and outsiders; and at some stage in their lives it is probable that almost all of the inhabitants had to appear before one of the many courts operating in medieval Durham. The administration of the law touched most aspects of a townsman's life, public or private, and it was enforced rigorously and persistently by the town's overlords.[1]

Medieval urban society was permeated with this concern to uphold law and order, for three main reasons. First, and most obviously, there was a need to maintain peace between individuals or groups wherever there was a concentration of people living and working together. A town depended for its life on its work-force, its industries and its trade; internal troubles could lead to the collapse of industries, the discouragement of outside traders and a reluctant work-force. A framework of rules, upheld by mutual consent as well as by legal sanctions, could both bolster the economic life of a town and preserve good relations between neighbours. Second, such rules provided a means for maintaining

---

[1] *VCH Warwicks.*, vol. 8, p. 210; R. B. Dobson (ed.), *The Peasants' Revolt of 1381*, 2nd edn (London, 1983), pp. 13–14, 267–8; Lobel, *Bury St Edmunds*; R. B. Dobson, 'Admissions to the freedom of the city of York in the later middle ages', *EcHR*, 26 (1973), 13; A. E. Butcher, 'English urban society and the revolt of 1381', in R. H. Hilton and T. H. Aston (eds.), *The English rising of 1381* (Cambridge, 1984), pp. 84–111.

a certain standard of life in a town for the well-being of all its inhabitants. Thus many borough by-laws attempted to improve the quality of town life by setting standards of public health and hygiene. Furthermore, the local courts enforced protective regulations to defend the population from rogues or from bad workmanship, to prevent the sale of sub-standard goods in the market and to control competition from outsiders. Third, the local courts were an effective mechanism through which an overlord could control and dominate his tenants. Many regulations which were enforced in the Durham courts were concerned less with keeping the peace between tenants than with establishing a soundly based relationship between a tenant and his lord. The rules concerning the milling of grain and the baking of bread show this aspect of the legal system at work, and such restrictions were perhaps the most rigorously enforced of all sections of urban legislation. In consequence, most notably in cases concerning grazing rights on common land, they were the source of the greatest resentment between the priory and its tenants.

This chapter attempts to explain the differences between the wide variety of courts operating in Durham, and surveys their personnel, the range of cases coming before them and the penalties which were imposed on offenders. There is no discussion here, however, of those pleas which were referred to the bishop's ecclesiastical courts or to the higher courts at York, which included disputes arising over the payment of mortuaries, breaches of ecclesiastical discipline by townsmen, and parochial matters such as the long-running battle by the inhabitants of the Old Borough to raise the status of their chapel (St Margaret's Chapel) to that of a parish church. With a few exceptions, such as cases involving criminous clerks, the machinery of the ecclesiastical courts and the operation of the canon law existed completely separately from the administration of secular law and order in Durham, which is the main concern of the following pages.[2] From this local evidence, it is possible to make some estimate of the extent of law-breaking in the community and to gauge the legal preoccupations of the overlords. This study also tries to

---

[2] For a typical case concerning disputed mortuary payments, see, for example, 4.15.Spec.56; *Depositions and other ecclesiastical proceedings from the courts of Durham*, ed. J. Raine, Surtees Society, vol. 21 (1845). For a case concerning an alleged criminous clerk, John Horne, see Loc.IV, no. 2 (1338).

bridge some of the gaps in a reconstruction of medieval Durham's society by looking at its lowest levels, the poor, the under-privileged and the criminal elements, whose history would otherwise remain obscure.

The prime documentary sources for this chapter are naturally the court rolls; and at least a few of these survive from each of the local Durham courts, except the tolbooth court in the market. In layout, the Durham rolls are similar to those generated by manorial and borough courts all over the country, but many are in such a fragmentary and fragile condition as to be only barely legible. Few cover a full year's sessions for any one court, although some of the Elvethall rolls are longer and include most of the court's annual proceedings. Some short rolls contain entries for only two or three sittings, as is the case with the rolls for the court of Elvet Borough. The largest roll to survive originates from the court of the Old Borough, although it is bolstered by documents relating to other special courts. This roll is composed of twelve membranes stitched together, not necessarily in chronological order.[3] Most of the surviving court rolls are to be found in the priory's archive,[4] and the greatest number, some fifty-four, relate to the prior's free court. These cover the period from 1305 to 1442, although the majority date from the late fourteenth century.[5] The records of the borough courts have fared less well; Elvethall again emerges well with nineteen rolls remaining.[6] Although these rolls date from 1356 to 1402, as with the prior's court rolls most relate to the late fourteenth century. There are only five surviving rolls from the Old Borough court,[7] but its proceedings between 1498 and 1524 were copied into the Crossgate Court Book, which is an invaluable source book for legal matters in late-medieval Durham. Elvet Borough court is the least well-documented priory court, with only two fragmentary rolls dating from 1329 and 1381 extant to provide a small sample of the business of this court.[8] Some stray survivors of special court sessions also remain, such as two rolls recording sessions of gaol

---

[3] Loc.iv, no. 229.

[4] Under the classification *Locellus* iv.

[5] Loc.iv, nos. 1–2, 4–5, 7, 10, 15, 20, 23, 25, 31, 33, 36–7, 40, 46, 48, 50, 52–3, 56, 66–8, 70–2, 75, 77–9, 81–4, 87, 144–5, 152, 154, 161, 188, 193–4, 197–8, 202–5, 207, 209, 212, 234.

[6] Loc.iv, nos. 96, 99, 101–4, 109, 116, 118–19, 124, 128–9, 131–2, 134, 235–6; Misc.Ch. 6796.

[7] Loc.iv, nos. 95, 120, 127, 201, 229.   [8] Loc.iv, nos. 123, 130.

delivery by the prior's court (for 1317 and 1346) and the Marshalsea rolls for 1311 and 1395.[9]

The evidence for those Durham courts which were not supervised by the priory is pathetically sparse. One book containing the proceedings of St Giles' Borough court survives, and it covers the period from 1494 to 1532, which is almost identical to that of the Crossgate Court Book. It begins with the proud statement 'This is my own boyk' and on the fly leaf, *pertinet Roberto Harvy*.[10] But one looks in vain for any earlier records of this court, which was administered by Kepier Hospital, through the mediation of its senior secular officer, the master. An indication of the scope of work carried out by the bishop's justices of assize when sitting in Durham is given in the surviving judgement rolls and in the sessions of oyer and terminer and gaol delivery.[11] The long series of chancery enrolments beginning with Bishop Bury's episcopacy also includes some litigation among other routine administrative matters.[12] Finally, the records of the bishop's halmote court, dating from 1348, contain references to tenurial matters in Durham under the entries for Chester (modern Chester-le-Street).[13] But none of these documents provides any indication of the day-to-day supervision of town life in the Bishop's Borough, or indeed of any business which arose as a result of trading in the market. This gap is a result of the absence of any surviving court rolls from the tolbooth court in the market place.

There are other documentary sources which can amplify the evidence of the court rolls, most notably the priory account rolls. These regularly record the income from courts in the form of fines and amercements under the miscellaneous receipts (*Varia Recepta*) or profits of the free court (*Perquisitiones Libere Curiae*) sections of the accounts; legal expenses, like the salaries paid to court officials, are to be found in the necessary expenses (*Expense Necessarie*) section. The sacrist's account rolls, for example, refer to his court in Alvertongate from 1361 and subsequently to his

[9] Loc.IV, nos. 60, 140, 157, 229, m.12.
[10] PRO, SC2, portfol.171, no. 6, henceforth referred to as St Giles Court Book.
[11] The surviving judgement rolls date from 1345 to 1531 but most are early sixteenth-century: PRO Durham 13, nos. 1, 221, 223, 228. See also, for example, PRO Pleas and Presentments, Durham 19, no. 1/1.
[12] PRO Durham Chancery Enrolments, 3/29–3/80.
[13] These survive in book form in the Public Record Office; PRO Halmote Court Books, Durham 3, nos. 12–23, 135.

court in Crossgate (from 1424 to 1535) when, presumably, it moved into the property called the tolbooth. The first surviving references to the Elvet Borough court occur in the hostillar's account for 1333. It has not proved possible, however, to find any earlier references to the holding of courts in Durham than those which occur in the cóurt rolls, and none of these are particularly early in date. This lack of early evidence should not be taken to imply that there were no borough courts in existence before 1300 in Durham; but rather it reflects the paucity of surviving thirteenth-century evidence.[14] The court rolls themselves seem to document a relatively advanced stage in the development of court procedure, a time when precedents and the organisation of business had become well established. The order of entries on the rolls as well as the diplomatic of the documents, with their heavy reliance on abbreviations, suggest this. Furthermore, it is unlikely that the Durham overlords neglected the close supervision of law and order, not to mention the collection of feudal dues from their tenants, before 1300. The borough court was the ideal forum for exerting their authority over their urban tenants.

THE LOCAL COURTS OF DURHAM

One of the most striking features of the administration of justice in medieval Durham is the proliferation of courts in a town which, even allowing for the hazards of calculation and estimates, was relatively small in area as well as population throughout the medieval period. At least seven courts were in operation in Durham by the fourteenth century on'a regular basis and, in addition, there were special courts meeting at irregular intervals for specific purposes.[15] All these courts can be divided, broadly speaking, into those of very local significance and limited competence, and those of more general application with wider powers. In the first category are the borough courts of Elvethall, Elvet Borough, the Old Borough (or Crossgate), St Giles and the tolbooth court in the market place. These courts were administered by the overlord of a particular borough, such as the priory

---

[14] This is the case in many other parts of the country: see *Manorial Records of Cuxham, Oxfordshire*, ed. P. D. A. Harvey, Oxfordshire Record Society, vol. 50 (1976), Introduction.

[15] For an explanatory diagram of the Durham courts, see appendix 5.

hostillar for Elvet and Elvethall courts and the priory sacrist for Crossgate court. The free tenants of each borough owed suit to these local courts, which dealt with a limited range of petty offences involving borough inhabitants and regulated borough life, rather as the wardmotes in London dealt with policing and public health in the wards.[16]

The second category of courts included the prior's court, *curia prioris*, and the bishop's courts, presided over by his justices of assize who were appointed to deal with specific cases involving Durham townsmen as well as the routine business of gaol delivery from Durham prison. These 'umbrella' courts came directly under the authority of the bishop or the prior, although both appointed officials to supervise the running of the courts. Through these courts of wider competence, they were able to enforce jurisdiction over any of their tenants, no matter in which borough they lived. These courts also had powers to deal with more serious offences committed in and around the town, such as the alleged misapplication of rents assigned to the maintenance of Durham bridges.[17] The prior's court was used for establishing matters of tenurial principle, such as suit of mill. Additional courts could be convened to meet the needs of special occasions or particular types of crime. The Marshalsea courts, for example, which probably operated in each borough, met at irregular intervals, primarily to check the weights and measures of traders in Durham and to make sure that brewers paid the customary dues to the borough overlord.[18] Lastly, the manorial jurisdiction exercised by the bishop through his halmote court for the Chester ward affected his tenants in Durham, many of whom owed suit to it and were admitted to, or surrendered, their holdings before the court.

Although there was a certain amount of duplication in the work of the Durham courts, it does appear that specific types of cases were confined to a certain level of court. For example, more serious crimes – such as theft, the receiving of stolen goods and murder – were tried at a higher level, in the prior's court or before the bishop's justices of assize, who could impose a harsher penalty on the offender.[19] Cases concerning some important incidents of

---

[16] *London Assize of Nuisance*, pp. xxvi–xxx; G. A. Williams, *Medieval London: from commune to capital* (London, 1963), p. 80.

[17] PRO Durham Chancery Enrolments, 3/31, m.3d (1371–2).

[18] See, for example, the Marshalsea court held in Elvet Borough on 13 October 1395: Loc.IV, no. 140.   [19] See, for example, Loc.IV, nos. 1, 15, 20.

tenure, such as suit of mill or suit of bakery, were dealt with in the prior's court because they affected priory tenants living in any Durham borough. At the lower level, nearly all the presentments and injunctions concerning public health, food and nuisances came before the borough courts, as did most of the minor agricultural offences such as animals wandering in priory fields or tenants taking brushwood from priory land. Consequently, there seems to have been a division of judicial business which could keep both levels of courts fully occupied on a regular basis.

The large number of local courts followed quite naturally from the division of the town into several administrative units. Each borough had a court to which its inhabitants owed suit and to which they had to apply for redress of grievances. A tenant living in Old Elvet could not be presented for an infringement of a borough by-law in Crossgate court. He had to appear in the court serving the area where he lived. It was in the interests of the overlords, in particular the priory, which had such a financial stake in the town, to maintain and staff these many courts to support a legal relationship with their tenants in the Durham boroughs. These tenants came to court to take up their holdings; thereby they acquired a legal title to land while at the same time they acknowledged their overlord's entitlement to certain services, including money rents. Moreover, even freeholders in these boroughs were required to attend certain court sessions each year, either in person or by proxy, to recognise that the prior was their overlord. The court provided a mechanism by which the priory could demonstrate its legal dominance over those holding land in its boroughs.

Direct financial gain was certainly not the motive for the overlords who operated so many courts throughout the town. The 'profits and perquisites' of justice, fines extracted for infringements of regulations, amercements of defaulting suitors as well as absentee parties to a case, landmale payments and the fines made to the court by freeholders or those admitted to tenements in a borough, were small indeed. The sacrist, for example, never received more than 11s. per annum from his court in Alvertongate between 1361 and 1423, and this income was at its lowest in 1378 and 1408 at 6d. After 1423, profits increased as his estate expanded, more tenants owed suit and the area of competence of the court increased: in 1424, for example, the sacrist's income from the Old Borough court was £2. 14s. 3d., a sum composed of £1. 3s. in landmale, 9s. 8d. in fines, 14s. 10d. in amercements and 6s. 9d. in alesilver, a customary toll or fine paid by brewers in the borough. But this total was never rivalled in the later fifteenth century; it had fallen to 11s. by 1486 and to 6s. 10d. by 1535.[20]

Moreover, this small income had to be offset against the considerable cost to the overlord of running a court. The salaries of the court's officers, principally the bailiff, were perhaps the largest regular items of expenditure. In 1413 the sacrist paid his bailiff, William Bolton, 6s. 8d. for holding the borough court and collecting fines in the borough; the income of the court that year was only 3s., so the Alvertongate court was running at a loss. By 1423 however, things had improved, for although Bolton's salary remained fixed at 6s. 8d., the sacrist's income from his court had increased to £2. 2s. Clerks and other legal representatives had to be paid from time to time for work done on specific cases. In 1376, the sacrist paid 8s. 8d. for a plea moved against John de Lethom and John de Baumburgh concerning a tenement in Alvertongate. In 1378 the sacrist acquired a writ for a suit at the tolbooth court costing 1s. 1d. and a writ against John de Wermouth for 4s. 4d. In 1424 he paid William Bolton an additional 3s. 4d. for the scribe's account and 3s. for parchment and paper. Even the bishop's assize courts were not very profitable. It has been shown that in 1420–1 less than 8s. was received from cases brought against twenty-six offenders and the income of the court was only 15s. 7d. in 1422–3.[21] Clearly, the annual costs of running the local courts were often greater than the income they brought an overlord; as Lobel wrote of the sacrist's court in Bury St Edmunds, 'there was more prestige than profit' in the running of a local court.[22]

It might be expected that the relationship between the bishop's courts and the court of the second most important landholder in Durham, the prior, would be fraught with difficulties and rivalries, leading to the sort of tensions and civil unrest characterising so many medieval towns which contained ecclesiastical franchises. This was not the case, and the remarkable *laissez-faire* that existed between the two in matters judicial can be attributed to that all-important agreement of the early thirteenth century, *le Convenit*. It gave the prior the right to hold his own

---

[20] All this information comes from the sacrist's account rolls, *Varia Recepta* or *Redditus Assise* sections.
[21] Storey, *Thomas Langley*, p. 64.   [22] Lobel, *Bury St Edmunds*, p. 40.

court with jurisdiction over tenants of his own fee: 'The prior will have his court freely, with Soc and Sac and Tol and Them and Infangenetheof...and writs of right'.[23] *Le Convenit* also established a special procedure for cases involving a priory tenant who had committed an alleged offence in the Bishop's Borough or elsewhere outside the prior's jurisdiction. This procedure relied on a passage of *le Convenit* in which it was agreed by the bishop and the prior that 'if any [man] either belonging to the land or the fee of the prior is in future attached by the bishop's bailiff for anything pertaining to the prior's court, the prior or his bailiff may demand his court'. In practice, what happened was that the alleged offender was summoned by the bishop's bailiff to appear before the bishop's court. If it was found that he was a priory tenant, the prior, through a representative, such as his steward or bailiff, was entitled to appear in the bishop's court and claim his man in an action which was known as the prior 'having his court'.

Several examples of this procedure can be found in the surviving rolls, proving that *le Convenit* had more behind it than legal theory. In 1336, for example, John Tunnak was accused of stealing hides both in Sadlergate in the Bishop's Borough and in South Street in the priory's Old Borough. He was summoned by the bishop's bailiff and appeared before the bishop's court, but, as the prior's court roll recounts, 'concerning this [case] the bailiff of the prior came and sought *Curiam Prioris* and he has it'. Tunnak was subsequently arraigned by the prior's steward and he appeared in the prior's court.[24] But this particular example of judicial cooperation did not mean that the prior's court had legal powers equivalent to the bishop's courts. The significant phrase in *le Convenit* is 'for anything pertaining to the prior's court'; in other matters there were severe limitations over the competence of the prior's court. Pleas of the crown and serious criminal matters were restricted to the bishop's courts. Since the bishop alone had the power to pardon convicted felons, for example, there were occasions when the prior had to request the bishop to pardon one of his own tenants, as in the case of William de Preston of Elvet, a carpenter, who had been found guilty of the killing of William Joliff in 1381.[25] More significantly for future relations, *le Convenit*

---

[23] *Feodarium Dunelm*, pp. 213–17.
[24] Loc.iv, no. 52; see also the case of Richard de Hett (1305), Loc.iv, no. 161.
[25] PRO Durham Chancery Enrolments, 3/31, m.10.

had stated that 'all easements and profit deriving from pleas of the crown and from assizes and all other pleas…concerning the land or the fee of the prior will be halved (*dimidiabuntur*)…between the bishop and the prior'. The prior had to pay to 'have his court'. Consequently, the income from court business which involved the bishop's jurisdiction could be severely restricted for the priory, as the hostillar's account of 1347–8 shows. That year, he received 9s. 3d. from the farmers of the Bishop's Borough, which was a half share of the amercements the bishop's court had trawled from the hostiller's tenants who had been summoned to appear before it.[26] As a result of *le Convenit*, the bishop reserved for his own courts the most important and profitable business and ensured that the prior's court was never able to assume an equal power or rival status in Durham.

The lack of surviving documentation concerning the bishop's courts tends to diminish or obscure what was a very complicated and sophisticated legal administration. Perhaps the clearest statement of the bishop's secular legal position was that made by Bishop Langley in 1433, which was based on the claims made by Bishop Bek in 1293. Langley argued that, among other privileges, he had his own chancery and court where all pleas were heard and assizes were held, and his own justices, sheriffs, coroners and escheators to supervise legal processes. In other words, he was claiming the right to administer justice in his bishopric without reference to the machinery of royal government.[27] How far this independence existed in practical terms is, of course, a moot point. Lapsley maintained that the bishop of Durham acted autonomously to keep the peace in his bishopric and illustrated this claim with examples such as the pardoning of convicted felons, the issuing of licences of amortisation, and the sequestration of land.[28] However, Lapsley was forced to admit that royal justice could and did infringe on the bishop's powers; the king could, for example, intervene where there was a default of justice and any tenant of the bishop could appeal to the royal courts over the head of the bishop's courts. The king also stepped in to run the courts during vacancies of the bishopric.[29] The bishop, just as the abbot

---

[26] Host. account, 1347/48, Receipts. See also Cart.IV, fol.29r, recording the now lost document, formerly 4.1.Spec.43; Reg.III, fol.178.

[27] Storey, *Thomas Langley*, p. 57.

[28] Lapsley, *County palatine of Durham*, chapter 2.

[29] See, for example, *CPR 1324–30*, p. 475.

of Bury, was 'a great feudatory with apparently almost unlimited powers, and yet bound hand and foot if he should fail to administer the king's justice well'.[30] The laws of England, as passed by Parliament, were observed in the bishopric and the royal writ did run there as, for example, when the *Quo Warranto* proceedings of 1311 were extended to the bishopric, and, as Mrs Scammell has commented, successive bishops of Durham seem to have been struggling 'not for the exclusion of the royal writ but for the monopoly of its execution'.[31] All the privileges they gained were by delegation from the king. Hence the surviving evidence shows the bishop upholding the laws of the rest of the realm by employing the legal practices current elsewhere in England, but using his own legal administration, which was in turn based on the model of the royal courts.

THE PERSONNEL OF THE DURHAM COURTS

The overall responsibility for running one of the Durham courts, whether it had local or general competence, lay with the overlord who took its profits. He it was who directed the business of each session and it was in his name that the court sat. The 1398 court roll for the local court of Old Elvet was headed 'the court of the prior and the hostillar of the Barony of Elvet held at Elvethall' and in 1480, St Giles' court was called 'the court of John Lund, master of Kepier Hospital'.[32] However, it is unlikely that the bishop or the prior presided personally in these courts on a regular basis, for the obvious reason that their many other duties and frequent travels would prevent them from taking such an active part in the administration of justice in one small town. The prior usually delegated the presidency to an obedientiary. On 5 March 1336, for example, the prior's court met chiefly to inquire into the lands which Margaret Walle held in Durham. The court roll was headed 'in the full court of the prior... before Walter de Skaresbrek, terrar'.[33] Alternatively, the prior was represented by his chief lay official, his steward or seneschal (*senescallus*). In 1346, at a special session of gaol delivery, Roger de Esshe, knight, the prior's seneschal, presided, and the case against John, son of

---

[30] Lobel, *Bury St Edmunds*, p. 117.
[31] *CChR 1307–13*, p. 345; Scammell, 'Origins and limitations of the liberty of Durham', pp. 449–73.
[32] Loc. IV, no. 101; St Giles Court Book.   [33] Loc.IV, no. 52.

William Salter, who was accused of burglary, was examined by Thomas Surteys, the prior's seneschal, in 1355.[34] The bishop also seems to have delegated the oversight of his local Durham court to his seneschal. In 1468, Richard Raket, seneschal, presided over the court of the Bishop's Borough where the quarrel between two factions of the weavers' trade was settled.[35] This office-holder was also responsible for the administration of the bishop's halmote court. According to his terms of appointment, Thomas Gray, seneschal, who presided over the halmote court in 1348, had to act as an archivist as well. He was to preserve all the bishop's court and halmote rolls as well as the rentals and muniments relating to these courts.[36] However, it seems that whenever cases concerning the prior's tenants came before the bishop's court, a senior official, the sheriff, presided. Tunnak's case, already mentioned, was heard before the sheriff and the coroner in 1336 and John Alman of Elvet was indicted for theft before William de Mordon, sheriff of Durham, in 1346.[37]

While the presidents of the Durham courts were drawn from either the ranks of the local gentry or from the growing class of full-time clerical advisers to the overlords, if not from among the priory obedientiaries themselves, the overlords relied on local townsmen to staff the lesser offices in the courts. By far the most important court official after the president was the bailiff, a man who may have been appointed by the overlord of the borough, as in Bury St Edmunds, from a fairly limited range of the wealthier property-holding tenants; however, no records of any selection or election procedure survive at Durham.[38] The names of many of these bailiffs are known from charters, where they usually appear near the head of the witness list, indicating a recognition of their status in the borough. In a survey of all the charters relating to property in Fleshewergate and Sadlergate, for example, out of fifty-eight charters dating from the 1280s to the early fifteenth century, the names of bailiffs headed witness lists in thirty-seven cases; seventeen names were in second place; seven were in third place; five were in fourth place and none were lower placed. It has already been shown that some wealthy

---

[34] Loc.IV, nos. 60, 154.
[35] PRO Durham Chancery Enrolments, 3/50, m.10.
[36] PRO Halmote Court Books, Durham 3, no. 12; PRO Durham Chancery Enrolments, 3/46, m.7.
[37] Loc.IV, nos. 52, 60, 154.   [38] Lobel, *Bury St Edmunds*, p. 62.

craftsmen became bailiffs of their boroughs and often held office for a number of years. This same tendency can be seen among those bailiffs whose occupation is not known; the same names recur frequently, suggesting that there was a fairly limited pool of suitable candidates for office. William de Heburne, for example, was bailiff of the Bishop's Borough four times (in 1302, 1312, 1315 and 1322) and Thomas de Coxside, Robert Olyver and Ralph de Warshopp were bailiffs three times each. In some years, two bailiffs were appointed, probably to share out the onerous and sometimes unpopular duties, as in 1295, when Gilbert de Querington and James Apotecarius were bailiffs of the same borough.

The bailiff's duties in court were limited to the implementation of instructions from the president; his was an essentially passive rather than an active, decision-making role. One of his main tasks was to summon people to hear or answer charges before the court. In a plea of debt brought against Richard Thornton, butcher, in the prior's court in 1442, the bailiff was instructed to 'summon him by his goods so that he will be at the next court'. At the next court session, Thornton did not appear and the bailiff was instructed to go a stage further and to 'attach' him, or apprehend him, to be at the next court.[39] If weights or measures of traders had to be checked, it was the bailiff who saw to it that all brewers, for example, were present in court.[40] As an alternative to a personal appearance by the accused, the bailiff was empowered to find people to act as pledges on their behalf. When, in 1442, the farmer of Scaltok Mill accused several men of withholding grain from his mill, the bailiff was instructed to appoint 'reliable pledges' as security for the men's appearances.[41]

Another of the bailiff's important tasks was to find and empanel sufficient men to form juries to investigate cases. In 1398 the Elvet-hall court instructed the bailiff to bring to court twelve men 'to investigate on oath if John Skalyng, webster, is guilty of various offences'.[42] The court of the Old Borough called on the bailiff to provide 'a good inquest' at the next court to investigate cases in 1392.[43] When he failed to find enough men to serve on a jury, or to empanel them properly, the whole case could be held up for

---

[39] Loc.iv, no. 46.
[40] *Present. ballivo hic quod venire fac. hic ad proximam omnes braciatores, pistores, regratores ... de excessibus per ipsos factis*: Elvethall court, 1398, Loc.iv, no. 96.
[41] Loc.iv, no. 46. [42] Loc.iv, no. 96. [43] Loc.iv, no. 120.

several court sessions. A case between the prior and John Sadbery, John Cage and others, which came before the prior's court, was adjourned to the next session for lack of jurors (1353). Another case brought by the prior against John de Belasys and others concerning a stolen horse was postponed repeatedly between 31 March and 28 July 1355 for the same reason, or because the bailiff did not return the list of prospective jurors.[44] The frequency of such delays, like the attempts by bailiffs to falsify jury returns,[45] indicates the difficulties they met in trying to raise sufficient men to adjudicate in local disputes.

None of the bailiff's responsibilities described so far were easy to discharge or popular with the average townsman, but probably his third main duty, to collect fines and distrain the goods of those the court found guilty, was the most difficult. In 1382, for example, he was asked by Elvethall court to distrain the goods of the debtor, William Sawer, but the outcome was not satisfactory: 'The bailiff testified that he had nothing except one brass pot.'[46] His attempts to seize goods on the instructions of the court occasionally rebounded on his head. Adam de Bille, the prior's bailiff, was summoned to court by Thomas Copper to answer a charge of taking two tin basins, one brass pot and one iron chain from Copper's house. Bille readily admitted the substance of the charge, but defended himself by arguing that he was acting for the prior in distraining Copper's goods because Copper had not paid the dues owed by all the borough's brewers to the priory.[47] In a similar case, the distraint of chattels by the bailiff had a more violent result. Robert de Whitton, junior, the prior's bailiff, summoned Hugh Cronan to appear before the prior's court in 1378 and accused him of assault. The alleged offence had taken place in Cronan's house when he resisted Whitton's attempts to distrain a brass pot on the orders of the court. Perhaps the brass pot had been used as the offensive weapon![48]

The practical difficulties of the bailiff's office were no doubt exacerbated by its unpopularity with his neighbours. His was an exposed position; he was, after all, the visible representative of the overlord acting on his orders to enforce measures which might be very unpopular, yet he was not protected by the authority of the

---

[44] Loc.IV, nos. 67, 68.
[45] See, for example, the instruction to the bailiff in the Crossgate court not to falsify the jury return, on penalty of a fine of 10s.: Crossgate Court Book, fol.7v (1529).
[46] Loc.IV, no. 104.   [47] Loc.IV, no. 145 (date unknown).   [48] Loc.IV, no. 71.

church. Furthermore, he was a townsman whose job it was to report on any infringements of borough by-laws or challenges to the feudal *status quo*, a kind of neighbourhood spy in what was a very small community. Consequently he was a suitable target for those with grievances against the overlords, and attacks on bailiffs seem to have been one of the hazards of the office. There are several examples of violent confrontations in the court rolls. Thomas Tuffan and William Pundar attacked the prior's bailiff in Elvet in 1316. In 1402, the prior's forester alleged that John del North 'spoke evil against the bailiff in the execution of his office, calling him false for carrying out the office of the court'.[49] William de Ryton, the prior's bailiff, and his servant Thomas le Hostelerman were attacked by John Baxster while they collected rents or other monies owed to the prior in Old Elvet in 1356, although here the motive might have been simply theft.[50] Given the dangers attendant on the office, it is hardly surprising that many townsmen tried to avoid it, although it brought some financial remuneration, as we have already seen. In 1401, for example, all cases had to be held over from the prior's court because the bailiff did not appear 'to respond to his office'.[51]

The other officers of the Durham courts had a far less exposed position in the administration of justice. The courts of more general competence, as could be anticipated, had more staff to cope with their business than had the local borough courts. The prior's court had its own coroner, not to be confused with the bishop's coroners, who worked in the four large wards – or legal divisions – of the bishopric. The prior's coroner may have sat regularly with the president of the prior's court (though not in the local courts), hearing all types of cases,[52] but his main function seems to have been the 'recognising' and swearing in of juries in the prior's court. A plea between the prior and Laurence Porter which came before the prior's court in 1356 was not heard because the coroner did not 'recognise' or approve the list of jurors. He may have had a hand in the selection of juries, because in 1337, 'the prior's coroner was ordered to be at the next court with twenty-four of the most worthy and law-abiding of the prior's fee' (24 *de probioribus et legalioribus de feodo*) to examine the case

---

[49] Loc.IV, nos. 37, 99.   [50] Loc.IV, no. 109.

[51] Loc.IV, no. 129 (Elvethall court).

[52] In Bury St Edmunds, the bailiff was also the coroner: Lobel, *Bury St Edmunds*, p. 62. See R. F. Hunnisett, *The medieval coroner* (Cambridge, 1961), p. 5.

against William de Barowe.[53] Other important officers of the prior's court were the clerks who acted as attorneys for parties to disputes, men who had, presumably, some specialised training in the law. Among the prior's legal representatives were John del Hay (1354), John de Elvet (1356) and William de Dalton (1356) who, as the court record says, 'followed for the prior'. The men who acted as farmers of priory mills often found it necessary to use attorneys to prosecute tenants for mill offences. In 1442, for example, John Horsle acted as attorney for Roger Milner, the farmer of Scaltok Mill.[54] Other clerks would be present in court to make a record of its proceedings and to advise the court on precedents. They are not mentioned by name in the rolls, although charges for scribes appear in the obedientiaries' account rolls.[55]

Indispensable to the workings of justice in medieval Durham was the jury, a group of borough inhabitants variously known as the 'free men', 'good men' or 'most law-abiding' (*probiores*) of the borough. The jury, inquest or *bona Inquisitio de visueto de Elvett* as it was called in the records of the different courts, was usually composed of twelve men, although occasionally the bailiff was requested to summon twenty-four.[56] It was common practice then as now for more men to be called up for service than were strictly necessary, presumably to ensure that, despite any objections to individuals or sickness among them, there would be enough for the case to go ahead. The list of jurymen attached in 1309 to appear in the prior's court included sixteen names, of whom twelve had the word *jurator* alongside to signify that they had been examined and selected.[57] Those chosen may have needed some residential qualification or at least to have been property-holders in the borough, and they do not seem to have been able to excuse themselves from duty without a specific pardon, such as the one given by the bishop to John Lewyn in 1370.[58] It is difficult to find any evidence of jury corruption in the surviving documents, although occasionally a jury was changed in the course of a case. During a common pasture dispute of 1360,

---

[53] Loc.IV, nos. 40, 203.
[54] For the prior's legal representatives, see Loc.IV, nos. 31, 40. For John Horsle, see Loc.IV, no. 46. Some private individuals also used attornies. In 1391, John Becley represented Thomas Bell in a plea of debt against Hugh Cronan: Loc.IV, no. 95.
[55] See, for example, Sac. account, 1424/25, *Expense Necessarie*.
[56] Loc.IV, nos. 2, 46.   [57] Loc.IV, no. 56.
[58] PRO Durham Chancery Enrolments, 3/31, m.2.

it emerged that certain jurymen had a vested interest in the outcome of the case because they claimed similar pasture rights by virtue of their landholdings. The jury was then changed to include *forinseci* from Darlington.[59] Juries were used for a wide variety of purposes; in civil cases they inspected disputed property boundaries and listed the holdings of wealthy freeholders who had died. In criminal cases, they heard the evidence of witnesses and decided the innocence or guilt of an accused person. In St Giles' court, they had even more power; it was the jury, acting through its foreman, which presented cases before the court and issued injunctions and instructions. In 1480, for example, the jury presented two men for an offence in Magdalenclose, and in the same session they set the prices for grain on market day.[60] Theirs was a partnership with the president of the court, a relationship expressed clearly in 1517: 'it is agreed both by the court and by the verdict of the jury'. In this court, the bailiff's role seems to have been outflanked by the jury.

It is clear from this survey of the personnel attached to the courts that many Durham townsmen would be involved in the administration of law and order in Durham, albeit in a part-time capacity as, for example, jurymen. However, it is likely that the main office-holders in the courts, especially in the prior's and bishop's courts, would have been drawn from a fairly restricted circle, a circle of those who had a legal education and probable connections with the households of the bishop and the prior in the case of the attorneys and clerks; and those with sufficient wealth or business success to be fitted for the office of bailiff. Yet although power might be in the hands of the few, the 'power of great acquaintance' complained against in fifteenth-century Southampton,[61] this power was greatly limited in Durham by the fact that all the officers were at the beck and call of the overlords of the boroughs. In turn, since the bailiffs or the coroners chose the juries, justice was heavily weighted in favour of the lord of the borough and open to a certain degree of manipulation. In other medieval towns, such as Hull, the inhabitants gradually came to have a greater share in the appointment of court officials as well

[59] 2.6.Spec.44; 3.3.Pont. 5. Compare this lack of evidence with Southampton, where there were several complaints of corruption: C. Platt, *Medieval Southampton* (London, 1973), p. 176.

[60] St Giles Court Book, fols.5,9.

[61] Platt, *Medieval Southampton*, p. 176; Hunnisett, *Medieval coroner*, p. 196.

as in the operation of the courts. In Durham, as in Bury and other church-dominated towns such as Tavistock, Abingdon and St Albans, the overlords retained this power in their own hands.[62]

THE BUSINESS OF THE DURHAM COURTS

The types of cases which were brought before Durham's courts, and the nature of the business there, can be used to illustrate certain themes of social and urban history which do not emerge so clearly from other documentary sources, and to amplify some which have been touched on earlier. Perhaps one of the most interesting of these is the apparently harmonious relationship between the townsmen and their ecclesiastical overlords. Surprisingly for a town so dominated by the clergy and by a religious corporation as powerful as the priory, there is little evidence in the court rolls of any animosity between the Durham townsmen and their overlords or of any civil disobedience. Whereas in York the wealthy and powerful St Mary's Abbey at times attracted urban riots and pitched battles around its walls, Durham Priory seems to have lived peaceably with its neighbours.[63] One incident suggests that a more serious source of unrest was the relationship between some members of the county gentry and the priory. In 1419, as they crossed the Old Bridge, the priory terrar and some of his servants were attacked by men wearing hauberks and brandishing crossbows, arrows, swords and other 'warlike arms'. Not unnaturally, the terrar beat a hasty retreat to the priory. It transpired that these men were servants of Thomas Billyngham of Sidegate manor, a gentleman who held a sizeable private estate in Durham, some of it within priory boroughs, as well as land and property in Billingham, in the south of the bishopric, from which the family took its name. His grievance was founded on a dispute with the priory over homage he was alleged to owe for his Billingham land, but there is also evidence that he was being used as an agent by another, wealthier tenant of the bishopric, Thomas Claxton, who was involved in a separate dispute with the priory about land in Castle Eden.[64] In the course of the quarrel, Billyngham laid siege to the priory for two months, and his servants were involved in other attacks on the prior's servants at

---

[62] *VCH Yorks., East Riding* 1, pp. 37–9; Lobel, *Bury St Edmunds*, p. 60; Platt, *English medieval town*, p. 139.

[63] Dobson, *Durham Priory*, p. 35; *VCH Yorks., City of York*, pp. 38–40.

[64] Burs. account, 1416/17, *Expense Necessarie*; Dobson, *Durham Priory*, p. 194.

the North Gate in the heart of the town.[65] This episode
demonstrates the difficulties faced by the cathedral priory in
extracting feudal dues and services from local landowners.
Members of Billyngham's class had little to fear from defying the
priory because they did not in any way depend on it for a living
or for their own ambitions and they knew that the priory had no
effective sanction against their intransigence. However, perhaps
one of the most significant aspects of this whole violent episode is
that the Durham townsmen seem to have offered no support to
the county gentry in their quarrel with the priory. Had they felt
a sense of grievance against their monastic overlords, surely they
would have seized on this opportunity to rebel.

The general level of violence in Durham's society, as reflected
in the cases coming before the courts, seems to have been fairly
low, although of course the most serious crimes would have been
investigated by the bishop's justices and few records of their
meetings survive. Full-scale urban unrest seems to have been
unknown in Durham. In 1396, some fifteen men, all tenants of the
prior, appeared before the court to take an oath that they would
'not make any affray'; this was followed by an injunction issued
by the Old Borough court that no tenants were to draw knives
against anyone, on penalty of a fine of 3s. 4d.[66] This isolated
incident seems to have been confined to one part of the town and
has more the appearance of a brawl than a riot. Evidence of
violent attacks on individuals can be produced from the court
rolls, but here the motivation was usually domestic or personal
and, with the exception of the attacks on court officials already
noted, it cannot be attributed to any concerted move against the
town's overlords. In 1338, for example, John Nouthird accused
John Potter and his wife of attacking him in Durham, with the
result that his clothes were torn, an assault which seems have hurt
his pride more than his body.[67] William Mayson's case was more
serious, however. He was attacked at night by John Clogh, who
was armed with a dagger. A blow in the left side of his stomach
was fatal: 'he received a mortal wound from which he
immediately died'.[68] Worse was the attack on Robert Batmanson
in Sadlergate in 1473 by Richard Whyte, James Trotter, Robert
Merley, William Hakforth and William Dalton, 'in a warlike

[65] Loc.xxi, no. 11; Cart.iv, fols.142–3; Dobson, *Durham Priory*, pp. 194–5.
[66] Loc.iv, no. 229, m.11.   [67] Loc.iv, no. 2.
[68] PRO Pleas and Presentments, Durham 19, no. 1/1 (1472).

fashion'. Batmanson was killed, but the jury had some difficulty in deciding who had struck the fatal blow. Was it Whyte, who 'with a stick called a "karlilaxe" struck him in the breast' or was it Trotter who 'with a stick called a "Bill" hit him on the back of the head'? Could it have been Merley who hit Batmanson on the back with an axe or Hakforth who with a stick 'called a "Walsshbill" hit him on the other side of the head'? Certainly, there was no doubting the murderous intentions of this group.[69]

There are two poignant examples of death by misadventure in the surviving documents. In the first, the bishop ordered an inquiry to be made into the case of John othe Castle, a cook, whose pregnant wife was knocked down by horsemen as she walked along the Bailey in 1345. 'She was suddenly thrown to the ground by the horses...so that Agnes...had an abortion.' A second tragic case concerned Walter Lewyn, who, while he was practising at the shooting butts in Framwelgate in 1398, accidentally overshot the target and hit a small boy who was sitting in the ditch next to the targets. The boy died, but in this case the bishop was able to exercise his prerogative of mercy and he pardoned Lewyn for this tragic accident.[70]

Theft was a much more common problem in Durham than armed violence, as the frequent cases of robberies, such as John de Byfield's alleged theft of a horse in South Street or John de Hovedon's taking of money and a knife from a man in the Old Borough in 1338, illustrate.[71] One of the more unusual items to be the subject of theft allegations in 1331 was a cross from St Giles' Church.[72] Occasionally, the articles taken amounted to a considerable sum, as in the case concerning Julia del Comunhous which was discussed earlier.[73] This alleged burglary in 1327 included a substantial amount of money and goods valued at £40. Such a case illustrates the wealth of some Durham inhabitants in comparison with the majority of their fellow citizens, and there is probably some significance in the fact that the victim of this last case lived in the Bailey, one of the more prosperous streets of the town. Other cases of theft show how desperate the less-fortunate Durham inhabitants were for food or for the means of making food and how near the subsistence level many of them lived. In 1324, Laurence Fullor of Elvet was accused of stealing corn in

---

[69] PRO Pleas and Presentments, Durham 19, no. 1/1.
[70] PRO Durham Chancery Enrolments, 3/29, m.16d; 3/33, m.20.
[71] Loc.IV, no. 2.   [72] Loc.IV, no. 20.   [73] See chapter 3, p. 89.

autumn from the field of the Old Borough, and William Mores was alleged to have taken two ears of wheat from the priory. Both men were, however, found not guilty.[74]

The Durham courts were used very regularly by all levels of society for the recovery of debts, with a preponderance of these cases concerning action taken by landlords or landowners to try to collect rent arrears arising on their properties. It was natural that the prior should use his own court to recover his rent arrears. In 1442, he recovered 8s. owed by Richard Thornton for his tenement in Elvet, and the court awarded him damages of 1s.[75] The Crossgate court, in particular, handled many such cases of rent recovery, not necessarily on behalf of the priory, but for private landlords who seem to have used it as a last means of recouping the money. In 1356, for example, John de Hert was accused by John Lewyn of not paying him 5s. 6d. owed for a property in the Old Borough.[76] But the local courts also dealt with private business debts as, for example, when items were sold to a client in good faith but the purchase money had never been handed over. In the Old Borough court in 1394, Richard Fyssher of South Street tried to recover a debt of 18d. owed by John Chestre for one pannier of haddock. John Dyconson accused John Tomson, 'tynkler', of not paying 11½d. owed to him for bread and ale in 1506.[77] Executors of wills formed another important group of plaintiffs in debt cases, as they tried to recover money owed to the deceased. Richard Arnburgh and his wife, executors of the will of James Tebson, summoned William Bell, shoe maker, before Crossgate court in 1504 on a plea of debt of 3s. 4d. which Bell had owed Tebson.[78] The debts claimed in court ranged from the small, a few pence, to the very large, and they indicate something of the cash-flow problems which traders must have encountered in Durham as well as the general difficulty of rent-collection.

The tenants' feudal obligations to their overlords are most clearly demonstrated in the court rolls. Freeholders such as John de Belassys in Elvet Borough came to court to do fealty personally to the hostillar in 1381, but in Old Elvet in 1398, John de Kendale preferred to excuse himself by essoinment and he paid a fine of 6d. for his suit of court. However, these were rare examples of law-

---

[74] Loc.IV, no. 79.   [75] Loc.IV, no. 46.   [76] Loc.IV, no. 40.
[77] Loc.IV, no. 229, m.2; Crossgate Court Book, fol.86r.
[78] Crossgate Court Book, 28 Feb. 1504.

abiding freeholders. In that same Old Elvet court session of 1398, when Gilbert de Hoton, John de Boynton and Gilbert de Elvet, who owed suit to the court, did not appear and did not send representatives or pay the fine for essoining, they were each amerced.[79] The independence of the freeholders' class of priory tenants has already been noted,[80] and the priory used their local courts to try to regulate and to maintain control over this uneasy tenurial relationship. The policing of fealty or suit of court owed by living freeholders was one concern; another was the recording of a deceased freeholder's obligations to the priory and the priory's interest in his property in inquiries held *post mortem*, so that his heir would not escape his responsibilities to the overlord by default. In 1332 the prior's court found that when Margaret de Hoveden died, she had been in possession of six burgages in Crossgate and Alvertongate which owed rent and fealty to the priory. It was ordered by the court that they be 'seised … into the lord's hand to inquire into their issues'.[81] The bishop's chancery court had wider powers still in dealing with his tenants-in-chief, and could assign wardships or dower to reward his servants, or keep land in hand as a source of income, as well as recover land either by escheat or from felons. In the eyes of this court, the prior was regarded as merely another tenant of the bishop, in feudal terms, albeit one of the most important. If he wished to expand the priory's urban estate by purchases of property in Durham, the prior or his representative had to appear before this court to seek a licence to alienate land in mortmain.[82] Thus the bishop in turn regulated the tenurial relationship with the priory closely through his courts.

Conveyancing matters occupied much of the time in the Durham courts. As in any manorial court, some tenements were surrendered there, new tenants were admitted to land and their title to it recorded on the court roll. In 1322, Hugh Knyth de Fery, a tenant-at-will, came before the prior's court and surrendered one messuage and twenty acres 'which are contained in le Landbuk' and Kathleen Robynson surrendered one burgage in St Giles Street to the use (*ad opus*) of Robert Symson in St Giles' Borough court in 1518. Symson took up the tenancy for a term of ninety-nine years at a rent of 6*d*. per annum and he paid an

[79] Loc.iv, nos. 123, 96.
[80] See chapter 4, pp. 113, 123–4.   [81] Loc.iv, no. 48.
[82] See, for example, PRO Durham Chancery Enrolments, 3/32, m.10.

entry fine of 6*d*. to the court.[83] One of the most important functions of all the Durham courts, but in particular the borough courts, seems to have been to act as a registry of deeds of title for tenants, the free as well as the unfree; and hence many charters were enrolled and confirmed in court, as they were in the London court of Husting and in the ward courts of Winchester and Canterbury.[84] The bishop's chancery was most popular with the freeholders, who had their title deeds enrolled there as a safeguard for their future interests.[85] In many cases, these enrolled deeds are the only remaining evidence for the tenurial history of some properties in Durham, particularly for land in the Bishop's Borough. Tenants could be asked to bring charters and other evidence of title to court in cases of disputed succession. In 1317, William de Chilton was ordered to produce his charter of enfeoffment to his land in Crossgate at the next court session.[86] By the later medieval period, contemporary developments in the land law were being reflected in the Durham courts. Tenants were beginning to bring entirely fictitious legal actions of common recovery before the bishop's courts to improve their titles to property. Robert Claregenet 'recovered' a tenement in the market place in this way in the early sixteenth century; but when the prior tried to use this device to 'recover' four tenements from William Highfeld, the bishop's justices of assize suspected collusion to avoid the penalties of mortmain. The land was taken into the bishop's hand pending an inquiry into the whole case by the sheriff.[87]

The prior's court was used to enforce and to re-state from time to time that all-important tenurial obligation, suit of mill. However, it was not just a matter of the tenants acknowledging the symbolic legal supremacy of their ecclesiastical overlord; it reflected the overlord's need to safeguard a source of income. This income came from the farmer of the mill, who raised it by exacting suit-of-mill payments from the priory's tenants. Consequently cases of tenants withholding this suit were pursued vigorously through the Durham courts as the farmers of mills tried to recoup any financial losses and also to have the court restate the important principle upon which their livelihoods

[83] Loc.iv, no. 5; St Giles Court Book, fol.19.
[84] Urry, *Canterbury*, p. 89; Keene, *Winchester*, vol. 1, part 1, pp. 11–19.
[85] See, for example, PRO Durham Chancery Enrolments, 3/29, m.3; 3/30, m.9d.
[86] Loc.iv, no. 36. [87] PRO Judgement Rolls, Durham 13, nos. 1, 228.

depended. It is significant that almost all the cases concerning milling in the prior's court rolls are annotated with later marginal notes such as 'Note that the tenants of the Old Borough were obliged to mill at Skaltou mill' (1339).[88] In 1333, John de Castro Bernardi, the farmer of Scaltok Mill, brought a case against Gilbert de Duxfeld, who had withheld suit from the mill. Acting on the principle that 'all the prior's tenants in the Old Borough owe multure to Scaltok', Castro Bernardi removed all the flour which he considered had been milled elsewhere from Duxfeld's house in Crossgate. The strong local feeling against the enforcement of suit of mill is borne out by Duxfeld's physical attack on Castro Bernardi and his subsequent recovery of all his milled flour.[89] However, once out of office, the erstwhile farmer was no more law-abiding than his fellow townsmen. In 1339, John de Castro Bernardi and William de Chilton were distrained to appear before the court to respond to the lord prior 'concerning suit withheld and grain carried from the mill'.[90] These milling cases and those concerning the duty of tenants to bake bread at the priory's ovens occupied many sessions of the prior's court. They were a recurrent theme, so demonstrating both the priory's difficulty in maintaining a monopoly of milling and baking and the townspeople's determination to avoid this obligation of tenure.

The many agricultural offences which were brought before the Elvet courts show how blurred were the boundaries between the south-eastern part of the urban area and its immediate countryside. Many townsmen kept animals, and it proved difficult for the borough courts to enforce controls on livestock in a town where the open fields intruded on street lines. The priory used its borough courts to check any attempts at incursions on its land by enforcing a series of by-laws which closely resemble contemporary village regulations found all over the country.[91] Most of the offences committed were for fairly minor infringements of these by-laws, which were made to protect the demesne lands of the priory, especially meadows and grazing areas like Smythalgh in Elvet Borough, into which animals strayed and ate off the grass, or woodland near Maiden Castle and Houghall,

---

[88] Loc.IV, no. 53.   [89] Loc.IV, no. 197.   [90] Loc.IV, no. 1.
[91] W. O. Ault, *Open-field farming in medieval England: a study of village by-laws* (London, 1972), p. 19; Raftis, *Estates of Ramsey Abbey*, p. 126, who demonstrates that the greatest number of infringements of such by-laws was for livestock wandering in the fields.

where tenants went for firewood and brushwood. In 1398, the bailiff of Elvethall court presented Mabel Porter and William de Thornburgh who had allowed their pigs (four and five respectively) to wander into Smythalgh. Thomas de Tyndale was presented because his horse was found in Elvetwood, and Robert Plummer had allowed twelve geese to stray into Smythalgh where they had 'trampled down and consumed' the lord's pasture land. All pleaded guilty and they were amerced.[92] Also in 1398, William Wryght was accused of cutting down oaks in Elvetwood without a licence and, worse still, of opening up the lord's beehive there to steal honey and wax from it![93]

This overlap between town and countryside was not confined to the Elvet area, and in other parts of the town, similar concerns were being voiced in the borough courts. All tenants of St Giles' Borough, for example, were ordered not to transport trees from Kepier's land or to take whins from the moor.[94] No doubt such cases could be duplicated if the documentary evidence for this court survived in greater measure. These agricultural offences of all types also provide incidental information about the nature of the countryside around Durham, the cultivation of the fields, the types of trees and the amount of undergrowth in the woods, and of current agricultural practices. Manuring of the priory land was taking place in Elvet Borough in the middle of the fourteenth century, for example. We learn about this because a case came before the prior's court in 1356 in which the servant of Laurence Porter prevented the prior's servants from carrying away cartloads of manure which was lying on priory land in Elvet.[95] In 1398, the bailiff of Elvethall court was ordered to attach Alan de Hayden and all those whose offence, seemingly, was to have dumped manure on the prior's land in 'le Lonyng'.[96]

A common source of dissension between tenants and their overlords from the fourteenth century onwards was over common pasture rights, a theme which occurs many times in late-medieval urban history in towns such as Coventry, Southampton and Norwich. Durham was not immune from this problem, yet whereas in Coventry and in Colchester in the early fourteenth century the townsmen had recourse to rioting and long-running disturbances in an attempt to effect change, the Durham tenants seem to have preferred a judicial confrontation, and brought a

[92] Loc.IV, no. 96.   [93] Loc.IV, no. 101.   [94] St Giles Court Book, fol.5.
[95] Loc.IV, no. 40.   [96] Loc.IV, no. 101.

series of test cases against the priory.[97] These cases were too important to be heard in the borough courts; and it was hardly likely that the tenants would receive a sympathetic or unbiassed hearing in the prior's court. Consequently, such cases were brought before the bishop's justices of assize and the judgements are preserved not only in original documents but in enrolments in the priory registers. The case of Alice othe Slade is typical of many. In 1334, she arraigned the prior by assize of novel disseisin concerning her alleged right of entry to forty acres of moor and pasture as a free tenant of the Old Borough. The bishop instructed his sheriff to assemble twelve men of the 'view' to inspect the land and, after many postponements, the case was decided in her favour in 1336. The court adjourned to the moor ('Beaureparemore') and in the sight of the justices Alice's right to common pasture was restored by the prior.[98] This right was subsequently claimed by another twenty-four tenants, and the priory built up a large dossier of notes and evidence in an attempt to rebut these claims. While the tenants of the Old Borough seem to have fought their claim to pasture rights solely through the courts, the freeholders of Elvet Borough used more unorthodox, but equally successful, methods. They and their animals made repeated small incursions on to the priory demesne lands, for which they were regularly presented in the Elvet courts. Gradually the prior's resistance was worn down and after lengthy negotiations, a legally binding agreement was made in 1442 between the priory and the free tenants such as Robert Danby and Thomas Claxton, members of the local gentry. This document stated that in future the tenants would not be amerced or their animals impounded if they entered priory land but 'amicably they will be driven away'. Furthermore, they were to be given the right to pasture their animals on Elvet Moor and within certain specified closes.[99]

Attempts were made to control the price and quality of food for the benefit of Durham consumers through the local courts and in special Marshalsea sessions. In 1398, the bailiff of Elvethall court was instructed to bring all brewers and regraters to court to inquire into any 'excesses' they had committed.[100] The borough

[97] Platt, *Medieval Southampton*, pp. 205, 218; *VCH Warwick.*, vol. 8, p. 210; Campbell, 'Norwich', p. 13; Phythian-Adams, *Desolation of a city*, pp. 254–7; Britnell, *Colchester*, p. 31.
[98] 2.6.Spec.58; Reg.III, fols.77–8.   [99] 4.16.Spec.26.   [100] Loc.IV, no. 96.

courts set the measures and the prices (the 'assize') to which brewers were supposed to conform, and a great deal of court business was tied up with enforcing these regulations. In 1402, the Elvethall bailiff presented Stephen Piper for selling ale by cups, measures and other vessels which were not the approved measures, and for selling a gallon more dearly than the assize allowed.[101] It was ordered by the Elvet Borough court in 1381 'by common assent' that 'all brewers show their mark and sell a gallon, pottle and quart and none sell ale in a house with measures' unless with the approved measures, or pay a fine of 3s. 4d. However, when William Barker was accused of selling ale at the wrong price against the assize, he defended himself by saying that John de Elvet, the hostillar's seneschal, sold *his* ale at that same price.[102] Bakers were urged to sell bread 'well fermented, salted…and fit for human use' and to ensure that it was of the right weight. As in the Norwich leet records, there were far fewer cases of bad bread presented before the Durham courts than breaches of the assize of ale.[103] The frequency with which tenants were presented for selling ale at the wrong price, for using incorrect measures and so on implies that the local courts were largely ineffective in controlling the food-and-drink trade. One explanation may have been the difficulties of detection when a court had so few officials to inspect the work places of the tenants; another may have been the small size of fines which the court was empowered to impose on offenders.

Borough hygiene was, naturally enough, a principal concern of the local courts as they sought to prevent or to control outbreaks of disease in areas of high population concentration and to enforce a certain minimum standard of living. Regular injunctions concerning public health were issued at court sessions, and these seem to have had the force of local by-laws. They fall into two main categories, the first regulating a tenant's responsibilities to maintain standards in his immediate surroundings, the streets, vennels and water supply, for example. The second category concerned a tenant's relationship with his neighbours. One of the most common injunctions in the first category was that tenants should enclose their 'frontes', probably meaning the boundaries of their properties, both along the street frontage and at its rear,

---

[101] Loc.IV, no. 99. [102] Loc.IV, nos. 123, 104 (1382).

[103] Loc.IV, no. 131; *Leet Jurisdiction in the City of Norwich*, ed. W. Hudson, Selden Society, vol. 5 (1892), p. xxxiv.

presumably to stop their animals wandering around.[104] The courts also issued frequent orders forbidding anyone from building out into the street or blocking water channels or vennels with rubbish. In 1401, Elvethall court instructed John Fabyan to deal with the water obstruction before the gate of Robert de Berall's house; and in Crossgate court in 1529, the tenants were ordered to mend the vennel called 'Litster chare' leading to the common oven in the borough.[105] Certain streams were to be kept clear of industrial or domestic waste so that the water would remain relatively free from pollution and could be used safely by householders. William Walker was instructed in 1500 that he should remove a dead and foetid pig lying in the Milneburn at the end of his orchard.[106] In 1501, all tenants who held land abutting the Milneburn stream had to remove any latrines and 'le wesshyngstonez' they might have had there; nor were wells to be polluted, as a by-law passed by Elvethall court in 1401 stated.[107] St Margaret's cemetery was not to be used by the borough inhabitants as grazing land for their pigs or horses.[108] All of these regulations were designed to improve the quality of street life in the town.

The second category of public health injunctions attempted to maintain good relations between all the Durham townsmen by improving living conditions in the boroughs. One important area of local legislation imposed restrictions on who could, or more importantly who could not, be accommodated by townspeople in their houses. In keeping with the general prejudice against Scots in the town, they were classed with vagrants, suspect characters and ungovernable women as being undesirable settlers. In October 1498, John Watson's wife was accused of entertaining Scots and women of a bad reputation at night and she was fined 1s. by Crossgate court.[109] In 1332, Geoffrey Marescallus of Elvet was accused of receiving and giving hospitality to Thomas Hardymarchand, in the full knowledge that he was a convicted thief.[110] The frequency of injunctions against vagabonds may reflect what had become a common theme in late-medieval

---

[104] See, for example, St Giles Court Book, fol.5.
[105] Loc.IV, no. 131; Crossgate Court Book, fol.7v.
[106] Crossgate Court Book, 7 October 1500.
[107] Crossgate Court Book, 13 January 1501; *pena ponit. est quod si quis maculet communem fontem quod solvat dominum 2d.*: Loc.IV, no. 131.
[108] Crossgate Court Book, October 1498.
[109] Crossgate Court Book, October 1498.   [110] Loc.IV, no. 20.

borough regulations, as in London (1475), Coventry from the 1490s and York from the early sixteenth century.[111] No one was to sub-let their 'bakdwellyngs', presumably in an attempt to reduce overcrowding or squatting. The ever-present fear of disease led to an injunction in St Giles' court in 1518 that no tenants were to receive any persons living in Crossgate or Elvet 'who are infected with *pestilencia*' and in Crossgate in 1498 no one was to receive visitors from Bishop Auckland where *pestilencia est regnans* unless they wished to incur the very heavy fine of £1.[112] One wonders just how successful such prohibitions were in limiting the spread of disease between the boroughs. On a more trivial level, those tenants whose wives were liable to be scolds were enjoined to guard them well, although the absence of any like injunctions on unruly men seems a little unfair.[113] In ways such as these the borough courts tried to intervene in the private lives of townsmen, relying, presumably, on the willingness of people to report reliable information or unreliable gossip about their neighbours to the bailiff, who would then bring them to court.

FINES AND OTHER PUNISHMENTS

The rate of success of Durham's courts in conquering crime, controlling the quality and prices of goods for sale in the town and combating disease and anti-social practices is, however, a matter for debate. Many cases brought before the courts were dropped for one reason or another, or postponed indefinitely. Alleged criminals were found not guilty by juries composed of their neighbours. The regularity of small amercements paid by brewers for breaking the assize of ale suggests that they were treated rather like an annual licence to offend.[114] The restatement of injunctions against illegal brewing or the withholding of suit of mill time after time implies that the courts were having a very limited effect. Why was this? The most obvious reason would seem to be the lack of effective sanctions. The punishments open to the lower courts were restricted to small money fines or

---

[111] See, for example, *VCH Warwick.*, vol. 8, p. 211; Reynolds, *English medieval towns*, p. 178.

[112] *Null...habeat aliquas personas manent. in tenur. viz. in domibus posterioribus*: Crossgate Court Book, 1508, fol.100v; St Giles Court Book, fol.1; Crossgate Court Book, ?April 1498.

[113] See, for example, Crossgate Court Book, 8 October 1505; Loc.IV, nos. 104, 109.

[114] As in Norwich: see *Leet Jurisdiction in Norwich*, pp. lxxiii–iv.

amercements and the confiscation or distraint of goods. The wide range of agricultural offences, from depasturing meadows to breaking down hedges, merited small fines such as 6*d*. for cutting and carrying away trees or wood for firewood in Kepier's demesne lands in 1528.[115] The fines for offences concerning wandering animals in Smythalgh ranged from only 1*d*. to 4*d*. and, like the amercements imposed by the Norwich leets, seem to have borne no relation to the numbers or to the size of the animals involved. The same fine was imposed on William de Thornburgh for his five pigs wandering in the demesne lands, on Thomas de Tyndale for one horse found in the wood and on Robert Plummer for twelve geese in Smythalgh in 1398.[116] The range of fines may have been related to the degree of damage done or to the wealth of the accused and his ability to pay, but it was hardly an effective deterrent. The breaking of regulations concerning brewing or baking also incurred only a small fine, such as, for example, 6*d*. in Elvethall court in 1398, although the actual injunction or by-law carried a theoretical penalty of 3*s*. 4*d*.[117] The stern tone of the injunctions was obviously not being supported by the sentencing policy of the court.

Larger penalties seem to have been imposed, or at least threatened, to stop certain specific abuses which had become common in the town or to prevent them from becoming a severe problem. The taking of another man's servants was treated severely in St Giles' court in 1528 (6*s*. 8*d*.) and the penalties for accommodating any one who might have been exposed to *pestilencia* were high (6*s*. 8*d*. in St Giles' Borough and, in the Old Borough, £1 in 1498).[118] The relative scarcity of such cases in the court rolls suggests it was a successful solution. Certain offences always carried a heavy penalty, especially where they were perceived as leading to potential civil unrest. Those who accommodated women of ill-repute or convicted criminals were fined heavily (6*s*. 8*d*. in St Giles and in the Old Borough).[119] The carrying of knives in the Old Borough could mean a fine of 3*s*. 4*d*. in 1396.[120] Yet in other cases, there seems no logic behind the scale of fines. The blocking of streets with dung or other

---

[115] St Giles Court Book, fol.5.
[116] Loc.IV, no. 96: *Leet Jurisdiction in Norwich*, p. xxxviii.
[117] Loc.IV, nos. 96, 131.
[118] St Giles Court Book, fols.1,5; Crossgate Court Book, ?April 1498.
[119] St Giles Court Book, fol.5 (1528); Loc.IV, no. 229, m.6 (1391).
[120] Loc.IV, no. 229, m.11.

rubbish, for example, was treated severely (3*s*. 4*d*. in Elvet Borough and in Elvethall), but the polluting of a well in Old Elvet, which on the face of it would appear to be a far more serious offence, would cost the inhabitants only 2*d*. for each infringement (1401), which seems a totally inadequate sanction.[121]

Small fines and amercements were also a characteristic of pleas concerning civil actions such as the withholding of goods or debt. In one case where William de Horsley admitted that he owed Alan de Tesdall 11½*d*., the court assessed damages at 4*d*. and also amerced Horsley (1391).[122] When the judgement of the court went against the accused, the plaintiff seems to have recovered the full amount of the debt, plus damages assessed by the court, and an amercement. At first sight, this seems to amount to a large sum of money, but the damages claimed by the plaintiff were usually considerably reduced by the court. In 1357, John Potter was accused of killing twenty-two sheep which the plaintiff valued at £1. 10*s*., and the plaintiff claimed damages of £2. The jury found Potter guilty, but the damages were reduced dramatically to 1*s*.[123] If a man failed to prosecute his plea, for whatever reason, he was amerced for a false claim, presumably to discourage frivolous litigation. Even if there was an out-of-court settlement, the accused was amerced so that the court's time was not entirely wasted. Robert Kirk came to court in 1499 for a licence to make an agreement with William Atkynson, and he was amerced for 4*d*.[124] There was an air of unreality about many such cases. Debtors were brought to court usually as a last resort by a plaintiff who was attempting to recover some of his losses. It was unlikely that fining them, charging damages and then amercing them would be of much benefit to the plaintiff if they could not afford to repay even the original debt.

When an offender refused to pay his fine, or, as in many debt cases, where he lacked the means to pay, the next course of action by the court was to instruct the bailiff to distrain his goods to the value of the fine or the damages awarded by the court. The objects distrained give some indication of the standard of wealth among the inhabitants. The more prosperous townsmen were usually dispossessed of their horses, commonly valued at 6*s*. 8*d*., or failing a decent horse, of any other animals they possessed. In

---

[121] Loc.IV, nos. 123, 131.
[122] Elvethall court: Loc.IV, no. 95.
[123] Loc.IV, no. 40. See also Loc.IV, no. 95 (1391).
[124] Crossgate Court Book, 18 Sept. 1499. See also Loc.IV, no. 95 (1391).

1501, the priory brought a case of debt against William Spark. He was attached to appear in court by the distraint of a black horse with a saddle and a full sack of coal.[125] The poorest inhabitants were distrained of their household goods, such as dishes, pitchers and bowls, which amounted to very little in value. In a few cases, the bailiff had to report that the sum of the man's goods did not meet the amount required for the distraint, and probably many of the poorest townsmen slipped through the judicial system altogether by having no chattels of any value.[126] Some of the poorer citizens may have been excused or pardoned payment altogether, as they were in Norwich. However, the wealthier inhabitants seem to have had scant regard for the court's decisions, even those made by a court of wider competence like the prior's court. Adam Mayson was accused of withholding suit of mill from Scaltok in 1339 and he failed to appear before the prior's court to answer the charge. His chattels, to the value of 2*s.*, were attached by the bailiff to ensure his appearance; but as he ignored even this order, the court then called on the bailiff to seize another possession, a tunic, worth 1*s.* Lack of surviving evidence from subsequent court sessions prevents an assessment of how successful this course of action was, but the case indicates the disrespect there was for the judicial procedures of the Durham courts among sections of urban society.[127]

The main conclusion to be drawn from most of this evidence is that the penalties which the lower courts could impose failed to act as a deterrent to those who broke borough regulations. Many tenants ignored the courts' rulings altogether despite the possibility of their goods being distrained. It seems there was little that a court or its main officer, the bailiff, could do either to compel attendance or to extract fines from offenders. On the other hand, the fact that these courts were truly local, and covered an area of only two or three streets each, meant that everyone's business would be known to the bailiff of the court and this may have discouraged potential offenders. The organisation of the local court was rather like a neighbourhood watch or 'vigilante' group, staffed by local men sitting in judgement and reporting on their neighbours. William Hudson's verdict on the power of the Norwich leet courts is apt for Durham: 'Although admirably adapted for the detection of crime or of breaches of the City

---

[125] Crossgate Court Book, 3 March 1501.
[126] See, for example, Loc.IV, no. 104.   [127] Loc.IV, no. 53.

custom, it is impossible not to be struck with its inefficiency in the way of *repression* and penalty.'[128]

The administration of justice in Durham was, on the evidence of the surviving documents, very similar to its operation in many other English medieval towns and many other courts, urban or rural. The law as it emanated from the king was observed in the bishopric of Durham, alongside local regulations and by-laws which resembled those of other urban communities and villages. These laws reflected the needs of the society they served: for peaceful co-existence, for the fostering of trade and for a reasonable standard of life in a place where there was a high concentration of people. Durham's court procedures and sentences or penalties were unremarkable, and, as elsewhere in the country, they and the laws they maintained were essentially conservative. The earliest surviving court rolls from the early fourteenth century show a system already well developed which was to continue to the end of the medieval period with no major innovations.

Yet the machinery of law and order in Durham appears, on the surface, at least, to be unique, because of the multitude of small courts which dealt with such a diversity of offences. It is perhaps the case that Durham had a greater variety of local courts before which its inhabitants could appear or make representations than any other medieval town outside London. However, the number of courts does not reflect any refinement of Durham's judicial administration or any improvement over the neighbouring towns in the area. It merely mirrors the administrative divisions of the town into several boroughs, each with its own miniature local government. If, as has been argued, the signs of flourishing urban life in medieval England are not just to be found in a town's trading activities but also in its growing administration or governing bureaucracy and such institutions as its courts, then, at first sight, medieval Durham displays all the characteristics of a lively and successful community.[129] But on the legal front, as elsewhere, these signs are totally misleading, for, if anything, the judicial apparatus simply reflects the dominance of all-powerful ecclesiastical overlords. There is a strong link between govern-

---

[128] *Leet Jurisdiction in Norwich*, pp. lxxiii–iv.
[129] *VCH Yorks., East Riding*, vol. I, p. 28; Platt, *English medieval town*, pp. 136–8; Reynolds, *English medieval towns*, p. 118.

ment and legal jurisdiction in the medieval town: whoever ran the town's courts controlled the town's government, and one of the marks of a town's growing independence from its overlord, lay or ecclesiastical, was the point at which its courts were taken over by its townsmen. This was never possible in Durham, and throughout the medieval period law and order was upheld primarily by the bishops and the monastic community of St Cuthbert, who both controlled the courts and ran the town's government.

Conclusion

Lordship and community: the relations between Durham and its ecclesiastical overlords in the later middle ages

This survey of the urban community at Durham between *c.* 1250 and 1540 was motivated by a wish to redress the balance of previous work, most notably to draw some attention away from its ecclesiastical rulers towards the town that lay at the heart of their temporal power. Furthermore, an attempt has been made to set Durham in the context of medieval urban history, to assess its economic and social status in relation to other English towns in the same period. Some broad general conclusions can be drawn from this study as a whole which, it is hoped, will be of significance to those working on, or interested in, the history of medieval towns. Clearly, Durham was a town whose period of physical growth had largely come to an end by the middle of the thirteenth century. The boundaries of the urban area were, more or less, established before 1250 and the borough divisions were already entrenched, and this urban landscape saw no dramatic changes in the later medieval period. Durham was a small market town with a restricted hinterland; it lacked good communications by land or water which benefited her neighbours, in particular Newcastle-upon-Tyne. Her trades and industries were small scale and produced goods primarily for a local market; consequently, the town probably did not exercise a powerful magnetic attraction towards the labouring poor from the surrounding region. Yet the very diversity of her trades and the lack of any one predominant manufacturing industry does mean, however, that Durham seems to have escaped the worst consequences of economic decline in the fifteenth and early sixteenth centuries. Starting from a very limited economic base and maintaining this low level of industrial activity, the town did not have so far to fall when times were hard. The population probably maintained a fairly stable level throughout the period, despite outbreaks of *pestilencia* and the warfare of the late thirteenth and early fourteenth centuries, although there is evidence that the overlords were finding some difficulties in recruiting tenants to occupy properties on the outskirts of the town in the fifteenth century. This evidence should be offset, however, by the indications of illegal squatting by Scots and labourers in the backs of tenements in the central urban area in the late fifteenth and early sixteenth centuries.

Perhaps the most important conclusion to be drawn from this study is that Durham's significance as an urban centre lay not so much in its economic development, or the lack of it, but rather in its political role as the centre of government for the bishop, with the castle as the visible sign of his power in the region. Furthermore, it was a significant religious centre containing a great Benedictine monastery and an important shrine. The town was created as a by-product of politics and religion: it came into existence as a result of a military decision to establish a stronghold behind the vulnerable frontier of Northumbria, to serve both the garrison and the religious community which was receiving protection there. It continued to depend almost exclusively on the clergy for its prosperity during the later middle ages. The church gave it a *raison d'être*, yet, paradoxically, it deprived the town of any real independence. Its courts were administered by ecclesiastical overlords and staffed by their loyal servants, or by townsmen who earned their livelihoods largely by service to the bishop or the prior. The inhabitants had little opportunity to participate in government: the number of offices open to them was severely limited and no merchant guild had developed to provide a forum for discussing issues affecting the town or for bargaining with their lords. Perhaps more significantly, no politically voluble section of town society emerged in Durham to compare with the merchant class of York or Newcastle which could represent the interests of the townsmen or act as a counterbalance to the all-powerful clergy. Although there were wealthy and influential Durham merchants, at least in the early fourteenth century, most of their prosperity appears to have stemmed from their involvement in, and connections with, international trade. This in itself would limit their interest in Durham's internal affairs which would have little bearing on their own careers. Thus Durham remained in a state of 'arrested development' to the end of the middle ages, with its ecclesiastical overlords making no concessions on self-government.[1]

[1] As at Bury St Edmunds because of opposition from the convent to any self-government by the townsmen: Lobel, *Bury St Edmunds*, p. 60.

Yet despite their political impotence, Durham's townsmen did not rebel against their overlords. Indeed, most of the evidence points to peaceful co-existence, even during periods of apparent economic difficulty in the early fifteenth century when it might be supposed that townsmen, who were struggling to make a living and to pay their rents, would come to resent more bitterly the tenurial yoke. For many years, it was the accepted wisdom among medieval historians that a characteristic of mesne boroughs, either with a lay or an ecclesiastical overlord, was the conflict between the governors and the governed. Pirenne saw this as the old world of demesne organisation, with its rigid system of feudal responsibilities, the services and dues owed by the tenants, meeting and clashing with the new world of the growing towns with the wants and aspirations of townsmen – identified by him as the desire for political autonomy and self-government.[2] The contrast between royal towns, where privileges were won relatively easily in return for political support, and towns under ecclesiastical control, where the struggle to gain autonomy was long and hard and was seen as a threat to the church's authority, was stark. This traditional interpretation continues to hold ground among several modern writers, who not only see the church as being 'very repressive to urban aspirations', but on the evidence from church-dominated towns such as Bury St Edmunds, Abingdon and St Albans, also make a link between local frustrations and wider political insurrections: 'It is ... notable how largely towns subject to ecclesiastical lords figured in the disturbances of periods like the 1260s, 1326–7 and 1381.'[3]

But was conflict inevitable in all towns which came under the control of ecclesiastical authorities? Is Durham the exception to a rule? Recently, Dr Rosser presented a very convincing case for the existence of smooth relations between the urban community of Westminster and its abbot in the later middle ages. As he says, the secular inhabitants of Westminster 'lived under monastic rule without recorded protest'.[4] Of course, the crucial word here is 'recorded', for the surviving archives of many smaller English towns are patchy, and for the mesne boroughs they are usually records which originated from the chancery of the overlord. The townsmen left few accounts of their challenges to authority, apart

[2] H. Pirenne, *Medieval cities* (Princeton, 1939), pp. 168, 170–1.
[3] Reynolds, *English medieval towns*, pp. 115–16.
[4] Rosser, 'The essence of medieval urban communities', p. 93.

from their royal petitions. The documents which reveal unrest may have been lost or even weeded out of the archive of the overlord because, after all, they provided what was evidence of misgovernment or a failure of authority. However, if the examples of St Albans and Bury St Edmunds are anything to go by, the outrage felt by the monastic lords at such challenges to their God-given authority is clearly reflected in the monastic chronicles, in the vigorous defence of their privileges before the king, and in the accumulation of dossiers of evidence against the townsmen. Such evidence for Durham is lacking: the extant priory propaganda, in the form of chronicles, concerns itself with vigorous defences against the powers of the bishops of Durham, not with the pretensions of the townsmen.

Why then were Durham's townsmen so apparently amenable to ecclesiastical control and why did the Durham overlords not run into more difficulties and opposition? In other church-dominated towns such as Bury St Edmunds and St Albans, the flash point of trouble seems to have come when the townsmen formed themselves into a representative body, a guild, for example, to demand change. As we have seen, apart from the actions of a group of freemen during the common pasture disputes in the early fifteenth century, there is no suggestion of co-operative protests by the Durham townsmen. The craft organisations developed too late in the day to take a lead in the search for municipal independence, if indeed there was ever such a search in Durham. The only other candidate for leadership was the Corpus Christi Guild, an organisation which was, in the fifteenth century at least, dominated by county gentry and members of the large class of notaries and clerical administrators who worked for the prior and the bishop. Hardly a revolutionary body! The importance of the 'professionals' in Durham society, the clerical officials serving both the bishop and the priory, should not be overlooked; they formed a sizeable proportion of the town's population and because of their education and background they, and not the craftsmen, were the town's natural leaders.

The lack of leadership among the townsmen to rally opposition to their overlords, if the need came, was crucial, but there was a further problem. Unlike the citizens of Bury St Edmunds, Abingdon or St Albans, who could unite against their respective abbots, the Durham townspeople faced no one common enemy. Authority in late-medieval Durham was shared between three overlords, and although the priory might have had control over the greater part of the urban area, the rights and privileges of the other overlords were supreme in their own boroughs. However, work on Winchester, Canterbury, Lincoln and York, for example, has shown that townsmen were prepared to struggle to overcome the privileges enjoyed by those who lived within ecclesiastical liberties in towns, often by taking to arms, even if such attempts ultimately proved futile. What seems to have been missing in Durham was the political will to rebel. Durham's overlords were not oppressive, arbitrary or unjust. The study of the priory's estate management policy undertaken earlier in this book, for example, shows that while the response to times of economic difficulties was slow and conservative, the priory was not unaware of its tenants' difficulties and tried, where possible, to meet them with equitable solutions. Nor was it possible for the townsmen to play off one overlord against another. The crucial agreement (*le Convenit*) made between bishop and prior in *c.* 1229 had ensured that there would be economic and legal parity between the boroughs. The united face presented by the overlords limited any opportunities for political agitation by the townsmen.

There were no economic grounds for unrest either, since so many livelihoods depended on the patronage of the overlords and the trade generated by pilgrims and other visitors to the centre of the bishopric. Nor should we underestimate the reverence and pride in which Durham people held their resident saint, the splendid cathedral which housed his remains and the community which surrounded his shrine with the rituals of prayer and celebration. For a variety of reasons, it was unlikely that Durham's townsmen would rebel against the lordship of bishop and prior. Their mutual interests lay in peaceful coexistence, and that, apparently, is the way they chose to live throughout the medieval period. Professor Dobson's comparison is apt: 'Like the residents of a modern university town, the inmates of fifteenth-century Durham may have sometimes looked askance at the impressive corporate monster in their vicinity; but they were wise enough to realise that it brought them less pain than profit.'[5]

For a town whose fortunes were so intertwined with those of the church, the dissolution of Durham Priory undoubtedly shook its security to the core. Durham was one of the last monasteries

[5] Dobson, *Durham Priory*, p. 50.

to be affected by the wave of reform that swept through England in the late 1530s. It was in December 1540 that the prior signed the deed of surrender to the Crown;[6] and by May 1541 a new foundation was established in Durham with a dean and eleven prebendaries. The old Durham overlords were gone; the basis of landholding in the city, the administrative divisions, the maintenance of law and order, were all affected. The communal life of the parishes was broken, the chantries were stripped of their plate after 1546 and the religious processions were ended by the suppression of the Corpus Christi Guild in *c.* 1547.[7] The Elizabethan writer of the *Rites of Durham* lamented the passing of the old order, the colourful ceremonies and the strong sense of community which came from the participation of townsmen in religious events. The lights that burnt before the high altar 'in token that the house was alwayes watchinge to God' were quenched and the bells sounding in 'the deep night that all was well' were silenced in the great abbey church.[8]

Yet was the impact on the town as catastrophic as one might expect? Were the changes revolutionary, in any sense, to the average townsman? Many seem to have been largely cosmetic; the titles of the former priory obedientiaries were changed to those of prebends, but they were the same men. Some twenty-six out of the original fifty-four monks remained at Durham.[9] The landed endowment of the priory was transferred to the new foundation. Those tenants who had formerly held their properties from the prior and paid rents to priory obedientiaries now had the dean and chapter as their landlords. The legal and financial relationship between the town and the new chapter was in many ways largely unchanged. Only very gradually were the townspeople able to share in the government of the city, and the bishop continued to retain his control over office-holding into the seventeenth century. Consequently, the town did not offer a very attractive prospect for future expansion or independence to would-be settlers as compared with, for example, Newcastle-upon-Tyne; no new or large-scale industries developed until the late eighteenth and nineteenth centuries and even then the urban

[6] Transcribed in Hutchinson, *Durham* 2, p. 132.
[7] *Injunctions and other ecclesiastical proceedings of Richard Barnes, Bishop of Durham, 1575–87,* ed. J. Raine, Surtees Society, vol. 22 (1850), appendix 3, pp. xiv–xlvii; *VCH Durham*, vol. 2, p. 33; *VCH Durham*, vol. 3, pp. 28–9.
[8] *Rites of Durham*, p. 14.
[9] D. Knowles, *Bare ruined choirs* (Cambridge, 1976), p. 278.

area expanded very slowly. It is plain to see, in Forster's plan of Durham of 1754, the medieval city still surviving in all its essentials. The town remained within its medieval boundaries until the industrial revival of the middle of the nineteenth century, and even then the visual core of the medieval urban area (the ecclesiastical and secular buildings on the peninsula), remained intact, as it does to this day.

Appendix 1

Maps and plans of Durham

Appendix 1

This is not the earliest plan of the town in existence: that distinction goes to Matthew Patteson's map of 1595, which was engraved by Christof Schwytzer, and is now in the British Library. However, the layout and the perspective representations of the buildings in Speed's plan are very similar to those of Patteson, which suggests that Speed used the latter as the basis of his own plan. Speed's plan shows the full extent of the urban area at the beginning of the seventeenth century, and gives some indication of the different land use in and around the town. The evidence gathered from the medieval title deeds and other documentary sources suggests that Speed's plan fairly represents the layout of the late-medieval town.

References: J. Speed, 'The bishoprick and cities of Durham', reprinted in *The counties of Britain. A Tudor atlas by John Speed*, ed. A. Hawkyard (London, 1988), pp. 74–5; P. M. Benedikz (ed.), *Durham topographical prints up to 1800* (Durham, 1968), pp. 1–2, 68; *Maps of Durham, 1576–1872*, catalogued by R. M. Turner (Durham, 1954), p. 5; R. A. Skelton, 'Tudor town plans in John Speed's *Theatre*', *Archaeological Journal*, 108 (1951), 113.

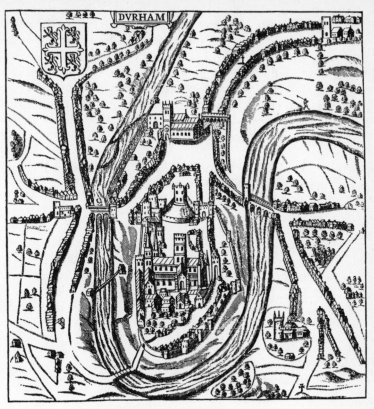

1 John Speed's plan of Durham, 1611

Appendix 1

2 JOHN WOOD'S PLAN OF DURHAM, 1820

This plan gives a very detailed depiction of the layout of the streets and the shape and size of individual tenements in Durham at the beginning of the nineteenth century. A comparison between Wood and Speed makes the point graphically that the urban area had changed very little in scale or organisation from the end of the medieval period to the industrial revolution. It is also possible that the tenement pattern shown on Wood's plan resembles closely that of the medieval period.

References: J. Wood, 'Plan of the City of Durham', in Durham University Library; *Maps of Durham*, p. 29.

2 John Wood's plan of Durham, 1820

Appendix 1

3 DURHAM IN *c.* 1250

This plan uses both Speed and Wood as its basis, and it draws on a number of documentary references to streets, boroughs and buildings in an attempt to reconstruct the appearance of the mid-thirteenth-century town. It demonstrates that, by 1250, Durham had already grown into a sizeable community with a range of public buildings to serve a thriving market town.

Legend:

Borough boundaries
Fortifications
+ Churches
◆ Gates

1. Cathedral
2. St. Oswald's Church
3. St. Nicholas's Church
4. St. Giles' Church
5. St. Mary's Church, N. Bailey
6. St. Mary's Church, S. Bailey
7. St. Margaret's Chapel
8. St. Mary Magdalen Chapel & jurisdiction
9. Castle
10. North Gate
11. East Gate
12. South-west Gate
13. Old Bridge
14. New Bridge
15. St. Giles' or Kepier Hospital & Chapel
16. ? Site of bishop's house
17. Mineburn mill
18. Monks' mill & weir
19. Fleshewergate
20. Saddergate
21. Souterpeth
22. Walkergate

3 Durham in c. 1250

243

Appendix 1

4 RECONSTRUCTION OF TENEMENTS IN CROSSGATE, ALVERTONGATE AND MILNEBURNGATE, OLD BOROUGH

These three streets within the Old Borough are particularly well documented in the priory archive because the majority of properties were in priory hands by the end of the fifteenth century. This schematic tenement plan has been compiled from the evidence of medieval title deeds, the priory rentals (in particular the sacrist's rental of 1500), and other documentary sources. As none of these sources gives any precise dimensions, no attempt has been made to draw the tenements to an accurate scale. The numbers refer to the order of tenements as they appear in the 1500 rental. This reconstruction shows the mixture of tenement shapes and sizes in the medieval town and in particular the congestion around the administrative and social centre of this borough, the church and the junction of Crossgate, Milneburngate and South Street.

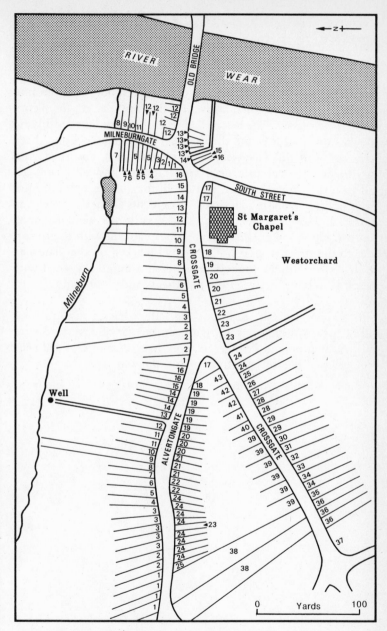

4 Reconstruction of tenements in Crossgate, Alvertongate and
Milneburngate, Old Borough

5 TENEMENT BOUNDARIES IN NEW ELVET, 1439–*c*. 1442

This sketch plan of the boundaries of sixteen tenements on the north side of the main road in the priory borough of Elvet (modern Old Elvet) was drawn up in the course of a legal battle over the disputed right of the borough's freeholders to common pasture in certain enclosed areas including Smythalgh, the priory hostillar's meadow. The priory had recently acquired a croft lying between this meadow and the river, a croft which had once been held by William Hesswell, and it had been absorbed into Smythalgh. Several title deeds relating to Hesswell's land are extant in the priory archive, and the history of the acquisition of this property, including Hesswell's tenements along the street, can be traced. This plan demonstrates the layout of tenements along the roadside in a regular, 'herringbone' pattern, with their short sides to the street frontage. The vennel marked on the plan may be identified with the modern lane which connects the street with a back lane lying between the tenements and the meadow.

References: Misc.Ch.5828/12; for the legal dispute, see Misc.Ch.5828/1–20; map 15, with commentary by M. G. Snape, in R. A. Skelton and P. D. A. Harvey (eds.), *Local maps and plans from medieval England* (Oxford, 1986), pp. 189–94.

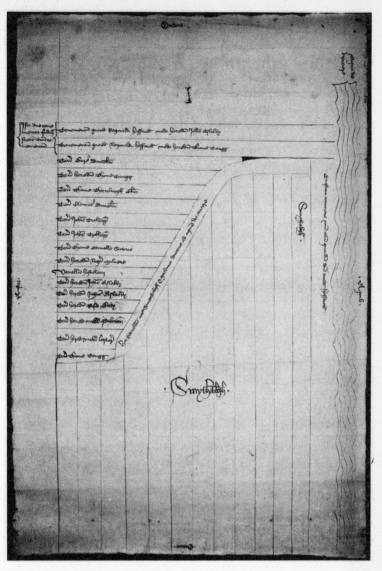

5 Tenement boundaries in New Elvet, 1439–*c.* 1442

6 PLAN OF THE SOUTH-EAST CORNER OF DURHAM
MARKET PLACE, *c.* 1567–8

This rough sketch plan of the boundaries of six burgages in the south-east corner of the market place was drawn up as a result of litigation concerning priory properties (or rather properties of the dean and chapter, as they were when the plan was compiled). The plaintiff in the case seems to have been Knighton, the tenant occupying Kyrkbye's burgage, and the defendant was Whytffeld, who occupied Aspor's burgage. The burgage which was in dispute, as indicated by the words *in traves*, was possibly Huton's burgage, which lay between Knighton and Whytffeld's land. The names of past and present tenants appear in the rough diagram, as does the name of the corner plot on the map, the 'Cornerboyth', and the rents owed for each burgage. There are some extant title deeds in the priory archive which can be associated with the plan to help trace the descent of these properties, and these, together with the documents concerning the legal dispute, enable an approximate date to be attached to the plan. The perspective of this plan is curious; it is a mole's eye view of the market place, seen as if from underground, with the east and west points of the compass reversed.

References: Loc.XXXVII, no. 113; for the associated documents concerning the case, see Misc.Ch.1699, 1714.

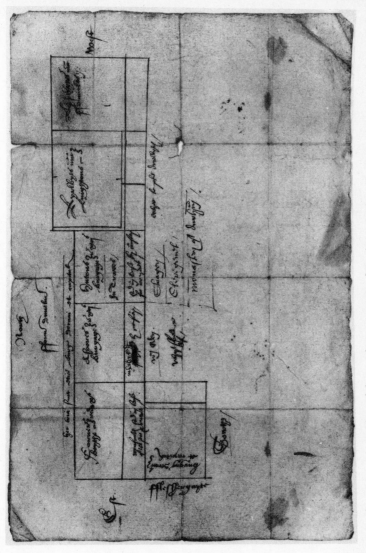

6 Plan of the south-east corner of Durham market place, c. 1567–8

249

Appendix 1

This plan is based on Speed's somewhat impressionistic depiction of the walls and gates of the town, and on documentary sources, in particular the monk Laurence's description of the fortifications in the middle of the twelfth century. It shows that the area which was most heavily defended, the peninsula, was not a truly urban area; it was the ecclesiastical and administrative centre of the town, containing the priory, the cathedral church and the bishop's castle, as well as some properties occupied by the retainers of the Durham overlords. The wall which enclosed the market place was a much later and poorer construction which, in military terms, was of negligible value to the Durham townsmen.

References: *Dialogi Laurentii Dunelmensis Monachi ac Prioris*, ed. J. Raine, Surtees Society, vol. 70 (1880), p. 10.

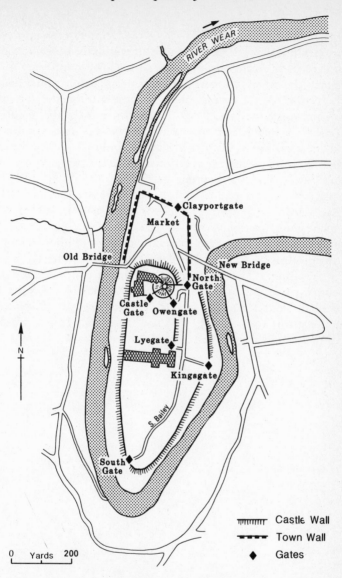

RIVER WEAR

Clayportgate

Market

Old Bridge

New Bridge

North Gate

Castle Gate

Owengate

Lyegate

Kingsgate

S. Bailey

South Gate

N

Castle Wall

Town Wall

Gates

0 Yards 200

7 Plan of Durham's fortifications, *c.* 1400

Appendix 1

8 PLAN OF DURHAM CASTLE

This plan illustrates the main developments in the construction of Durham castle during the medieval period. The complexity of the military design of the castle and its relationship to Durham's fortifications is clear, and helps to account for the fact that Durham castle never fell to an enemy during the medieval period. What had been simply a military headquarters in the early middle ages was transformed into a bishop's palace by the fifteenth century, with the addition of guest quarters, kitchens and other purely domestic buildings.

References: Symeon, *Historia Ecclesiae Dunhelmensis*, pp. 113–14; Symeon, *Historia Regum*, pp. 199–200; Laurence, pp. 11–12; G. Simpson and V. Hartley, 'Excavation below Bishop Tunstal's Chapel, Durham Castle', *Antiquaries Journal*, 33 (1953), 56–64; C. E. Whiting, 'The castle of Durham in the middle ages', *ArchAel*, 4th ser., 10 (1933), 123–32; *VCH Durham*, vol. 3, pp. 65, 69–70; D. Pocock and R. Gazzard, *Durham: portrait of a cathedral city* (Durham, 1983), p. 45; P. A. G. Clack, *The book of Durham City* (Buckingham, 1985), p. 50.

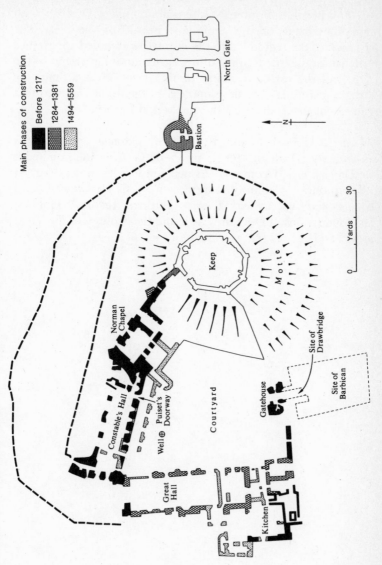

Main phases of construction

■ Before 1217
▓ 1284–1381
░ 1494–1559

North Gate

Bastion

Keep

Motte

Norman Chapel

Constable's Hall

Well ⊕ Puiset's Doorway

Courtyard

Great Hall

Kitchen

Gatehouse

Site of Drawbridge

Site of Barbican

N

0   30
Yards

8 Plan of Durham Castle

Appendix 1

It is only possible to interpret the topography of Durham with some knowledge of the geological profile of the area. The glaciation of the region led to the distinctive rounded appearance of the landscape, the fertility of the agricultural hinterland of the town, and the tortuous course of the River Wear around the Durham peninsula. The development of the town plan was to a large extent determined by this geological history.

References: D. Pocock and R. Gazzard, *Durham: portrait of a cathedral city* (Durham, 1983), pp. 7–9; G. A. L. Johnson (ed.), *The Durham area*, Geologists' Association Guides, no. 15 (1973); P. Beaumont, 'Geomorphology', in J. C. Dewdney (ed.), *Durham county and city with Teesside* (Durham, 1970); A. Holmes, 'The foundations of Durham Castle and the geology of the Wear gorge', *DUJ* 25 (1928), 319–26.

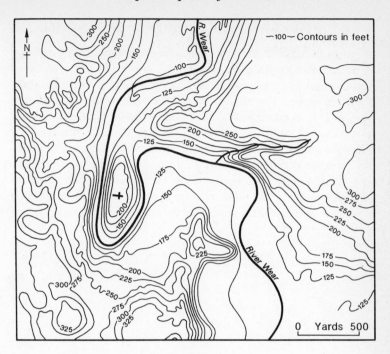

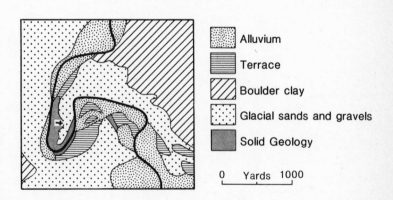

9 The site and geology of Durham

Appendix 1

This plan uses Speed as its basis, and incorporates all the medieval documentary references to bridges and mills. The river was used to maximum effect by a series of water mills along its banks, some of which served the town's overlords and some the borough tenants. Two were fulling mills – one of the two mills below the priory and the South Street mill. The rest were corn mills. The bridges were crucial to the development of Durham's trade as they connected the neck of the peninsula where the market place was situated with the surrounding countryside. The Durham street plan was heavily influenced by the position of these crossing points, on which routes converged.

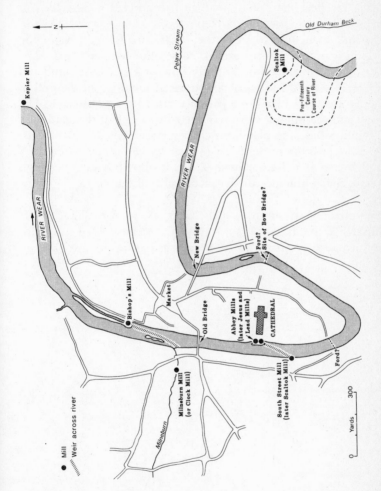

10 Late-medieval Durham: bridges and mills

Appendix 1

This plan was drawn up as a result of a legal dispute involving the extent of the priory's responsibility for maintaining the road which ran near the mill. This road had flooded, it was alleged, because earth had been taken from it to shore up Scaltok Mill dam. The mill itself suffered from the vagaries of the current of the river flowing beneath the promontory called Maiden Castle. The difficulties of maintaining a steady flow of water to the mill and of keeping its dam in repair led to the abandoning of the mill in about 1462, at the foot of a partially dried-up ox-bow lake. The name and the milling were transferred to a mill at the south end of South Street. The plan is the clearest documentary evidence for the exact position of the Elvet mill, at the eastern extremity of a road which is modern Green Lane. It also shows, in a rough sketch, the appearance of the medieval mill building.

References: Misc.Ch.7100; Misc.Ch.5828/9; Misc.Ch.6794(b); Bursar's accounts, 1458/59, 1462/63, receipts; Map 17, with commentary by Snape, in *Local maps and plans*, pp. 203–9.

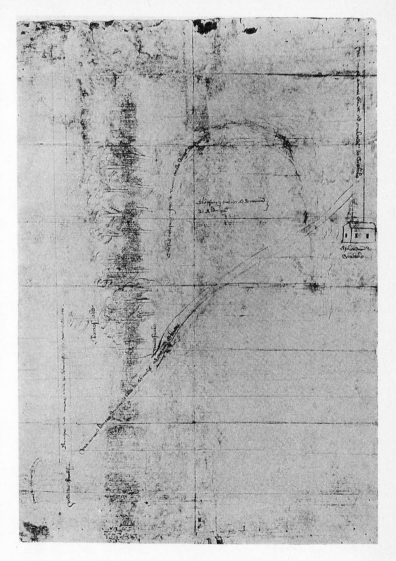

11 Scaltok Mill *c.* 1440–5

Appendix 2

Tables

Table 1. *The income of the bursar from Durham rents, 1270–1539*

	1270 £ s. d.	1335[b] £ s. d.	1347[b] £ s. d.	1382 £ s. d.	1396 £ s. d.	1427 £ s. d.
Bailey	—	10.10	1. 13. 0	4. 3. 6	5. 5. 6	3. 19. 0
Elvet	1. 16.10[a]	2. 7. 3	2. 4. 3	6. 1. 0	5. 19. 3	7. 4. 0
Elvet bakehouse	—	6. 8	13. 4	?1. 10. 0	1. 10. 0	1. 4. 0
Borough of Durham	14. 0	9. 0	9. 0	1. 0. 8	2. 0. 0	2. 5. 4
South Street	—	—	—	13. 8	13. 8	12. 8
Crossgate	—	19. 5	1. 11. 5	5. 15. 3[b]	4. 16. 9	1. 8. 8
Old Borough	4. 13. 4[a]	3. 0. 0	—	3. 6. 8	2. 13. 4	2. 13. 4[c]
St Giles	—	—	—	15. 12. 6	20. 0. 6	9. 13. 2
Scaltok Mill	29. 6. 8	19. 6. 8	13. 6. 8	11. 0. 0	12. 0. 0	—
Total income	36. 10.10	26. 19.10	19. 17. 8	49. 3. 3	54. 19. 0	29. 0. 2

	1446 £ s. d.	1464 £ s. d.	1495 £ s. d.	1508 £ s. d.	1517 £ s. d.	1539 £ s. d.
Bailey	3. 2. 4	4. 1. 4	5. 2. 8	3. 12. 8	3. 15. 4	4. 19. 0
Elvet	5. 1. 8[d]	4. 16. 8[d]	5. 17. 0	7. 13. 6	5. 13. 4	4. 18. 4
Elvet bakehouse	—	—	1. 6. 8	1. 11. 8	1. 6. 8	1. 6. 8
Borough of Durham	1. 11. 4	2. 7. 4	4. 16. 2	5. 3. 4	5. 16. 0	7. 1. 0
South Street	—	—	—	—	—	—
Crossgate	2. 8. 0	7. 19. 4	1. 12. 10	1. 13. 2	2. 17. 0[g]	2. 11. 1
Old Borough	—	—	—	—	—	—
St Giles	12. 2. 8	11. 3. 10	6. 3. 4	5. 1. 4	4. 19. 4	5. 16. 10
Scaltok Mill	6. 0. 0[e]	—[f]	10. 0. 0	13. 6. 8	13. 6. 8	13. 6. 8
Total income	30. 6. 0	30. 8. 6	34. 18. 8	38. 2. 4	37. 14. 4	39. 19. 7

Notes:

[a] Farm of borough, not individual rent

[b] Approximate rent income

[c] Pension received from sacrist in exchange for farm of borough

[d] Includes Elvet bakehouse

[e] Repairs needed

[f] Mill lay waste

[g] Old Borough missing from rental. Rent income supplied from 1519 account roll

Sources: Bursars' rentals; Bursars' account rolls.

Table 2. *The growth of the hostillar's estate in Durham, c.1300–1480 :*
income received from the farms of Old and New Elvet

	Old Elvet £ s. d.			New Elvet £ s. d.			Total £ s. d.		
130[2]–3[a]	5.	6.	8	5.	0.	0	10.	6.	8
1333–5	10.	2.	$10\frac{1}{2}$	4.	0.	0[b]	14.	2.	$10\frac{1}{2}$
1354–5	13.	4.	7	4.	0.	0	17.	4.	7
1364–5	12.	14.	$5\frac{1}{2}$	5.	6.	8[b]	18.	1.	$1\frac{1}{2}$
1377–8	15.	0.	0	3.	6.	$2\frac{1}{2}$	18.	6.	$2\frac{1}{2}$
1384–8	10.	9.	$2\frac{1}{2}$	4.	9.	$7\frac{1}{2}$	14.	18.	10
1405–6	10.	15.	$4\frac{1}{2}$	4.	19.	8	15.	15.	$0\frac{1}{2}$
1416–17	11.	14.	$4\frac{1}{2}$	—			—		
1424–5	11.	10.	$5\frac{1}{2}$	—			—		
1440–1	13.	18.	0	—			—		
1455–6	13.	18.	0	4.	18.	$6\frac{1}{2}$	18.	16.	$6\frac{1}{2}$
1479–80	˙13.	18.	0	—			—		

Notes:
[a] Possibly one term only
[b] This total includes profits of the borough court

Source: Hostillar's account rolls

Table 5. The growth of the hostillar's estate in Durham: acquisitions of land, 1305–1512

	Description of land	Income
1377	William Heswell's land, Smythalgh	?
1383[a]	Thomas de Bricby's kiln	3s. 4d.
1389	Simon Alman's meadow	6s. 8d. (13s. 4d.: 1390)
1391	Feretrar's tenement	13s. 4d.
1392	William Alman's estate. Old Elvet	£2. 5s. 9½d.[b] (£4. 2s. 10d.: 1417)
1394	Simon Alman's tenement etc.	£4. 18s. (£5: 1417)
1394	William Alman's 2 burgages. New Elvet	£2. 1s. 3d. (£2. 2s. 8d.: 1447)
1398	Tenement leased to chaplain of St Andrew's Chapel. New Elvet	10s.
1398	William Masham's dovecot	2s.
1407	Almoner's tenement	?
1415	Tenement near St Oswald's Church. Old Elvet	13s. 4d.
1435	Tenements in Old and New Elvet	£1. 7s. 6½d.
1440	Master of Infirmary's tenement. New Elvet	6s. 8d.
1440	Master of Infirmary's tenements. Old and New Elvet	£1. 6s. 8d. (£1. 4s. 4d.: 1447)
1443	Feretrar's tenements. Old and New Elvet	£5. 2s. 4d.
1470	Thomas Aspour's 7 burgages	?
1471	William Aspour's 4 tenements. Old and New Elvet	19s. 4d.
1474	Richard Lumley's tenement in Old Elvet	?
1487	Marion Tomson's 2 tenements. New Elvet	£1. 4s. 4d.
1488	John Berhalgh's 5 tenements. Old Elvet	£1. 9s. 0d.
1488	William Hyfeld's 2 tenements. Old Elvet	3s. 0d.
1505	Thomas Wright's tenement. New Elvet	13s. 4d.
1512	Thomas Popley's burgage (feretrar).	18s. 8d.

Notes:
[a] One term only
[b] Income was low at first because William Alman's widow held the principal tenement

Source: Hostillar's account rolls

Table 4. *The income of the almoner from Durham rents, 1290–1537*

	1290 £ s. d.	1313 £ s. d.	1325 £ s. d.	1333 £ s. d.	1344 £ s. d.	1424 £ s. d.	1501 £ s. d.	1533–7 £ s. d.
South Street	3. 18. 10	8. 9. 2	7. 4. 8	7. 9. 6	6. 18. 0	3. 9. 10	3. 1. 2	2. 1. 2
Alvertongate	4. 0	4. 0	4. 0	4. 0	4. 0	3. 6	3. 6	3. 6
Crossgate	15. 0	15. 0	2. 0. 2	2. 0. 2	2. 3. 4	11. 7	2. 13. 3	2. 18. 0
Framwelgate	2. 2. 6	2. 11. 10½	2. 19. 6	2. 19. 6	2. 19. 6	3. 7. 4	3. 11. 11	4. 8. 8½
Clayport	—	2. 5. 10	2. 7. 4	2. 7. 4	2. 7. 4	8. 0	8. 0	8. 0
Market place	—	3. 6. 6	3. 6. 6	3. 6. 6	3. 6. 6	—	—	—
Souterpeth	—	1. 6. 8	8. 0	17. 0	1. 2. 0	1. 16. 0	1. 9. 0	1. 10. 0
Bailey	—	2. 18. 10	3. 5. 6	2. 11. 10	2. 18. 9	10. 10. 2	8. 4. 10	9. 19. 4
Ratonrawe	—	4. 10	6. 10	8. 5	5. 6	5. 1	5. 1	4. 7
Elvet	—	1. 16. 4	1. 15. 0	1. 13. 6	1. 0. 0	1. 5. 0	1. 4. 0	1. 3. 8
Old Elvet	—	4. 2. 0	10. 8	1. 13. 8	2. 9. 4	3. 5. 4	3. 12. 2	3. 9. 2
St Mary Magdalen	—	—	—	—	—	2. 3. 6	10. 13. 8	16. 2
Total income	7. 0. 4	28. 1. 0½	24. 8. 2	25. 11. 5	25. 14. 3	27. 5. 4	35. 6. 7	27. 2. 3½

Sources: Almoner's rentals; Almoner's account rolls

Table 5. *Rent arrears and decayed rents in the Durham estates of the bursar, the hostillar and the almoner, 1325–1533*

Bursar

	1348	1359	1395	1404	1412	1429	1446	1464
Number of rents lost	5	23	6	—	—	18	—	—
Value of rents lost	18s. 5d.	£4. 0s. 2½d.	£1. 7s. 0d.	£2. 4s. 9d.	£4. 10s. 4d.	£6. 7s. 8d.	12s. 0d.	£2. 12s. 4d.

Hostillar

	1325	1396	1398	1412	1424	1440	1509
Number of rents lost	21	—	24	9	14	4	32
Value of rents lost	£1. 2s. 6½d.	12s. 8d.	£3. 2s. 5d.	£1. 10s. 8d.	£1. 17s. 2d.	4s. 8d.	£4. 3s. 7d.

Almoner

	1353	1391	1408	1428
Number of rents lost	47	48	76	39
Value of rents lost	£5. 7s. 5d.	£5. 0s. 4d.	£13. 18s. 6½d.	£2. 18s. 11½d.

Almoner

	1432	1448	1501	1515	1533
Number of rents lost	25	24	70	32	41[a]
Value of rents lost	£5. 16s. 2½d.	£3. 1s. 8d.	£6. 19s. 10d.	£4. 1s. 10d.	£5. 18s. 9d.[a]

Note:

[a] Total of decayed rents only, not arrears

Sources: Account rolls; rentals

Table 6. *Waste rents in the Durham estates of the bursar, the hostillar and the almoner, 1352–1515*

Bursar

	1395	1396	1397	1400	1404
Number of waste rents	3	8	7	15	10
Value of waste rents	17s. 6d.	£2. 5s. 6d.	£1. 8s. 2d.	£3. 1s. 2d.	£3. 10s. 10d.

Bursar

	1406	1412	1418	1434	1446	1464
Number of waste rents	8	—	—	—	32	
Value of waste rents	£2. 2s. 10d.	£1. 19s. 0d.	15s. 10d.	£2. 5s. 0d.	£7. 6s. 8d.	£4. 9s. 10d.

Hostillar

	1396	1397	1398	1400	1401	1405
Number of waste rents	8	9	9	10	8	8
Value of waste rents	£1. 18s. 0d.	£2. 16s. 11d.	£2. 1s. 0½d.	£3. 13s. 8d.	£1. 19s. 8d.	£2. 3s. 4d.

Hostillar

	1413	1417	1422	1437	1440	1448	1509
Number of waste rents	7	10	14	7	30	20	14
Value of waste rents	£1. 4s. 10d.	£1. 14s. 0d.	£3. 12s. 4d.	18s. 5d.	£9. 9s. 11d.	£4. 19s. 10d.	£2. 16s. 3d.

Almoner

	1352	1353	1391	1411	1412	1428	1448	1515
Number of waste rents	1	6	6	11	13	20	26	32
Value of waste rents	1s. 9d.	13s. 5d.	9s. 10d.	£3. 14s. 2d.	£1. 14s. 9d	£3. 19s. 0d.	£4. 4s. 2d.	£3. 6s. 10½d.

Sources: Account rolls; rentals

Table 7. *Trades and crafts mentioned in Durham deeds pre-1300*

Victualling	*Textiles*
Baker	Dyer
Brewer	Fuller
Butcher	Hosier
Cook	Tailor
Fisherman	Weaver
Gardener	Woolpuller
Miller	
Poulterer	*Building*
Spicer	Carpenter
Vintner	Charcoal burner
	Dauber
Leather and fur	Glazier
Barker	Mason
Cordwainer	Painter
Currier	Plumber
Felter	Quarrier
Furrier	Roofer
Pelterer	Waller
Saddler	
Scabbard maker	*Miscellaneous*
Souter	Apothecary
Tanner	Barber
	Carter
Merchants and mercers	Cooper
	Forester
Metal workers	Palmer
Arrow/razor smith	Parchment maker
Cutler	Parker
Farrier	Porter
Goldsmith	Shepherd
Sivewright	
Smith	
Turnwright	

Appendix 2

Table 8. *Trades and crafts mentioned in Durham deeds, 1300–1400*

Victualling	*Textiles*
Baker	Draper
Butcher	Lister
Cook	Tailor
Miller	Weaver
Poulterer	?Whitetailor
Salter	
	Building
Leather and fur	Carpenter
Barker	Mason
Currier	Painter
Glover	Sawyer
Pelterer	Slater
Saddler	Tiler
Scabbard maker	
Skinner	*Miscellaneous*
Souter	Barber
Tanner	Chapman
	Cooper
Merchants and mercers	Forester
	Porter
Metal workers	
Cutler	
Girdler	
Goldsmith	
Moneyer	
Smith	
Wheelwright	

Table 9. *Trades and crafts mentioned in Durham deeds, 1400–1500*

Victualling	*Textiles*
Butcher	Lister
	Walker
Leather	Weaver
Barker	
Currier	*Building*
Glover	Carpenter
Saddler	Mason
Shoe maker	Plumber
Skinner	
Tanner	*Miscellaneous*
	Barber
Merchant	Chapman
	Hardwareman
Metal workers	
Smith	

The dates of the bishops of Durham from 995 to the Dissolution

Appendix 3

Note. See transferred from Chester-le-Street 995

Aldhun		d. 1018
	See vacant for 3 years	
Edmund	acc. *c*. 1020	d. *c*. 1040
Eadred	acc. *c*. 1040	d. *c*. 1040
Æthelric	cons. 11.1.1041	res. 1056
Æthelwine	acc. 1056	depr. 1071
Walcher	cons. 1071	d. 14.5.1080
William de St Calais	cons. 27.12.1080 or 3.1.1081	d. 2.1.1096
Ranulf Flambard	cons. 5.6.1099	d. 5.9.1128
Geoffrey Rufus	cons. 6.8.1133	d. 6.5.1141
William de St Barbara	cons. 20.6.1143	d. 13.11.1152
Hugh du Puiset	cons. 20.12.1153	d. 3.3.1195
Philip de Poitou	cons. 20.4.1197	d. 22.4.1208
Richard Marsh	cons. 2.7.1217	d. 1.5.1226
Richard Poore	temp. 22.7.1228	d. 15.4.1237
Nicholas Farnham	cons. 26.5 or 9.6.1241	res. 2.2.1249
Walter Kirkham	cons. 5.12.1249	d. 9.8.1260
Robert Stichill	cons. 13.2.1261	d. 4.8.1274
Robert de Insula	cons. 9.12.1274	d. 7.6.1283
Anthony Bek	cons. 9.1.1284	d. 3.3.1311
Richard Kellaw	cons. 30.5.1311	d. 9.10.1316
Lewis de Beaumont	cons. 26.3.1318	d. 24.9.1333
Richard de Bury	cons. 19.12.1333	d. 14.4.1345
Thomas Hatfield	cons. 1.6.1345	d. 8.5.1381
John Fordham	cons. 5.1.1382	trs. Ely 3.4.1388
Walter Skirlaw	temp. 13.9.1388	d. 24.3.1406
Thomas Langley	cons. 8.8.1406	d. 20.11.1437
Robert Nevill	temp. 8.4.1438	d. 9.7.1457
Lawrence Booth	cons. 25.9.1457	trs. York 1.9.1476
William Dudley	cons. 1.9 × 12.10.1476	d. 29.11.1483
John Shirwood	temp. 16.8.1485	d. 14.1.1494
Richard Fox	temp. 8.12.1494	trs. Winchester 1501
William Sever	temp. 15.10.1502	d. 1505
Christopher Bainbridge	temp. 17.11.1507	trs. York 20.9.1508
Thomas Ruthall	cons. 24.6.1509	d. 4.2.1523
Thomas Wolsey	temp. 30.4.1523	trs. Winchester 8.2.1529
Cuthbert Tunstall	temp. 25.3.1530	res. 28.9.1559

The dates of the bishops of Durham

Key to abbreviations

acc.	accession
cons.	consecration
d.	death
depr.	deprivation
res.	resignation
temp.	restitution of temporalities by the Crown
trs.	translation

Source: *Handbook of British chronology*, E. B. Fryde, D. E. Greenway, S. Porter and I. Roy (eds.), 3rd edn, Royal Historical Society (London, 1986), pp. 216, 241–2.

The obedientiaries of Durham Priory

By the later middle ages, Durham Priory had evolved a complex administrative structure, as befitted a leading Benedictine house of considerable wealth and influence with important temporal and secular roles. There were a number of administrative departments, each presided over by a monk (an obedientiary) who was usually assisted by other brethren in the house, lay and ecclesiastical. Eleven of these offices (or obediences) had a greater importance than the others, simply because they had wider responsibilities and so dealt with a larger annual budget. The obedientiaries holding these offices had a duty to account for their income and expenditure at the annual chapter held in June and to draw up annual statements of their finances. However, even within this group of eleven obediences some had far weightier duties than others, most notably the bursar's office, which was involved in the financial management of the prior's household as well as that of the whole monastic community and so its operations affected all the other obediences. Changes in the number and names of these offices occurred throughout the medieval period; some offices were amalgamated from time to time and held by one monk, as, for example, the offices of terrar and hostillar in the fifteenth century. The prior could, and did, redistribute the duties attached to some offices: Wessington divided the bursar's duties between three monks, the bursar, the cellarer and the granator between 1438 and 1445. Some of the offices found in other monastic houses do not appear at Durham: there was no pittancer or anniversarian, for example. Many of the obedientiaries were selected by the prior without any consultation with the other monks, but the commoner, for example, was appointed by the sub-prior and the convent without the need to refer to the prior. But the prior could not appoint or remove the sacrist, hostillar, almoner or chamberlain without the consent of the other monks in chapter.

The eleven most important office-holders of Durham Priory, who drew up regular account rolls, are listed below, with their principal duties:

the bursar: he was assigned the greater share of the monastic revenues to cope with his many financial obligations and he presided over the central receiving office of the priory. He was responsible for the provisioning of the prior and his household as well as the whole monastic community. He delegated the provision of food and drink to the cellarer and granator, under his budgetary control, but he bought wine.

He provided cloth for the liveries of members of the monks' household. He paid the pensions and stipends of the prior's servants and counsellors.

the terrar: in the thirteenth century, he was principally a land-agent acting on behalf of the prior. As the duties of the bursar expanded, the terrar became his deputy, and collected revenues for him throughout priory lands. By the early fifteenth century, with the leasing of the priory's demesnes, the terrar's role was diminished and the office was often held jointly with that of the hostillar.

the hostillar: he was responsible for the accommodation and entertainment of guests in the priory. He supervised the operations of Elvethall Manor on the outskirts of Durham. He kept the chancel of St Oswald's Church in Old Elvet in repair, paid the stipend of its vicar (and of the chaplains who served St Margaret's Chapel in the Old Borough) and provided the vestments for the church. In the fifteenth century, this office was often held jointly with that of the terrar.

the cellarer: he was responsible for acquiring food and drink for the kitchen of the monastic community, including that most important commodity, meat, but usually excluding the buying of wine, which was undertaken by the bursar. He it was who saw that meals were served on time in the refectory. Both the cellarer and the granator were dependent on the bursar for an allocation of funds to discharge their offices.

the granator: he was responsible for supplying the priory with wheat, barley and malt, under the financial control of the bursar.

the chamberlain: he was responsible for the provision of clothing for the monastic community. He had a tailor who made up woollen cloth and linen into shirts, socks and sheets for the novices and monks. He also provided leather for boots.

the almoner: his main duties were to look after the poor and infirm, and so he administered the two almshouses in Durham (the infirmary outside the priory gatehouse in the Bailey and the *Domus Dei* in the North Bailey) and two hospitals (one at Witton Gilbert and the other, St Mary Magdalen, in Durham). He also ran the almonry school by the infirmary, where a schoolmaster supervised the teaching and feeding of the pupils.

the commoner: he was responsible for looking after the common house beneath the monks' dormitory, providing fuel and candles for it. He purchased spices for the monks during Lent.

the master of the infirmary: he looked after sick, elderly and dying monks within the priory infirmary (not to be confused with the almoner's infirmary outside the priory). He was responsible for the upkeep of the fabric of the infirmary. Another duty was the supervision of the priory prison, or lying house, where monks or people in holy orders who had broken their vows were kept.

the sacrist: he was responsible for the upkeep of the fabric of the cathedral church, including its bells and windows, and he supplied all the wax, wine, bread and incense which was necessary for liturgical purposes. He also looked after all the vestments for use in the cathedral.

the feretrar: he kept the keys of St Cuthbert's shrine, and he was responsible for looking after it and the shrine of the Venerable Bede. He accounted for all the receipts and gifts presented at these shrines. This office was often combined with that of third prior.

The second tier of administration in the priory included the following office-holders, who did not present formal accounts:

the sub-prior: he performed the duties of the prior in his absence. He exercised a disciplinary role over the other monks in the priory and had custody of the priory keys at night. He was responsible for seeing that all the monks were in the dormitory at night. He was master of the refectory, and presided at mealtimes. One of his main responsibilities, which he shared with the precentor and the succentor, was to organise the rota of monks saying masses at chantries and altars in the cathedral church.

the third prior: he performed the duties of the prior in the absence of the prior and the sub-prior.

the sub-sacrist: the understudy for the sacrist, who helped him with his considerable duties.

the sub-feretrar: the understudy for the feretrar.

the chancellor: his most important responsibility was to give legal advice to the prior and to represent the priory's interests in, for example, the York consistory court. He helped to audit the accounts of the other obedientiaries. He was also the custodian of the library, and looked after the official seal of the prior and chapter.

the refectorer: he was responsible for the upkeep of the fabric of the refectory in the priory.

the precentor: he helped the sub-prior with the organisation of the rota of monks saying masses at chantries and altars in the cathedral church. He was responsible for the production of the obituary roll and the organisation of prayers for the souls of dead monks.

the succentor: he was associated with the precentor and the sub-prior in organising the saying of masses at chantries and altars in the cathedral church.

two prior's chaplains: one was a domestic chaplain, who prayed and said mass with the prior in his private chapel. He acted as the prior's personal secretary, witnessing his business transactions and accompanying him on all business journeys. He also kept the prior's letter-book and made copies or memoranda of his correspondence. He kept the prior's privy purse and was empowered to make small payments to, for example, minstrels. The second chaplain was sometimes called the prior's steward. He acted as the receiver of all the money which the bursar handed over to provision the prior's household. He provided all the food, clothing and furnishings for the prior's household at Durham and Bearpark. He supervised the work of the members of these households and hired them and paid their wages.

Sources: *Extracts from the account rolls of the abbey of Durham*, ed. J. T. Fowler, 3 vols., Surtees Society, vols. 99, 100, 103 (1898–1901). For an account of the duties of individual obedientiaries and brief notes on the content of their account rolls, see in particular vol. 103.

Rites of Durham, ed. J. T. Fowler, Surtees Society, vol. 107, no. 2. (1902).

R. B. Dobson, *Durham Priory, 1400–1450* (Cambridge, 1973).

Appendix 5

The Durham courts

The Durham courts

This diagram includes courts of secular jurisdiction only, which affected Durham townsmen

(a) Courts of wider judicial competence

ASSIZE COURT OF BISHOP	HALMOTE COURT OF BISHOP	PRIOR'S COURT
(includes special sessions of gaol delivery and oyer and terminer) President: chief justice	(exercised manorial jurisdiction over tenants in Framwelgate as part of Chester ward) President: bishop's steward	(exercised jurisdiction over priory tenants throughout the town) President: prior's steward or monastic terrar

(b) Local courts of limited judicial competence

TOLBOOTH (for BISHOP'S BOROUGH)	ST GILES	OLD BOROUGH	ELVET BOROUGH	ELVETHALL (for BARONY OF OLD ELVET)
President: bishop's steward or sheriff	President: master of Kepier Hospital	President: monastic sacrist	President: monastic hostillar	President: monastic hostillar

Bibliography

MANUSCRIPT SOURCES

(a) Muniments of the dean and chapter of Durham (held in Prior's Kitchen, Durham): charters, rolls and other documents

  (i) Documents catalogued in the *Repertorium Magnum* (*Rep. Mag.*):

    Pontificalia (Pont.)

    Regalia (Reg.)

    Specialia (Spec.) a most important category including title deeds and other legal documents concerning priory property in Durham and elsewhere. The documents are arranged under place names.

  (ii) Miscellaneous Charters (Misc.Ch.)

    A truly miscellaneous class of documents, formed and catalogued, unsystematically, by J. Stevenson and W. Greenwell in the middle of the nineteenth century. It contains many title deeds relating to Durham properties.

  (iii) Locelli (Loc.)

    Of especial value to this study are:

    Locellus IV: court rolls of the Durham borough courts and the prior's court.

    Locellus XXXVII: miscellaneous property deeds relating to Durham.

  (iv) Account rolls of the following Durham obedientiaries:

    Almoner (Alm.) includes rent rolls of the early fourteenth century

    Bursar (Burs.)

    Commoner (Comm.)

    Hostillar (Host.)

    Master of the Infirmary (Infirm.)

    Sacrist (Sac.)

  (v) Special Collections, containing mainly title deeds which are grouped according to the obedientiary or the Durham cell within whose estate the land lay:

    Elemosinaria (Elem.)

    Sacristaria (Sac.)

    Finchale deeds (Finch.)

(b) Muniments of the dean and chapter of Durham: records mainly in book form

    Registrum I (Reg. I) to *c.* 1400

    Registrum II (Reg. II) 1312–1401

Registrum III (Reg. III) 1401–44
Cartuarium II (Cart. II) written c. 1407–10
Cartuarium IV (Cart. IV) written c. 1500
Rentals of the Almoner: 1424, 1501, 1533
Rentals of the Bursar: 1340, 1342, 1382, 1396, 1397, 1427, 1432, 1495, 1507, 1508, 1517, 1538, 1539
Rentals of the Hostillar: 1523–34
Rentals of the Sacrist: fourteenth century and 1500
Rentals of the Commoner: fifteenth century
Inventories of the Bursar: 1446, 1464
Receivers' Book II, 1542 (Rec.Book II)
Crossgate Court Book, 1478–1524

(c) London, Public Record Office: Records of the Palatinate of Durham
Chancery Enrolments, Bishops Bury to Tunstall (Durham 3/29–3/80)
Abstracts & Registers of Inquisitions *post Mortem* (Durham 3, Reg. vols. II, III, IV; Portfolios 164–91)
Halmote Court Books (Durham 3, nos. 12–23, 135)
Entry Book of Leases (Durham 8/78)
Book of Leases (Durham 3/10)
Judgement Rolls (Durham 13, nos. 1, 221, 223, 228)
Pleas & Presentments (Durham 19, no. 1/1)
London, Public Record Office: Special Collections (SC)
St Giles Court Book, 1494–1532 (SC2, portfolio 171, no. 6)

(d) Durham County Record Office
Salvin family title deeds (D/Sa/D)

PRIMARY SOURCES (PRINTED)

Anglo-Saxon chronicle, ed. G. N. Garmonsway, London, 1953.
Anglo-Saxon chronicle, ed. D. Whitelock, London, 1961.
Bishop Hatfield's survey, ed. W. Greenwell, Surtees Society, vol. 32, 1857.
Boldon Buke, ed. W. Greenwell, Surtees Society, vol. 25, 1852.
British borough charters, 1042–1216, ed. A. Ballard, Cambridge, 1913.
Calendar of charter rolls, 1307–13, Public Record Office.
Calendar of close rolls, 1337–9, Public Record Office.
Calendar of the Greenwell deeds, ed. J. Walton, *ArchAel,* 4th ser., 3 (1926).
Calendar of the patent rolls, 1226–1553, Public Record Office.
Coventry leet book, ed. M. D. Harris, EETS, vols. 134–6, 146, 1907–13.
Depositions and other ecclesiastical proceedings from the courts of Durham, ed. J. Raine, Surtees Society, vol. 21, 1845.
Dialogi Laurentii Dunelmensis Monachi ac Prioris, ed. J. Raine, Surtees Society, vol. 70, 1880.
Dobsons Drie Bobbes, ed. E. A. Horsman, Durham, 1955.
Durham episcopal charters, 1071–1152, ed. H. S. Offler, Surtees Society, vol. 179, 1968.

Bibliography

Early records of medieval Coventry, The, ed. P. R. Coss, Records of social and economic history, new ser., vol. 11, 1986.

English historical documents, 1042–1189, ed. D. C. Douglas and G. W. Greenaway, 2nd edn, London, 1981.

Extracts from the account rolls of the abbey of Durham, ed. J. T. Fowler, 3 vols., Surtees Society, vols. 99, 100, 103, 1898–1901.

Feodarium Prioratus Dunelmensis, ed. W. Greenwell, Surtees Society, vol. 58, 1872.

Historiae Dunelmensis Scriptores Tres, ed. J. Raine, Surtees Society, vol. 9, 1839.

Historia Ecclesiae Dunhelmensis, Continuatio Prima, Continuatio Altera and *De Obsessione Dunelmi*, in T. Arnold (ed.), *Symeonis Monachi Opera Omnia*, Rolls Series, 75, vol. 1, 1882.

Historia Regum, in T. Arnold (ed.), *Symeonis Monachi Opera Omnia*, Rolls Series, 75, vol. 2, 1885.

Injunctions and other ecclesiastical proceedings of Richard Barnes, bishop of Durham, 1575–87, ed. J. Raine, Surtees Society, vol. 22, 1850.

Itinerary of John Leland, ed. L. Toulmin Smith, vol. 1, London, 1906.

Leet jurisdiction in the city of Norwich, ed. W. Hudson, Selden Society, vol. 5, 1892.

Libellus de Vita et Miraculis S. Godrici, Heremitae de Finchale, ed. J. Stevenson, Surtees Society, vol. 20, 1845.

London assize of nuisance, ed. H. M. Chew and W. Kellaway, London Record Society, vol. 10, 1973.

Manorial records of Cuxham, Oxfordshire, ed. P. D. A. Harvey, Oxfordshire Record Society, vol. 50, 1976.

Memorials of London life, ed. H. T. Riley, London, 1868.

Memorials of St Giles, Durham, ed. J. Barmby, Surtees Society, vol. 95, 1896.

Public works in medieval law, vol. 2, ed. C. T. Flower, Selden Society, vol. 40, 1923.

Records of the borough of Leicester, 1103–1327, ed. M. Bateson, vol. 1, London, 1899.

Regesta Regum Anglo-Normannorum, 1066–1100, ed. H. W. C. Davis, Oxford, 1913; *Regesta Regum Anglo-Normannum, 1100–1135*, ed. C. Johnson and H. A. Cronne, Oxford, 1956.

Reginaldi Monachi Dunelmensis Libellus de Admirandis Beati Cuthberti Virtutibus, ed. J. Raine, Surtees Society, vol. 1, 1835.

Registrum Palatinum Dunelmense, ed. T. D. Hardy, 4 vols., Rolls Series, 62, 1873–8.

Rites of Durham, ed. J. T. Fowler, Surtees Society, vol. 107, no. 2, 1902.

York memorandum book, ed. M. Sellers, Surtees Society, vols. 120 and 125, 1912 and 1915; ed. J. W. Percy, Surtees Society, vol. 186, 1973.

SECONDARY SOURCES

Ault, W. O. *Open-field farming in medieval England: a study of village by-laws*, London, 1972.

Barlow, F. *Durham jurisdictional peculiars*, Oxford, 1950.

Barron, C. M. 'The parish fraternities of medieval London', in C. M. Barron and C. Harper Bill (eds.), *The church in pre-Reformation society*, London, 1985, pp. 13–37.

Barrow, G. W. S. 'Northern English society in the early middle ages', *Northern History*, 4 (1969), 1–28.

Bartlett, J. N. 'The expansion and decline of York in the later middle ages', *EcHR*, 12 (1959/60), 17–33.

Bean, J. M. W. *The estates of the Percy family, 1416–1537*, Oxford, 1958.

Beaumont, P. 'Geomorphology', in J. C. Dewdney (ed.), *Durham county and city with Teesside*, Durham, 1970, pp. 26–45.

Benedikz, P. M. (ed.), *Durham topographical prints up to 1800*, Durham, 1968.

Beresford, M. W. *New towns of the middle ages*, London, 1967.

Biddle, M. 'Towns', in D. M. Wilson (ed.), *The archaeology of Anglo-Saxon England*, Cambridge, 1976, pp. 99–150.

(ed). *Winchester in the early middle ages*, Oxford, 1976.

Biddle, M. and Hill, D. 'Late Saxon planned towns', *Antiquaries Journal*, 51 (1971), 70–85.

Bolton, J. L. *The medieval English economy, 1150–1500*, London, 1980.

Britnell, R. H. *Growth and decline in Colchester, 1300–1525*, Cambridge, 1986.

Brown, R. A. *English castles*, 3rd edn, London, 1976.

Butcher, A. E. 'Rent, population and economic change in late medieval Newcastle', *Northern History*, 14 (1978), 67–77.

'English urban society and the revolt of 1381', in R. H. Hilton and T. H. Aston (eds.), *The English rising of 1381*, Cambridge, 1984, pp. 84–111.

Cambridge economic history, vol. 1, M. M. Postan (ed.), 2nd revised edn, Cambridge, 1966.

Cameron, K. *English place-names*, London, 1961.

Campbell, J. 'Norwich', in M. D. Lobel (ed.), *The atlas of historic towns*, vol. 2, London, 1975, no. 4, pp. 1–25.

Carter, H. 'The geographical approach', in M. W. Barley (ed.), *The plans and topography of medieval towns*, CBA Research Report no. 14, London, 1976, pp. 7–19.

Carus-Wilson, E. M. 'The first half-century of the borough of Stratford-upon-Avon', *EcHR*, 2nd ser., 18 (1965), 46–63.

Carver, M. O. H. 'Excavations in New Elvet, Durham City, 1961–73', *ArchAel*, 5th ser., 2 (1974), 91–148.

'Three Saxo-Norman tenements in Durham City', *MedArch*, 23 (1979), 1–80.

'Early medieval Durham: the archaeological evidence', in *Medieval art and architecture at Durham Cathedral*, BAA Conference Transactions for 1977, London, 1980, pp. 11–17.

Carver, M. O. H. and Gosling, P. F. 'The archaeology of Durham City', in P. A. G. Clack and P. F. Gosling (eds.), *Archaeology in the north: the report of the Northern Archaeological Survey*, HMSO, 1976, pp. 133–45.

Clack, P. A. G. 'The origins and growth of Darlington' in P. Riden (ed.), *The medieval town in Britain*, Gregynog Seminars in Local History, no. 1, Cardiff, 1980, pp. 67–84.

Bibliography

'Rescue excavations in County Durham, 1976–8', *TAASDN*, new ser., 5 (1980), 56–70.

The book of Durham City, Buckingham, 1985.

Clark, P. and Slack, P. (eds.). *Crisis and order in English towns, 1500–1700*, London, 1972.

English towns in transition, 1500–1700, London, 1976.

Colvin, H. M. 'Domestic architecture and town planning', in A. L. Poole (ed.), *Medieval England*, vol. 1, Oxford, 1958, pp. 37–93.

Conzen, M. R. G. *Alnwick, Northumberland: a study in town plan analysis*, Transactions of the Institute of British Geographers, vol. 27, London, 1960.

Cooper, J. 'The dates of the bishops of Durham in the first half of the eleventh century', *DUJ*, 60 (1968), 131–7.

Cramp, R. J. 'A cross from St Oswald's church, Durham, and its stylistic relationships', *DUJ*, 57 (1966), 119–24.

'The pre-conquest sculptural tradition in Durham', in *Medieval Art and Architecture at Durham Cathedral*, BAA Conference Transactions for 1977, London, 1980, pp. 1–9.

Craster, H. H. E. 'The patrimony of St Cuthbert', *EHR*, 69 (1954), 177–99.

Darby, H. C. *The Domesday geography of Eastern England*, Cambridge, 1971.

'Domesday England', in H. C. Darby (ed.), *A new historical geography of England*, Cambridge, 1973, pp. 39–74.

Davies, J. Conway, 'The muniments of the dean and chapter of Durham', *DUJ*, 44 (1951–2), 77–87.

Dobson, R. B. *Durham Priory, 1400–1450*, Cambridge, 1973.

'Admissions to the freedom of the city of York in the later middle ages', *EcHR*, 26 (1973), 1–22.

'Urban decline in late medieval England', *TRHS*, 5th ser., 27 (1977), 1–22.

'Cathedral chapters and cathedral cities: York, Durham and Carlisle in the 15th century', *Northern History*, 19 (1983), 15–44.

(ed.). *The Peasants' Revolt of 1381*, 2nd edn, London, 1983.

Dodds, M. H. 'The bishop's boroughs', *ArchAel*, 3rd ser., 12 (1915), 81–185.

Douglas, D. C. *William the Conqueror*, London, 1966.

Ekwall, E. *The concise Oxford dictionary of English place-names*, Oxford, 1960.

Streetnames of the city of London, Oxford, 1965.

Fraser, C. M. *A history of Antony Bek, bishop of Durham, 1283–1311*, Oxford, 1957.

'The pattern of trade in the north-east of England, 1265–1350', *Northern History*, 4 (1969), 44–66.

'The medieval period', in J. C. Dewdney (ed.), *Durham county and city with Teesside*, Durham, 1970, pp. 207–13.

Fraser, C. M. and Emsley, K. *Tyneside*, Newton Abbot, 1973.

Fryde, E. B. *Some business transactions of York merchants*, Borthwick Paper no. 29, York, 1966.

Fryde, E. B., Greenway, D. E., Porter S. and Roy I. (eds.), *Handbook of British chronology*, 3rd edn, Royal Historical Society, London, 1986.

Gooder, A. and E. 'Coventry before 1355: unity or division?', *Midland History*, 6 (1981), 1–38.

Medieval Coventry: a city divided?, Coventry and Warwickshire Pamphlets, no. 11, Coventry, 1981.

Gosling, P. F. 'Carlisle – an archaeological survey of the historic town', in P. A. G. Clack and P. F. Gosling (eds.), *Archaeology in the north: the report of the Northern Archaeological Survey*, HMSO, 1976, pp. 165–85.

Gottfried, R. S. *Bury St Edmunds and the urban crisis, 1290–1539*, Princeton, 1982.

Gransden, A. *Historical writing in England, c. 550–c. 1307*, London, 1974.

Greenwell, W. 'Durham Cathedral', *TAASDN*, 2 (1869–79), 182–8.

Halcrow, E. M. 'The decline of demesne farming on the estates of Durham Cathedral Priory', *EcHR*, 2nd ser., 7 (1955), 345–56.

'The administration and agrarian policy of the manors of Durham Cathedral Priory', unpublished BLitt thesis, University of Oxford, 1949.

Hall, R. A. 'The topography of Anglo-Scandinavian York', in R. A. Hall (ed.), *Viking age York and the North*, CBA Research Report no. 27, London, 1978, pp. 31–6.

Harbottle B. and Clack, P. A. G. 'Newcastle-upon-Tyne: archaeology and development', in P. A. G. Clack and P. G. Gosling (eds.), *Archaeology in the North: the report of the Northern Archaeological Survey*, HMSO, 1976, pp. 11–31.

Harvey, B. *Westminster Abbey and its estates in the middle ages*, Oxford, 1977.

Harvey, J. *English mediaeval architects: a biographical dictionary*, London, 1954.

Hassall, J. M. and Hill, D. 'Pont de l'Arche: Frankish influences on the West Saxon burh?', *Archaeological Journal*, 127 (1970), 188–95.

Hatcher, J. *Plague, population and the English economy, 1348–1530*, London, 1977.

Hawkyard, A. (ed.), *The counties of Britain: a Tudor atlas by John Speed*, London, 1988.

Hegge, Robert. *The legend of St Cuthbert* (1626): ed. George Smith, Darlington, 1777; ed. J. B. Taylor, Sunderland, 1816.

Hill, J. W. F. *Medieval Lincoln*, Cambridge, 1948.

Holmes, A. 'The foundations of Durham Castle and the geology of the Wear gorge', *DUJ*, 25 (1928), 319–26.

Holt, S. B. 'A note concerning Russell's estimate of the population of Durham City in the 14th century', *Durham County Local History Society Bulletin*, 22 (1978), 43–4.

Honeybourne, M. B. 'The pre-Norman bridge of London', in A. E. J. Hollaender and W. Kellaway (eds.), *Studies in London history*, London, 1969, pp. 17–59.

Hoskins, W. G. *Provincial England*, London, 1963.

Local history in England, 2nd edn, London, 1972.

Hughes, E. *North country life in the eighteenth century*, Oxford, 1969.

Hunnisett, R. F. *The medieval coroner*, Cambridge, 1961.

Hutchinson, W. *The history and antiquities of the County Palatine of Durham*, 3 vols., Newcastle, 1785–94.

James, M. E. 'Ritual, drama and the social body in the late medieval English town', *Past and Present*, 98 (1983), 3–29.

Bibliography

Jarrett, M. G. 'The Maiden Castle excavations', *TAASDN*, 11 (1958), 124–7.

Johnson, G. A. L. (ed.), *The Durham area*, Geologists' Association Guides, no. 15, 1973.

Johnson, M. 'The great North Gate of Durham Castle', *TAASDN*, new ser., 4 (1977), 105–16.

Johnson, P. *The National Trust book of British castles*, London, 1978.

Jones, B. C. 'The topography of medieval Carlisle', *Transactions of the Cumberland and Westmorland Antiquarian and Archaeological Society*, 76 (1976), 77–96.

Jones, S. Rees, 'Property, tenure and rents: some aspects of the topography and economy of medieval York', unpublished DPhil thesis, University of York, 1988.

Jones, W. T. 'The walls and towers of Durham', *DUJ*, 22–3 (1920–3), 6 parts.

Keene, D. J. 'Suburban growth', in M. W. Barley (ed.), *The plans and topography of medieval towns in England and Wales*, CBA Research Report no. 14, London, 1976, pp. 71–82.

  Survey of medieval Winchester, vol. 1, part 1; vol. 2, parts 2 and 3 and appendices, Oxford, 1985.

  'Some aspects of the history, topography and archaeology of the north-east part of the medieval city of Winchester, with special reference to the Brooks area', unpublished DPhil thesis, University of Oxford, 1972.

Kelly, S., Rutledge, E. and Tillyard, M. *Men of property: an analysis of the Norwich enrolled deeds, 1285–1311*, Norwich, 1983.

Kermode, J. I. 'Urban decline? The flight from office in late medieval York', *EcHR*, 2nd ser., 35 (1982), 179–98.

King, E. *Peterborough Abbey, 1086–1310: a study in the land market*, Cambridge, 1973.

Knowles, D. *Bare ruined choirs*, Cambridge, 1976.

Lancaster, J. 'Coventry', in M. D. Lobel (ed.), *The atlas of historic towns*, vol. 2, London, 1975, no. 3, pp. 1–13.

Lapsley, G. T. *The county palatine of Durham*, Harvard Historical Studies, vol. 8, New York, 1900.

Lobel, M. D. *Bury St Edmunds*, Oxford, 1935.

  'Salisbury', in M. D. Lobel (ed.), *The atlas of historic towns*, vol. 1, London, 1969, no. 8, pp. 1–9.

  'Bristol', in M. D. Lobel (ed.), *The atlas of historic towns*, vol. 2, London, 1975, no. 1, pp. 1–27.

Lomas, R. A. 'The priory of Durham and its demesnes in the 14th and 15th centuries', *EcHR*, 2nd ser., 31 (1978), 339–53.

  'A northern farm at the end of the middle ages: Elvethall Manor, Durham, 1443/44–1513/14', *Northern History*, 18 (1982), 26–53.

  'Durham Cathedral Priory as landowner and landlord, 1290–1540', unpublished PhD thesis, University of Durham, 1973.

Lomas, T. 'Land and people in south-east Durham in the later middle ages', unpublished PhD thesis, Council for National Academic Awards, 1977.

Bibliography

Longstaffe, W. Hylton Dyer (ed.), 'Local muniments from the vestry of St Margaret, Durham', *ArchAel*, new ser., 2 (1858).

Loyn, H. R. *Anglo-Saxon England and the Norman conquest*, London, 1962.

MacGregor, A. 'Industry and commerce in Anglo-Scandinavian York', in R. A. Hall (ed.), *Viking Age York and the North*, CBA Research Report no. 27, London, 1978, pp. 37–57.

McClure, P. 'Patterns of migration in the late middle ages: the evidence of English place-name surnames', *EcHR*, 2nd ser., 32 (1979), 167–82.

McKinley, R. A. *Norfolk and Suffolk surnames in the middle ages*, London, 1974. *The surnames of Oxfordshire*, London, 1977.

Marcombe, David (ed.), *The last principality: politics, religion and society in the bishopric of Durham, 1494–1660*, Studies in Regional and Local History, vol. 1, Nottingham, 1987.

Meade, D. M. 'The medieval parish of St Giles', *TAASDN*, new ser., 2 (1970), 63–9.

Meehan, B. 'Outsiders, insiders and property at Durham around 1100', in D. Baker (ed.), *Church, society and politics*, Studies in Church History, vol. 12, 1975, pp. 45–58.

Munby, J. 'Medieval domestic buildings', in J. Schofield and R. Leech (eds.), *Urban archaeology in Britain*, CBA Research Report no. 61, London, 1987.

Offler, H. S. *Medieval historians of Durham*, inaugural lecture, University of Durham, Durham, 1958.

Palliser, D. M. 'A crisis in English towns? The case of York, 1460–1640', *Northern History*, 14 (1978), 108–25.
Tudor York, Oxford, 1979.
'The medieval period', in J. Schofield and R. Leech (eds.), *Urban archaeology in Britain*, CBA Research Report no. 61, London, 1987.

Pantin, W. A. 'Medieval English town house plans', *MedArch*, 6–7 (1962–3), 202–39.

Parker, V. *The making of King's Lynn*, London, 1971.

Phythian-Adams, C. V. 'Ceremony and the citizen: the communal year at Coventry, 1450–1550', in P. Clark and P. Slack (eds.), *Crisis and order in English towns, 1500–1700*, London 1972, pp. 57–85.
Desolation of a city: Coventry and the urban crisis of the late middle ages, Cambridge, 1979.

Pirenne, H. *Medieval cities*, Princeton, 1939.

Platt, C. *Medieval Southampton*, London, 1973.
The English medieval town, London, 1976.
The castle in medieval England and Wales, London, 1982.

Pocock, D. and Gazzard, R. *Durham: portrait of a cathedral city*, Durham, 1983.

Raftis, J. A. *The estates of Ramsey Abbey*, Toronto, 1957.

Reynolds, S. *An introduction to the history of English medieval towns*, Oxford, 1977.

Richmond, I. A. and others, 'A civilian bath house of the Roman period at Old Durham', *ArchAel*, 4th ser., 22 (1944), 1–21; 29 (1951), 203–12; 31 (1953), 116–26.

Rogers, A. 'Medieval Stamford', in A. Rogers (ed.), *The making of Stamford*, Leicester, 1965, pp. 34–57.

Rosser, A. G. 'The essence of medieval urban communities: the vill of Westminster, 1200–1540', *TRHS*, 5th ser., 34 (1984), 91–112.

Rubin, M. *Charity and community in medieval Cambridge*, Cambridge, 1987.

Rumble, A. R. 'The personal name material', in D. J. Keene, *Survey of medieval Winchester*, vol. 2, appendix 1, Oxford, 1985.

Russell, J. C. *British medieval population*, Albuquerque, 1948.

Salter, H. E. *Medieval Oxford*, Oxford Historical Society, vol. 100, 1936.
  Survey of Oxford, ed. W. A. Pantin and W. T. Mitchell, 2 vols., Oxford Historical Society, new ser., vols. 14, 20, 1960, 1969.

Salzman, L. F. *Building in England*, 2nd edn, Oxford, 1967.

Scammell, G. V. *Hugh du Puiset, bishop of Durham*, Cambridge, 1956.

Scammell, J. 'The origin and limitations of the liberty of Durham', *EHR*, 81 (1966), 449–73.

Schofield, J. and Leech, R. (eds.), *Urban archeology in Britain*, CBA Research Report no. 61, London, 1987.

Simpson, G. and Hartley, V. 'Excavation below Bishop Tunstal's Chapel, Durham Castle', *Antiquaries Journal*, 33 (1953), 56–64.

Skelton, R. A. 'Tudor town plans in John Speed's *Theatre*', *Archaeological Journal*, 108 (1951), 109–20.

Skelton, R. A. and Harvey, P. D. A. (eds.), *Local maps and plans from medieval England*, Oxford, 1986.

Smith, R. A. L. 'The *Regimen Scaccarii* in the English monasteries', *TRHS*, 4th ser., 24 (1942), 73–94.
  Canterbury Cathedral Priory: a study in monastic administration, Cambridge, 1943.

Snape, R. H. *English monastic finances in the later middle ages*, Cambridge, 1926.

Storey, R. L. *Thomas Langley and the bishopric of Durham, 1406–1437*, London, 1961.

Surtees, R. *The history and antiquities of the County Palatine of Durham*, 4 vols., London, 1816–40.

Swanson, H. *Building craftsmen in late medieval York*, Borthwick Paper no. 63, York, 1983.
  'Crafts and craftsmen in late medieval York', unpublished DPhil thesis, University of York, 1980.

Tatton-Brown, T. 'Canterbury's urban topography: some recent work', in P. Riden (ed.), *The medieval town in Britain*, Gregynog Seminars in Local History, no. 1, Cardiff, 1980, pp. 85–98.

Thrupp, S. L. *The merchant class of medieval London*, Chicago, 1948.

Turner, H. L. *Town defences in England and Wales*, London, 1971.

Turner, R. M. (ed.), *Maps of Durham, 1576–1872*, Durham, 1954.

Urry, W. *Canterbury under the Angevin kings*, London, 1967.

Veale, E. M. 'Craftsmen and the economy of London in the 14th century', in A. E. G. Hollaender and W. Kellaway (eds.), *Studies in London history*, London, 1969, pp. 133–51.

Victoria County History, Durham, 3 vols., London, 1905–28.

Victoria County History, Northamptonshire, vol. 3, London, 1930.

Victoria County History, Oxfordshire, vol. 4, London, 1979.

Victoria County History, Warwickshire, vol. 8, London, 1969.

Victoria County History, Yorkshire, City of York, Oxford, 1961.

Victoria County History, Yorkshire, East Riding, vol. 1, London, 1969.

Whitelock, D. 'The dealings of the kings of England with Northumbria in the 10th and 11th centuries', in P. Clemoes (ed.), *The Anglo-Saxons*, London, 1959, pp. 70–88.

Whiting, C. E. 'The castle of Durham in the middle ages', *ArchAel*, 4th ser., 10 (1933), 123–32.

'Durham trade gilds', *TAASDN*, 9, part 2 (1941), 143–262; part 3 (1943), 265–415.

Whitworth, T. 'Deposits beneath the North Bailey, Durham', *DUJ*, 61 (1968), 18–31.

Wilkinson, B. 'Northumbrian separatism in 1065 and 1066', *Bulletin of the John Rylands Library*, 23 (1939), 504–26.

Williams, G. A. *Medieval London: from commune to capital*, London, 1963.

Wood, M. *The English medieval house*, London, 1965.

Young, A. *William Cumin: border politics and the bishopric of Durham, 1141–1144*, Borthwick Papers, no. 54, York, 1979.

Index

All references are to places or people in Durham, unless otherwise stated

Index

domestic buildings (*cont.*)
   medieval survivors, 79; partitions,
   89; repairs, priory policy, 76,
   138–40; solars, 86; stables, 80; terms
   used in documents, 79; windows,
   89; *see also* building materials;
   building techniques
Doncastre, William, vicar of St Oswald's
   Church: overseer of road repairs for
   priory, 65; trustee for priory in
   conveyancing, 65
Dryng, Peter, mason: property, 176;
   rewarded with land, 176
Durham: agricultural community, 29–30,
   47, 67, 117, 128, 145, 186, 218–19;
   geology, 38–9, 254–5; market town,
   10, 16, 145, 147, 169–74, 192–4, 229;
   origins, 9–10, 12–17; settlement
   antedating town, 9–10, 13–14;
   shrinking, 67, 128; site, 1, 7, 37–9;
   social composition, 157, 196–7;
   standard of living, 103; status of
   town, 35–6, 194; topography, 7,
   254: influence on site, 7, 14, 37–40,
   67; urban area, extent of, 229, 235;
   writers on, 1, 11
Durham fair, *see* Cuthbert, St: fairs

Elvet Borough (*see also* New Elvet), 86,
   89–90, 105, 126–8, 132–3, 140, 147,
   159, 189, 203, 209, 215, 223, 262–3,
   266
   attempt by prior to have market there,
   27, 29; boundaries, 29, 54; charters
   given by prior, 29, 46, 60, 168;
   common pasture disputes, 220, 246;
   manuring, 219; road repairs, 65–6;
   Smythalgh, 218–19, 224, 246, 265;
   subdivision of tenements, 72
Elvethall manor, 29–30, 47, 98, 100–1,
   119–20, 145, 279
   agricultural services, 116; repaired and
   maintained by hostillar, 100, 139, 279
Elvetwood, 81, 219
de Essh, William, son of Walter, butcher,
   179
   heir, lack of male, 177; lived in
   Fleshewergate, 162; property, 162,
   175, 177; wealth, 162
Exeter, 51

fairs, regional, 155, 171–2, 174
   purchases of cloth, fish, haberdashery
   and wine by bursar, 155, 171–3

feretrar: duties, 280; receives pension
   from almoner, 136
fires in town, 22, 28, 33–4, 141
fish: purchases by priory, 171–2
Fleshewergate, 44, 47, 59, 113, 124, 147,
   151, 159, 166, 206
   alternative street names, 61; butchers'
   quarter, 45, 61, 63, 162, 175, 177;
   Cornerbooth, 73, 98, 157, 163, 248;
   domestic buildings, 79;
   encroachments, 62; 'le Colhole', 70,
   73; tenement patterns, 70
flood damage, 33, 50, 66
fortifications, 14–15, 18–20, 250
   bridges incorporated into, 52; duty of
   merchants in Old Elvet to contribute
   to, 28; effect on town, 22, 70, 164;
   lanes to walls to be kept clear, 63;
   see also castle; North Gate;
   walls
Framwelgate (modern Framwellgate), 44,
   59, 61, 68, 85, 90–1, 112, 114, 141,
   147, 154, 175–6, 266, 284
   bishop's meadow ('le Milnmedowe'),
   112; guild house ('le Gildehouse'),
   94–5, 97; outbuildings in
   tenements, 88; shooting butts, 214;
   signs of decline, 45, 75–6; tanners'
   quarter, 45, 63, 153, 164–6; timber-
   framed houses, 82

Gateshead, 27, 37
goldsmiths, 269–70
   bailiff of Old Borough, 181; craft
   regulations, 184–6, 188, 192;
   location, 158, 163–4, 168; market
   for their goods, 163–4, 194;
   property investment, 164, 175
de Gretewych, Robert, merchant, 170
   cloth sold to priory, 158
guild halls and houses, 77, 94–7, 103
   absence of craft guild halls, 97, 103;
   converted from domestic buildings,
   97; converted to inn, 97; dating of,
   95–6; decline of, 97; stone-built,
   96–7; used as borough court house,
   98, 100

Halifax, 173
Hartlepool, 37, 158, 193
   merchants, 157, 172; wine imports,
   153
Hegge, Robert, 1, 39
Hereford, 44

Index

Index

saddlers, 269–71
 burgesses, 181; family relationships,
  162–3; location, 153, 162–3; places
  of origin, 179–80
Sadlergate (modern Saddler Street), 59,
  61, 69–70, 87–8, 113, 118, 137, 140,
  166, 175–6, 203, 206, 213
 alternative street names, 61;
  encroachments, 62; goldsmiths, 63,
  163–4; 'le Barkhousyarde', 73;
  saddlers, 153, 162–3; tanneries, 63,
  88, 165; tenement patterns, 69–70;
  tenements destroyed, 71–2
Salisbury, 161
salt: purchases by priory, 173
Scots: attacks on town, 18–19, 26, 63,
  187; by-pass town, 22; local
  injunctions against, 222; prejudice
  against, 179, 187–8
services: agricultural, 116, 136–7;
  commutation of rents, 137; military,
  80; suit of court, 136–7; suit of mill,
  56–7
service industries, 145, 150, 157, 160; see
  also luxury trades; victualling trades
sheriff: of bishop, 206, 220
Shields, 172
 fish purchases by bursar, 172
shops, 64, 87
 on or around bridges, 53, 176
Sidegate, 155, 166
 land and spring held by Thomas
  Billyngham, 51
Silver Street, 44, 59, 79, 90, 92, 128
 misleading occupational street name,
  163–4
smiths, 90–1, 155, 269–71
 locksmiths, 91; served castle garrison,
  155
Smythalgh, see Elvet Borough
Souterpeth, 59, 61, 66, 81–2, 86, 96, 128,
  140–1, 154, 163, 266
 'Herthall', 86, 96;
Southampton, 83, 211, 219
South Bailey (see also Bailey), 79, 80,
  82–4, 92, 136
South Street, 36, 44, 59, 61, 67, 86, 88,
  90, 156, 203, 214–15, 262–3, 266
 borough court, 99, 106; evidence of
  decline, 71–2, 75–6, 125; freehold
  tenements, 69, 112; 'le Byre' and
  'le Haverbarn', 73; lack of repair
  work, 140; 'Mevhanthouse', 73;
  possible manor at south end, 29–30,

47; quarries for building stone, 81,
  85, 102, 166; stone houses, 80;
  tenement patterns, 71; vennel kept
  open by court order, 63–4; waste
  tenements, 45, 71, 127–8
Speed, John: plan of town, 1611, 39–40,
  62, 79, 238
spices: bought in market place, 170; ·
  purchases by priory 170, 172–3
stalls, 64, 87, 100
Stamford, 6, 35, 146
 crafts, 154, 161
steward (or seneschal): of bishop, 206; of
  hostillar, 221; of prior, 205–6
stipends: of priory servants, 117
Stockton, 35, 37, 59
Stratford-upon-Avon, 179
street names: alternative and variant
  names, 61; dating, 161; derivations,
  61; occupational, 61, 154, 161–4;
  stable, 60–1
street plan, 49, 58–9
 origin, 60; permanent and stable, 59,
  62
streets: encroachments, 62, 222;
  functions, 63–4; hierarchy, 59–60;
  material used for repairs, 66; repair
  and maintenance work, 64–7
surnames: derived from place names, 170,
  178–80; occupational, 90, 146–8,
  151, 155–6
Surtees, Robert, 2, 100, 184, 192
Symeon of Durham, 1, 11, 13, 15, 18

tanning, 45, 58, 88
 barkers, 150, 153, 180, 269–71;
  continuity of trade in one tenement,
  164–5; equipment, 165; lack of
  regulation, 165; location, 45, 63,
  153, 164–6; need for water, 165–6,
  167; numbers, 153; tanners, 153,
  159, 181, 269–71
tenants: absent from town, 120–1;
  baking, 100–2; customary, 116;
  freeholders, 125, 163, 201, 215–17,
  220, 232, 246: independence of, 113,
  120, 123, 216; milling, 100, 217–18;
  leaseholders, 163; obligations of
  tenure, 94, 98, 100, 137, 215–16,
  218; pasturage or grazing rights,
  112, 219–20; priory, 107; repair
  work to offset rents, 129; rents
  owed, 108, 111–14, 120–1; retain
  legal interest in property, 135; sick